DEEP CONVICTION

DEEP CONVICTION

TRUE STORIES

of Ordinary Americans

Fighting for the Freedom

to Live Their Beliefs

STEVEN T. COLLIS

SHADOW
MOUNTAIN

For Jerusha.
She alone understands the meaning of this book.

For Mathew, Jonah, Joshua, and Autumn.
May you all be peacemakers.

Visit us at shadowmountain.com

Library of Congress Cataloging-in-Publication Data

Names: Collis, Steven T., 1978– author.
Title: Deep conviction : true stories of ordinary Americans fighting for the freedom to live their beliefs / Steven T. Collis.
Description: Salt Lake City, Utah : Shadow Mountain, [2019] I Includes bibliographical references and index.
Identifiers: LCCN 2018056381 I ISBN 9781629725536 (hardbound : alk. paper)
Subjects: LCSH: Freedom of religion—United States—History—21st century.
Classification: LCC BR516 .C685 2019 I DDC 323.44/20973—dc23
LC record available at https://lccn.loc.gov/2018056381

Printed in the United States of America
Lake Book Manufacturing, Inc., Melrose Park, IL

10 9 8 7 6 5 4 3 2 1

CONTENTS

INTRODUCTION

S he wasn't getting better.

It was the middle of 2010. In a hospital room in Kansas, sixty-four-year-old mother of eight Mary Stinemetz lay in a bed while doctors, once again, drained her chest. In recent months, her body had withered. Her abdomen had swelled. As the fluid pooled in her alveoli, it clipped her breathing. Her illness had caused her immune system to fail, so common sicknesses stalked her now, waiting for an opening. Her face had aged so dramatically she could have passed for someone twenty years older. She was weak, so just leaving the house to come to the hospital was a challenge. Anemia left her feeling cold all the time.

Twenty years earlier, she had received the diagnosis that led to this bleak point. It was primary biliary cholangitis. A chronic disease, caused by both genetic and environmental factors, was slowly destroying the bile ducts in her liver. And it was finally overtaking her.

As fate would have it, all hope wasn't lost. Researchers had discovered a cure. It would have saved her and given her decades more to play with her grandchildren and serve in her church. It was a liver transplant, but there was just one problem. A devout Jehovah's Witness, Mary couldn't accept a procedure that involved a blood transfusion. Citing numerous biblical verses, she believed it violated God's commands to accept blood from another person. No matter how foolish the doctors might have thought her religious convictions, she couldn't ignore them. Like millions of others, if forced to choose between life and her deeply held religious beliefs, she would choose the latter.

The good news was that medicine had developed a bloodless procedure that would work. The bad news was that the Kansas Health Policy Authority refused to authorize it. They could have. The difference in patient outcomes was largely insignificant. It didn't cost any more than the traditional procedure. In fact, some estimates indicated it might have been cheaper. But they didn't believe her "religious preference" rose to the level of being a medical necessity.

They demanded that Mary choose: forget her religious beliefs . . . or die.

Mary sued. Her argument was that the state couldn't constitutionally put her in such an impossible position.

Although the clock on her life was ticking with the stilted regularity of each of her struggling gasps, the state refused to back down.

The number-one factor that would determine whether Mary would live or die wasn't what most people think. It wasn't doctors or medical procedures. It wasn't money. The single greatest influence wasn't even a person or lobbying group. It was an idea, an experiment, something that has been brewing on this continent since before the founding of the United States. It was the notion that religious freedom for all, truly cherished, would allow justice and protection for everyone.

Religious liberty[1] is a complicated topic. Some attack it, some defend it, and most mischaracterize it. The principles aren't obvious. The best path is to walk alongside a few of the intrepid travelers who have put their reputations and livelihoods at risk to preserve it. Seeing what they saw, hearing what they heard, feeling what they felt, we can appreciate its relevance to our own lives.

Of course, we could lose ourselves in thousands of stories. I have picked just four. I chose them for their universality, for the broad principles they teach us. Together, they show why this very important of human liberties should matter to everyone.

In many respects, the individuals in this book couldn't be more different: a Catholic priest who faced prison just after the country's founding, in the humid courtrooms of a still-rural New York City; during the middle of the Cold War, an atheist who pushed his seemingly mundane attempt to become a Maryland notary public all the way to the United States Supreme Court; thirty years later, a Klamath Indian man who had used his faith to climb out of the depths of despair only to have the state of Oregon try to punish him for it; and finally, a gay couple and a cake maker in the Mile High City who peered at each other from opposite sides of a chasm seemingly impossible to cross.

What binds the stories together, from a dusty prison in 1813 Manhattan to a cake shop in Lakewood, Colorado, is one unbreakable thread that stretches and twines across the United States: the principle that religious liberty is a liberty for all of us, one that births other liberties, one that allowed the formation of the most religiously diverse country on earth, one that protects us regardless of our beliefs, and one we must not take for granted. That thread pierces both time and geography.

———

Lying in her hospital bed, needles and tubes stretching from her lungs, Mary Stinemetz had only the vaguest sense of where she fit into America's experiment with religious freedom. As her case progressed and her body destroyed itself from the inside out, she would learn. Her family would as well. And the stories in this book shed light on the principles they would come to understand, which in turn would determine whether Mary would live or die.

They begin with an Alsatian Jesuit priest shouldering the burden of a people not entirely his own.

NOTE

1. Throughout this book, I use the terms "religious liberty" and "religious freedom" interchangeably.

PART 1

THE SEAL OF
THE CONFESSIONAL

T orrents of blood have been spilt," James Madison wrote at
the time of the founding of the United States. Like all the
Founders, he faced an opportunity few others had ever or will
ever experience: the chance to form the laws for a completely new nation. And he was describing what had occurred in the centuries before,
when a lack of religious freedom had led to unimaginable human suffering. He looked back through time, and he wondered how this new
nation could avoid the same tragedies that had plagued people everywhere else.

It was a legitimate concern. Human history—and especially the
European history the Founders knew so well—has seen some of its
worst atrocities when one group of people has attempted to use the
powerful hand of government to bolster its religious views over others'. In the 1500s, what we now call the Reformation saw the rise
of Protestantism—groups of Christians who formed to *protest* the
then-dominant Catholic Church. What followed for centuries was one

attempt after another by Catholics and Protestants to use the power of the state to win their religious arguments. The result was nothing but bloodshed, and virtually no one was left unscathed. History had confirmed through sad experience that it was the nature of almost all people to abuse power once they had it, to use the power of government to force their beliefs on others, and to crush those with differing views.

The question for Madison and the other Founders was whether their new nation could protect against that very human—and nearly universal—instinct. To that end, they drafted protections into the United States Constitution. They debated over how the individual states should treat religion. They penned letters to each other seeking the solution.

And after they had devised an answer they hoped would work, with the rules set, they watched their fledgling country begin to grow. In that setting, while some of the Founders still lived, one of the first known challenges of America's promise of religious freedom began not with captured prisoners in the then-raging War of 1812, nor with an attention-grabbing headline in *The New York Evening Post*; it didn't even begin with a law explicitly burdening religion; it started with a jewelry theft.

Chapter 1

THIEVES IN THE NIGHT

During the winter of 1812, James Keating stood in awkward silence before the questioning glares of a police panel. They wanted information. He refused to give it.

They met in the grandeur of New York City's newly constructed city hall. It was an imposing building, and a commoner like Keating would have no doubt felt humbled to stand inside it, as if his very clothes might blemish its ornate, Georgian steeple. Completed the year before, it was now the largest building in the fledgling city, modeled after the French *hôtels particuliers*, with a central pavilion flanked on either side by two large wings. Grand steps met Corinthian and Ionic pillars and pilasters that stood before the entrance like centurion guards. The glowing marble façade reflected the aspirations and wealth of the budding nation, even if Keating and his people had yet to fully experience it.

Keating, a Catholic coppersmith and merchant, eked out a living in New York City. Weeks earlier, he had reported the theft of some of his jewelry. The police had investigated the crime and indicted a married couple for ultimately receiving the jewelry, but they still didn't know who the actual thieves were.

They had also learned something odd: after all of this, someone had returned the stolen goods to Keating. Nevertheless, a punishment for the theft was still in order, so the panel had summoned Keating and demanded to know how he had gotten the jewelry back.

He clammed up. The simple thing would have been to lie and tell them he had misplaced it, but he didn't take the easy path.

Who had given it to him?

Again, he wouldn't answer.

They interrogated him. Every silent breath made the mystery more compelling. They needed to know. He was clearly afraid to speak, and they demanded to know why.

His silence was infuriating.

They began to suspect that perhaps he was the one who had received stolen goods, that perhaps his report of a theft was simply part of a larger, ingenious plot to save himself from suspicion when he was eventually found with the jewelry. Perhaps it had never been his after all.

Whatever the case, Keating couldn't bring himself to open his mouth. He begged the police to let him go in peace.

But he had a duty, they told him, to reveal the whole truth, and it was their duty to peel back the layers of secrecy and ensure obedience to the law. As well as punishment for breaking it.

Keating remained silent.

If he refused to comply, they threatened, he would be sent to Bridewell Prison.[1]

The prison was an institution that could strike fear into even the most seasoned criminal. Bridewell had a nefarious history. Designed to hold debtors and other felons, the prison had been built decades earlier on the plot next to the newly constructed city hall, with construction beginning in 1775. The Declaration of Independence and Revolutionary War had interrupted its completion, and after the fighting erupted, the British used Bridewell to house American prisoners of war. Their treatment was less than humane. During the long fight for independence, the building contained nothing but iron bars on the windows to keep out the elements. Too hot in the summer, too cold in the winter, it allowed the icy winds to creep in like ghostly tendrils and take the lives of hundreds of American patriots.

Apparently, the threat of being relinquished to a building so affiliated with death was too much for even Keating to withstand. He caved, admitting that he was a parishioner at St. Peter's Catholic Church and that his priest, Father Anthony Kohlmann, had returned the jewelry to him. The thief had given it to Kohlmann as part of penance during confession.

Keating's reticence was understandable. In 1813, native New Yorkers considered Catholics to be foreign and un-American, not to be trusted.[2] That his jewelry had been returned was miraculous enough. That it had come through a sacrament alien to the police would make anyone afraid to draw attention to it.

Who was the thief? the police demanded.

Keating didn't know.

In the splendor of city hall, in their new majestic chambers, emanating grandeur and power, it is easy to imagine the authorities, their curiosity now piqued to insatiable levels, leaning back in their chairs, arms behind their heads, saying, "Bring us Father Kohlmann." Indeed, they demanded exactly that. One way or another, they were going to get to the bottom of this mystery; they were going to flush out the thief.

The Catholic priest was the key.

———

The police issued a summons for Father Kohlmann.

After receiving it, Kohlmann likely slipped on whatever he had to stay warm and ventured out into the frigid air. We don't know precisely where he was when the summons arrived, just that he complied quickly. The summons demanded he appear at the police office. If he had been at St. Peter's, the only Catholic church in the city, it would have been a short walk down Barclay Street, across the hardened dirt of Broadway, and to the office, which was little more than a block away.

If he had been elsewhere in the city, or even in the meadows, farmers' fields, and woods that made up most of the island of Manhattan at the time, the journey would have been far more arduous. Most likely, he would have traversed through filth. New York City had not mastered trash removal or street cleaning yet,[3] and he would have navigated a labyrinth of stinking paths filled with garbage, human and beast excrement, stagnant pools of water and urine covered in scum and ice, carts of putrid vegetables, and rotting fish.[4] Eventually, he would have reached the wealthier part of town, where the fashionable, three-story stone row houses of the city's higher strata lined Broadway. Across from them sat the Common, the park directly in front of city hall, its young elms, poplars, willows, and catalpas standing like pillaged skeletons, stripped but defiant against the winter breeze.[5]

As he traveled, Kohlmann likely knew what the police would ask him. He no doubt had considered his answer and pondered the possible reactions. He marched up the steps and soon stood before them.

The question came as expected: How had he gotten the jewelry?

Peering at them through wire-rimmed glasses, Kohlmann explained that a repentant member of his congregation had admitted the crime to him during confession. Kohlmann had explained to the confessor that if truly penitent, he or she would restore the jewelry. The thief did so, giving it to Kohlmann, who had returned it to Keating.

The police demanded to know who the confessor was.

Kohlmann refused to give them a name, explaining that, for Catholics, confession was a sacrament and that one of the most important aspects of it was secrecy. He could not and would not break that secrecy, no matter the consequence.

The police were not satisfied. This was not their religion. It was a foreign practice to them, as were so many other Catholic traditions, and the priest's refusal was nothing more than obstruction of justice, undermining their ability to do their job and enforce the rule of law so prized by new Americans. The general law was simple: anyone with knowledge regarding a legal affair needed to provide it to the police or, if necessary, to a court of law. Failure to do so was a crime.

But Kohlmann wouldn't—couldn't, in his mind—compromise his religious beliefs. He would go to prison before he would violate his sacred duties.

His interrogators tried another tack, hoping to piece together the thief's identity through roundabout questions.

They asked for the thief's sex.

Kohlmann refused to give it.

They asked for the skin color.

Again, Kohlmann refused. This man, whose life in many ways had prepared him for a moment just like this, would not be fooled by indirect questions, and he would not be intimidated. The seal of the confessional was absolute, he said, and he could not break it.

The police let Kohlmann go, but their investigation was not over. The priest had laid down a challenge. From the investigators' point of view, Kohlmann believed that no matter what the law required of everyone else, he should be exempt from it. It was a problematic request. If they allowed Kohlmann to walk away simply because of his religious beliefs, they would be failing in their duty, and if they did that too often, the rule of law would collapse.

One way or another, they were coming for him. He couldn't hide behind his religion forever.

NOTES

1. For the details of Keating's conversation with the police, see William Sampson, *The Catholic Question in America* (New York, 1813), 1.
2. Paul A. Gilje, *The Road to Mobocracy: Popular Disorder in New York City, 1763–1834* (Chapel Hill: University of North Carolina Press, 1987), 28, 130–31.
3. Raymond A. Mohl, *Poverty in New York: 1783–1825* (New York: Oxford University Press, 1971), 10–11.
4. Ibid., 11.
5. Augustine E. Costello, *Our Police Protectors: History of the New York Police from the Earliest Period to the Present Time* (New York, 1885), 59–60.

Chapter 2

MARTYR OF CHARITY

In later years, behind high, solid cheekbones and a jutting nose that projected poise, people would see a pain in the eyes of Father Anthony Kohlmann. And no wonder. His birthplace was symbolic of where his life would lead, of the disease and death and heartache he would not only see but actually wade through in his earlier years. He was born in Kaysersberg, Alsace, the border region between France, Germany, and Switzerland. It was a verdant, lush part of Europe, with plains nestled between the Vosges Mountains to the west and the Black Forest Mountains to the east, the Rhine River feeding the soil and making it rich and fertile. Not surprisingly, in the agricultural centuries of humanity's past, it was a highly sought-after area, regularly invaded and annexed. Every neighboring empire that had risen to power eventually tried to conquer it and make it part of their kingdom. Representative of the schism that was Alsace, it was part of France at the time of Kohlmann's birth in 1771; but the people largely spoke Alsatian, a German dialect.

Kohlmann's years prior to arriving in New York included the faithful quality of a martyr stepping into the fog. About his childhood, we know little. His father died when he was nine, leaving a wife and five children under eighteen. In the years and even decades that followed, Kohlmann's would be a hero's journey of an Odysseun nature. Even at an early age, he'd been attracted to spiritual pursuits, and by his early twenties, he

12

had joined the order of Catholic friars known as Capuchins, a monkish group that practiced solitary penance, wore humble brown habits, and placed great emphasis on preaching and ministering to the poor.

It seemed his desire to serve drove him from one of humanity's horrors to the next. Trying to escape the extremes of the French Revolution, he crossed the Rhine to Fribourg in Switzerland, where he sought asylum and completed his theological studies. He was ordained a priest at the age of twenty-five, in 1796. As the century turned, he sought to heal when the rest of Europe seemed bent on war.

In 1799, as a result of various European conflicts, an epidemic ravaged the countryside in Austria. The strain of flu was highly contagious and left scores sick or dying. Kohlmann plunged in to do his duty despite the deathly toll the outbreak wreaked among the populace and the risk it posed to him. He ministered to the sick on a daily basis. Maneuvering among them, tending to their needs as they lay in cots and makeshift beds, the young priest cemented his reputation as someone who was not only interested in theology but who was also willing to act on it. The survivors in one Austrian city began referring to him as the "Martyr of Charity."[1]

In time, he found himself on assignment in Padua and Pavia, Italy, where his superiors had asked him to serve as chaplain. There, in the military hospitals, he tended to scores of bloodied and broken men. The effects of the epidemic in Austria had been heartbreaking, but the ravages of war were downright devastating. Broken, bruised, battered, and beaten, soldiers from all across Europe crammed into the Italian hospitals. In Pavia alone, more than three thousand men tried to recover in just four overrun, makeshift hospitals. There were only two priests. In that bastion of death, where typhus left men shaking with fever and overridden with rash, where hygiene was nonexistent, Kohlmann was exposed to men from all walks of life. They hailed from across Europe, young men who spoke different languages and believed in different religions, caught up in wars and revolutions many of them couldn't possibly understand.

In the evenings, when he struggled to sleep amidst the moans of the injured, the scratching of the vermin, and the overwhelming stench of human excrement, Kohlmann navigated among the soldiers, who were piled on top of one another for lack of space, often lying in their own and each other's filth. He heard confessions. He administered the Catholic sacraments to those who requested them. He tended to the sick and wounded. He preached to those not of his faith. No doubt he saw many die. This was no minor temporary assignment for Kohlmann, nor was it a feel-good mission trip that would allow him to return to the comforts of his childhood home. For two years, he labored among the ravished, bleeding, infected men in Padua and Pavia, witnessing, even touching and grasping, the horrific fruits of the twin trees of war and conflict, unaware that he was also drawing attention to himself.

———

Just as Kohlmann was establishing a reputation for charity and sacrifice, he was also developing his intellect and shrewdness. His superiors noticed. They asked him to take charge of not one, but two educational institutes. In time, he became a Jesuit. This was an important and crucial decision for Kohlmann and, it would turn out, for the lives of the many Catholics who would later immigrate to New York.

The American Revolution had triggered something in Europeans of the day, a sense of boundless opportunity and a vast new world where all people could escape the stifling conflicts of the past. In 1789, the Jesuits opened Georgetown College in the relatively young Washington, DC, to train Catholic novices. Though Kohlmann was still considered a novice himself, the Jesuits in Russia, who were helping to support the movement across Europe and the other side of the Atlantic, asked him to go to Georgetown to teach philosophy. He embarked in July 1806 and set sail from Hamburg, Germany, on August 20. For the new Jesuit, nothing would ever be the same.

Kohlmann sat in the undulating belly of a ship for three months, plowing west through the waves of the Atlantic, the horrors of wars and sickness fading behind him, the opportunities and challenges of a new world growing closer and more realistic. With the ascent of every wave, Kohlmann's ambitions for the Jesuits in the United States swelled. His vision was as expansive as the vast American continent. "I have no doubt," he wrote several months after arriving, "that in the new order of things that there is no country in the world at this time more ready to give foundation to the society than" the United States.[2] His grandiosity would later prove crucial when the justices of the peace came knocking regarding the Keating jewelry theft.

At the time, his enthusiasm led only to disappointment. His ship docked in Baltimore, and after maneuvering down the gangplank in the crisp autumn air in early November 1806 and traveling to Georgetown, he found the college in disrepair. Bare, unplastered walls and boarded, glassless windows disguised a "superb building" that was now more potential than reality.[3] A structure designed to house more than two hundred students held only twenty-six, and lack of funds made any improvements impossible. Still, Kohlmann would prove to be a man driven by vision, not necessarily practicality. He was penniless, but he set to work.[4]

As before, his demeanor inspired confidence in his superiors. In a relatively short period, Bishop John Carroll asked that Kohlmann travel north to New York, where he would oversee the affairs of a fledgling diocese while it awaited a new bishop stranded in Europe. Kohlmann had two missions: tend to the struggling parish, which had been rocked by scandal, and build a school to educate the youth. Neither would prove easy.

NOTES

1. *The New International Encyclopedia* (New York: Dodd, Mead and Company, 1905–16), 11:580.
2. In Robert Emmett Curran, *The Bicentennial History of Georgetown University: From Academy to University 1789–1889*, vol. 1 (Washington, DC: Georgetown University Press, 1993), 59.
3. Ibid., 59–60.
4. Ibid., 59.

Chapter 3

RIOTS, GANGS, SCANDALS, AND SCHOOLS

In early October 1808, when a hesitant Kohlmann docked in New York Harbor with five men from Georgetown, neither he nor his companions had a penny in their pockets.[1] Seagulls likely glided just above the licking waves, scouring for morsels. That time of year, the air would have been pleasant, but the looming winter would have made her presence known, providing just a tinge of cold, a gentle reminder of her imminent arrival. Kohlmann's journey had all the compelling qualities of the ancient tales of reluctant heroes. He didn't want to be there, had even argued with Carroll about sending him,[2] and every passing landmark had the potential to mock him, as if placed there intentionally to remind him of how hard his tasks truly were. On Bedloe's Island in the harbor, close to the lighthouse, amidst the grass, clams, rabbits, and shacks, laborers toiled to build a granite defensive fort in the shape of an eleven-point star, with mountings for twenty-four guns*—a sign of American fears that the Napoleonic Wars would spread from Europe. The poverty and unemployment that ravished his new parish would have been evident everywhere.

---

* There is no way Kohlmann could have known it then, but decades after his death, the fort would become the base of the Statue of Liberty, an icon whose symbolic significance would, because of cases like Kohlmann's, mean so much more to the millions of immigrants who cast their eyes upon it for the first time when they sailed into New York Harbor from their troubled homelands.

Foremost, Kohlmann would have been aware of the tension between the majority nativist Protestants and the minority, mostly immigrant, Catholics. As he navigated his way from the docks to St. Peter's, the only Catholic church in the city, it would have lingered in the air like a toxic, unseen gas waiting to ignite.

Fewer than two years before, on Christmas Eve, many Catholics in the city had gathered at St. Peter's, on the corner of Barclay and Church Streets, to celebrate midnight mass. Although the Catholics had enjoyed relative peace to that point, they knew they were still outsiders. In their homelands, midnight mass had been cause for elaborate public processions and celebrations. Not in New York City. The Catholics kept their ceremonies quiet, within the walls of their church, for fear that "the novelty, by attracting crowds at an untimely hour of the night, might terminate in broils and riots."[3] Their hesitancy would prove well-founded. As the number of Catholic immigrants streaming into the city had swelled in recent years, so too had nativist Protestant fears. Their worry: that Catholics would be more loyal to the pope than to the United States, eventually resulting in an overthrow of the fledgling republic.

While the Catholics celebrated mass inside, a gang of nativists, calling themselves Highbinders, gathered in the street, hoping to see some of the Catholic rituals for themselves and to taunt the churchgoers at the first opportunity.[4] They were a motley crew of dock workers, apprentices, and sailors, drunk and feeling brutish, perhaps from a night of celebrating the holiday. When they realized the parishioners didn't intend to hold any ceremonies outside, they pounded on St. Peter's doors, demanding to see the service. The group of protestors swelled to more than fifty people. The parishioners inside heard the demands, the angered shouts. Many were unsure how to respond. Others were no doubt fearful. Someone had the wherewithal to send for Andrew Morris, a new alderman and the first Catholic ever to be elected to public office in New York City. Morris arrived before the mob turned violent and convinced them to disperse without incident.

In the wee hours of the morning, many of the parishioners feared the Highbinders would return, so they took a defensive posture. Arming themselves, they surrounded St. Peter's, determined to protect their only building. With guns, knives, whatever other weapons they could find in hand, they waited, their panting breath hanging in the air like signal smoke. It's hard to say if the Catholics' actions provoked the Highbinders to return or if the parishioners had simply anticipated what the gang would inevitably do, but return they did. There were no politicians this time. Shouting led to fighting, which led to an all-out brawl. Soon, Irish Catholics and Highbinders were rioting in the streets, "from the door of the church to Irish town," a distance of nearly seven Manhattan blocks.[5] In the melee, at least one of the Catholics is alleged to have stabbed to death a member of the city watch named Christopher Newfanger.

The Highbinders responded with equal fury, and the fighting lasted into the night.

Other rabble-rousers heard the commotion. A group of six or seven men streamed from a nearby tavern, where they had been dancing.[6] They stumbled to the church to spy the "Irish and the sailors . . . engaged in deadly conflict."[7] Upon learning of the murdered watchman, they plunged into the fray as well, attacking the Catholics. They and other rioters erupted through the city streets. On Augustus Street, just northeast of Bridewell Prison, nativists bashed in the windows of an Irishman's grocery store, charged into the building, and smashed his liquors. The men from the tavern ended up in Irish Town, which was in the Sixth Ward, on the then-edge of the city. It was where the poorest Irish immigrants lived. The group barged into an Irish grogshop like teenagers looking for a fight and demanded a half pint of rum from the barkeep and owner.[8]

"Clear out," he ordered, calling them a "set of rascals."[9]

They pounced, beating and waling on him. Two other men tried to defend the helpless barkeep, but the Highbinders lunged at them as well, faces red, fists flying. They pummeled and defeated any and all challengers.

The barkeep's wife fled to the cellar.

The ruffians locked the cellar door on her, preventing her escape, then took control of the shop. The other Irishmen bolted from the pub into the riotous streets and chilly Christmas air. The thugs were now alone with the drinks. They took advantage. One of them, William Otter, recalled, "We drank as much as we pleased" while the barkeep's wife no doubt trembled in the frigid and dark air below, her husband unconscious on the floor above her. The mob outside eventually spilled into the conquered shop and joined in the reverie. Drunk, victorious, high on the adrenaline of the fight, the Highbinders began to smash bottles, glasses, and pitchers. They bashed in barrels and destroyed "all and everything they could find in the shop."[10] The barkeep and his wife were left with nothing.

When the drink was gone and there was nothing left to damage, they charged back into the streets as if the taste of blood and alcohol fueled a desire for more. In Otter's words, they fought through the night, "laying all Irishtown waste; a great deal of property was destroyed by the mob, and a great deal of human blood shed."[11] The fighting stopped only when Mayor Dewitt Clinton, backed by a sizeable contingent of the city watch, arrived on the scene and ended the chaos. Clinton witnessed firsthand how easily religious persecution, when allowed, could ignite. That witness would prove crucial in the case against Anthony Kohlmann.

For Kohlmann, standing before St. Peter's on the first day of his New York ministry, perhaps unaware of Mayor Clinton at all, the riots were simply a reminder of one more pit-infested labyrinth he would need to navigate. He no doubt was grateful he hadn't come alone. By his side was his traveling companion Benedict Fenwick, a fellow priest and novitiate with the Jesuits. Also with him were four scholars and faculty from Georgetown. They carried a decent number of books from that college's library.

Still, signals of even more challenges continued to spring up at seemingly every turn, taunting reminders of why Kohlmann had not wanted to be there in the first place. The nativist prejudice and bloody Protestant-Catholic history that hounded the Catholics were flaming, daunting demons to be sure, but they were external, even dormant at times. What caused far more damage were the acts of clergy who awoke them. In the years prior to Kohlmann's arrival, the priests of St. Peter's had engaged in open and public battles both with themselves and with church hierarchy, at one point even temporarily banning Bishop Carroll from entering the church.[12] That had been problematic enough. Now something far worse had happened. Distant rumors and accusations had been swirling for years that the priests of St. Peter's had engaged in sexual misconduct, fanning the nativists' worst fears and mistrust about Catholics. From Baltimore, Bishop Carroll had learned the rumors were true.

He had demanded Kohlmann go and try to clean up the parish.

For Kohlmann, his first day in the city made one thing abundantly clear: on fledgling New York's stage of strife, the Catholic Church's survival was an open question. In a city of roughly one hundred thousand people, fourteen thousand were Catholics, but they were a disjointed group, fresh off the boat, mostly poor and out of work, mainly "Irish, some hundreds of French, and as many Germans."[13] They had been described as a public nuisance and relegated to the city slums. Immediately after his arrival, Kohlmann wrote to a mentor, "The scandals given in this congregation . . . by the clergymen, have brought it very near its ruin."[14] "The parish was so neglected in every respect, that it goes beyond all conception."[15] Despite his hesitancy, he and Fenwick set to work.

———

Kohlmann's visionary nature didn't abandon him. He soon saw each boulder in his path not an obstacle but as a step to climb to a greater height. Over time, he came to treat them as God-given opportunities. The Jesuits had no presence in New York yet—and within weeks, Kohlmann shook off the rust of reluctance and came to believe he had been sent to "diffuse the good odor"[16] of their society and to build their reputation by healing the ills of the congregation and serving its citizens. "May we be so happy as to produce these desirable effects upon the public mind!" he wrote at the time.[17]

Kohlmann learned that even the most neglected vineyard has potential if nurtured properly. His bore fruit. By the time the new year turned, he had raised more than $3,000 to help the poor, a staggering figure since so many in his congregation were, in fact, poor.[18] People lined up for confessional. Sunday masses exceeded capacity. By June 1809, he had lain the cornerstone for a new church on the outskirts of town amidst the woodlands, meadows, and foxes.[19] He had started an academy, the New York Literary Institution, which grew quickly and which he anticipated would one day overshadow Georgetown and "rivalize any college in this country."[20] With all the successes, Kohlmann rejoiced in his letters, and Carroll praised him, writing, "Incalculable good is done there"[21] and "It is hard to imagine the improvement which occurred in the Church of New York, ever since Father Kohlmann has been its Vicar-General."[22]

NOTES

1. Anthony Kohlmann, Letter to Rev. Strickland, September 14, 1810, in *Historical Records and Studies, vol. 1* (New York: United States Catholic Historical Society, 1900), 72.
2. Robert A Maryks and Jonathan Wright, eds., *Jesuit Survival and Restoration: A Global History, 1773–1900* (Leiden, the Netherlands, Koninklijke Brill, 2015), 379–80.
3. Jason K. Duncan, *Citizens or Papists?: The Politics of Anti-Catholicism in New York, 1685–1821* (New York: Fordham University Press, 2005), 133.
4. Ibid.
5. Ibid., 134.
6. William Otter, *History of My Own Times, or, The Life and Adventures of William Otter, Sen* (Emmitsburg, MD, 1835), 82.
7. Ibid.
8. Ibid., 82–83.
9. Ibid., 83.
10. Ibid.
11. Ibid.

12. Maryks and Wright, *Jesuit Survival and Restoration*, 379.
13. Anthony Kohlmann, Letter to Rev. Strickland, November 7, 1808, in *Historical Records and Studies, vol. 1* (New York: United States Catholic Historical Society, 1900), 70.
14. Ibid., 71.
15. Kohlmann, Letter to Strickland, November 1808. Quoted in J. Wilford Parsons, "Rev. Anthonthy Kohlmann, S.J. (1771–1824)," *The Catholic Historical Review* 4, no. 1 (April 1918): 42.
16. Kohlmann, Letter to Rev. Strickland, November 7, 1808, *Historical Records and Studies, vol. 1*, 71.
17. Ibid.
18. J. Wilford Parsons, "Rev. Anthony Kohlmann, S.J. (1771–1824)," *The Catholic Historical Review* 4, no. 1 (April 1918): 43.
19. This church is located at the corner of Prince and Mott Streets, just east of the SoHo neighborhood in Lower Manhattan, and is now known as the Basilica of St. Patrick's Old Cathedral.
20. Letter to Rev. Strickland, September 14, 1810, *Historical Records and Studies, vol. 1*, 73.
21. In Parsons, "Rev. Anthony Kohlmann, S.J. (1771–1824)," 43.
22. John Carroll Letter to John Peemans, January 8, 1813, *The John Carroll Papers*, vol. III (1807–1815) (Notre Dame: University of Notre Dame Press, 1976), 211.

Chapter 4

"INSTANTANEOUS DEATH"

K ohlmann's biggest challenge yet began with the summons—
scrawled on an unassuming slip of paper—to stand before the
justices of the police. In January 1813, that single paper became the amalgam of all his other problems rolled into one: thievery
among his parishioners, as the poorer stole from the less poor; the economic hardships of the Embargo Act replaced with depression from
the War of 1812; nativists who still looked at Catholics as if they were
a foreign enemy and a threat to the American way of life; Protestants
who didn't understand holy Catholic sacraments and who, even worse,
viewed them with suspicion, even claiming they were of the devil.[1]
That little slip of paper was going to bring all of it to the surface.

For the next few weeks, after his initial refusal to give the police
any information, Kohlmann continued in his duties, perhaps hoping
that the police would simply leave him alone. During the weekdays, he
tended to the poor, both spiritual and temporal. On Saturdays, he traveled the road to the Literary Institution, where he visited with board-
ers, heard confession from students, and oversaw the school. He and
Fenwick tried to balance their respective duties. At one point, Fenwick
had been out at the school full-time while Kohlmann managed the affairs of the parish, but Kohlmann acknowledged that trying to "attend
about fourteen thousand souls is too heavy a work for one man."[2] Still,
he labored on.

The police continued their investigation, hunting for the thief, their eyes never far from Kohlmann, the one man with all the answers locked away in his own mental vault. The evidence they uncovered without him was mounting, pieces of a puzzle that gave them parts of a picture, but they needed the priest to bring it all together. He refused to participate. Their frustration must have been excruciating. By the end of February, the officers finally had enough to involve a grand jury.

Grand juries in 1812 were groups of citizens called on to engage in impressive inquests, to dig as deep as possible into any and all facts without being hindered by rules of evidence, court procedure, privilege, or anything else that might prevent them from determining whether someone should be indicted for a crime. On the surface, they were to stand as bulwarks between the people and the prosecutors and police. If a prosecutor was eager to bring a case for political or other reasons, he had to convince a grand jury there was enough evidence to justify it. Oftentimes, not surprisingly, they were the targets of politicians and officials alike who would regale them about the importance of various laws in an effort to convince them to either indict someone or let them go free. To do their job, the jurors needed total access to the facts. They demanded, and received, what they wanted from prosecutors and law enforcement. When they called for documents, they received them. When they subpoenaed witnesses, they came. And they required witnesses to speak freely without fear of reprisal. Perhaps the most significant power they possessed was the ability to compel people to testify, under the long-standing and highly respected notion that it was the duty of all citizens to disclose all their knowledge in legal proceedings on matters connected with the public good.

If someone refused to testify for fear of incriminating themselves, the grand jury had the power to grant them immunity so they could go after a bigger fish. Those who refused to cooperate or to testify when asked faced severe reprisals, including indefinite prison time and a contempt-of-court ruling. If citizens' minds were dark, mysterious caves, the grand jury was the legally authorized spotlight.

They subpoenaed Kohlmann. If he thought he had escaped scrutiny, the grand jury subpoena put any such notion to rest. Once again, we have no evidence that he hesitated to stand before them. He respected the process and the role of the grand jury, even the requirement that ordinary citizens provide everything they knew. But he would not be intimidated.

Kohlmann appeared before them.

They, like the police, demanded that he give up the name of the thief.

From the moment he rose, Kohlmann was Kohlmann. The grand jury couldn't get even a morsel from him for the same reasons he had given the police.

We don't know the precise makeup of the grand jury, but it was likely fifteen or twenty men, mostly, if not all, Protestant. They either didn't respect Kohlmann's position or they hoped he would abandon it. Otherwise, they wouldn't have summoned him in the first place. His view was already clear.

They had reason to be exasperated. They had pieced together enough evidence, clue by clue, to craft a credible story of what had happened: two men, Charles Bradley and Benjamin Brinkerhoff, had broken into Keating's shop and stolen his jewelry. Both were black. They had then sold the jewelry to Daniel and Mary Phillips. But suspicions weren't enough. The evidence was circumstantial at best. Some witnesses could provide a few details, perhaps place certain people in the right places at the right time, but to get a conviction, prosecutors would need more. They needed the confession given to Father Kohlmann. The grand jury demanded it. Who had come to him? Who had given him the stolen jewelry?

He politely declined to answer.

Despite their frustrations, they did not yet move to hold him in contempt or to force jail upon him for his refusal. They still had other options. He left them that day with a victory—he had stood his ground, and they had respected him enough not to throw him in prison, but the success was fleeting.

On March 3, 1813, the grand jury approved two indictments, one against Bradley and Brinkerhoff for theft and one against Daniel and Mary Phillips for receiving stolen goods. All four pleaded not guilty, which meant the case would go to trial. The court combined all four cases into one and scheduled it for just two days later. Based on what the grand jury had found, the district attorney wrote the names of all witnesses on the back of the indictments. Despite Kohlmann's repeated insistence that he would not testify, his name was on the list, which meant he had no choice but to appear in court. It seems that either the district attorney or the judge believed he could get the priest to give up the thief.

On Friday, March 5, 1813, Kohlmann ascended the steps of city hall. Inside the doors, a grand staircase led to the second floor and to the Court of General Sessions. It was stately enough to intimidate even the most seasoned orator. Crimson draperies with gold edges framed the windows, and the ornately carved alcove ceiling portrayed a dark-blue sky penetrated by golden rays of sunshine and clouds. The rosewood-like judge's bench loomed above the rest of the room, flanked by white ionic columns and backed by striking red curtains.

The galley was packed. In that day, court cases were not just about the individuals involved—they were a form of entertainment. Newspapers covered them like sporting events. People appeared who were interested in the outcome of the case, but others came simply for the spectacle, to witness the arguments, the passionate oration, the drama of thefts and murders and intrigue, the probability of someone being sentenced to Bridewell. For the Keating jewelry case, the room was especially electric. Several Protestant ministers had caught wind of both the trial and of Kohlmann's refusal to testify. They were incensed. They had come to put pressure on both him and the judge and had already been maneuvering behind the scenes to ensure the Catholic priest not be allowed to shirk his civic duties. Other lawyers filled the room as well.

The judge that day was Pierre C. Van Wyck, who was sitting in for Mayor Dewitt Clinton while he attended to his duties in the state capital of Albany.[3] Twelve men filled the jury box. An attorney named George Wilson represented the four defendants. As far as we know, Kohlmann sat in the back of the room with no lawyer to represent him—at the time, Catholic lawyers were not admitted to the bar.[4] Richard Riker was the district attorney. He was an intelligent man, balding, with a large beaked nose, thin lips, and oversized ears. A regular player in New York's political arena for most of his professional career, he appeared to be well-connected in the city. His gaze portrayed both kindness and duplicity.

It's hard to guess what thoughts frolicked in the various participants' minds as the trial got underway. Kohlmann no doubt knew he would be called to the stand, and we can only guess at what anxiety he felt as he watched the judge ease into the bench, his authoritative robes a potentially ominous black.

The defendants—a married white couple and two black men— must have known that their freedom depended on Kohlmann's ability to honor the seal of the confessional. Would he reveal what he'd been told? Would the threat of prison or worse compel him to back off the stance he had taken? Would he be willing, for the sake of his religious beliefs, to endure prison and punishment in their place? These residents of Irish Town may have seemed like an odd group. But the name "Irish Town" was actually only partly accurate. Every rejected group in the city had been thrust into those slums. Free blacks settled into the Sixth Ward alongside the low-income Irish, Germans, and Jews. Over time, the neighborhoods saw the African Free School and black churches rise up alongside the Irish grocers and tenements. The economics and bigotry of the day connected them, but their predicaments couldn't have been more different. For the Phillipses, if Kohlmann broke his vows of secrecy, the penalty may have been prison, a fine, even lashings; severe to be sure, but for Bradley and Brinkerhoff, those punishments were just the beginning.

Antebellum New York City was notorious for kidnapping and selling free black men, women, and children to the South as slaves. Oftentimes, the children would simply disappear, tragically vanishing from the streets just as they have from history, their parents left searching through despair for ghosts. Black men often lost their freedom through much more devious tactics: prosecutors, judges, magistrates, and police stripped their rights from them through sham court hearings where the judge would rule against them as to some criminal charge and then declare they were no longer free, placing them into the hands of unscrupulous underground slave traders, proof that the underground railroad was a heartbreaking two-way track. In fact, it was rumored that the prosecutor, Richard Riker, was part of the group who engaged in such tactics. Whether Van Wyck did is an open question, but it is no doubt one that haunted the minds of Bradley and Brinkerhoff.

———

Once the jury, the judge, the witnesses, and the audience were settled and the preliminaries resolved, Riker, his domed cranium reflecting the light in the room, called Kohlmann to the stand. He was sworn in and agreed to tell the truth.

Riker immediately began asking him about the jewelry, the theft, and how he had received the stolen goods.

Kohlmann did not give any answers. Turning to the judge, he instead pleaded that he be allowed to leave without testifying. "Were I summoned to give evidence as a private individual," he said, "I should not for a moment hesitate. . . . But if called upon to testify in quality of a minister of a sacrament, in which my God himself has enjoined on me a perpetual and inviolable secrecy, I must declare to this honorable Court, that I cannot . . . and that it would be my duty to prefer instantaneous death or any temporal misfortune, rather than disclose the name of the penitent in question."[5]

With everyone in the room watching, he continued, "For, were I to act otherwise, I should become a traitor to my church, to my sacred ministry and to my God. In fine, I should render myself guilty of eternal damnation."[6] Kohlmann provided a deeper doctrinal explanation for the sacrament of confession, but he lacked any legal basis for why he should be allowed to avoid a duty that applied to almost everyone else. More importantly, he didn't have a lawyer to make the argument for him. His was an argument of conviction, and while those can be persuasive on an emotional level, they rarely give a judge a legal foundation for ruling in someone's favor.

Before the judge could respond or even give his thoughts, Wilson, the lawyer for the defendants, stood and objected on behalf of his clients as well. To do otherwise would have been nothing short of legal malpractice. Kohlman's religious convictions had given him an escape route. This was Wilson's best and most powerful opportunity to keep the key damning evidence against his clients from coming in. Still, if he provided the judge any legal basis for ruling in Kohlmann's favor, we have no record of it.

When Wilson finished, all eyes turned to the judge, who wielded the contempt power like a king of old. It was the universal law of the land that individuals participating in court proceedings were bound to obey the court, its orders, and processes.[7] First and foremost, this meant telling the truth when called to do so. Those who didn't could be held in contempt simply at the whim of the judge. The punishment: a fine, prison, or both. Theoretically, the judge could probably have made the consequences even worse if he were so inclined, but the bottom line was that he had the unchecked authority to push Kohlmann into the impossible space between a cold, dark prison cell and an eternally scorching flame, with no other avenue of escape.

The time had come. Van Wyck appeared to hesitate. This was a new and novel question, one that had never been addressed in

American courts.[8] He had little legal argument to follow beyond the default rule that everyone must testify. Bradley and Brinkerhoff looked on, the Phillipses as well. Of everyone in the room, Kohlmann appears to have been the most at peace. The specter of Bridewell loomed over him like a hooded figure, but he didn't cower or run from it. If that was where his faith led him, just as it had into the plague-infested homes of Austria or to the fever-induced moans of broken soldiers in Italy, so be it. Everything he had been building in New York would likely begin to crumble, he had to know, but he had already determined his course, and, as one modern-day jurist has noted, "the decided are always gentle."[9] It would be inaccurate to suggest he didn't feel anxiety. He and others had been writing about the case, expressing their whispered concerns, but his unease was the same felt by anyone soaring through the air after taking a leap of faith: nervous or not, he had already made an irrevocable choice.

As the judge was preparing to issue his decision, something occurred that was as unlikely as it was unexpected. Ordinarily, the only participants in a courtroom proceeding are the lawyers, the witnesses, the judge, and possibly a jury. Those in the galley remain silent. But this time, before the judge could issue an order, a man sprung from the crowded benches. In a thick Irish accent, he introduced himself as William Sampson and asked to address the court. All eyes turned to him. His general air of confidence suggested he was comfortable in the courtroom. He was mature, nearly fifty, and his skin and the bags under his eyes revealed a life of wear. The curls on his head bore an uncanny resemblance to vines in a thicket creeping over one another for light and freedom. His left eye was lazy, but his high cheekbones, strong nose, and disarming smile made it easy not to notice.

The judge, perhaps grateful for the temporary reprieve, granted the newcomer an opportunity to speak.

Sampson declared himself an *amicus curiae*, a legal term meaning "friend of the court." It was common then, and remains so today, for parties not officially in a lawsuit to bring briefs and arguments to help sway a court in one legal direction or another. They call themselves "friends of the court" because, at least on the surface, their role is to help inform judges of key philosophical, scientific, or sociological considerations before they make difficult, precedent-setting decisions. If Kohlmann knew who the man was, it was not through church. He was not a Catholic. In early-nineteenth-century New York, the odds meant that he was an engaged Protestant or someone who pretended to be. Most likely, neither Kohlmann nor any of the defendants had ever seen Sampson before. He was clearly a lawyer, given his demeanor and familiarity with the process, but beyond that, it would have been impossible to know who he was, why he was there, or what his intentions were.

With a rapt courtroom looking on, Sampson explained to the judge that in all of his travels, in every country he had visited, whether Protestant or Catholic, even in his native Ireland, where the Catholic religion was legally barred, he had never heard of a time where a priest was forced "to reveal the solemn and inviolable secrecy of sacramental confession."[10] This was an important question, he argued, and it deserved "deliberate argument."[11] Perhaps to Kohlmann's shock and relief, the stranger asked if he could argue the question on behalf of the priest. He requested that Van Wyck postpone ruling until the attorneys could return with prepared arguments. The case was "novel and without precedent," and it deserved more than an impromptu ruling.[12]

Riker, for reasons unknown, did not object. Van Wyck also didn't hesitate. He postponed the trial, let the jury go, then announced that the court would hear argument the following Monday, after the weekend. As the courtroom cleared, Sampson and Kohlmann would have seen each other through the dispersing audience. They stood on different rims of a vast religious canyon. Kohlmann was the lone representative of the despised Catholics; Sampson was a Protestant thriving in New York. But they were both blessed with the uncanny vision and ability to build bridges where others saw only impassible expanses. Kohlmann had needed legal help that simply didn't exist among his own congregants. Sampson, this stranger from Ireland, had stepped into that crowded courtroom like Moses wandering in from the desert to demand that Pharaoh let his people go. How he arrived there, in that moment, is a story almost as epic as the biblical shepherd happening upon a burning bush.

NOTES

1. Paul A. Gilje, *The Road to Mobocracy: Popular Disorder in New York City, 1763–1834* (Chapel Hill: University of North Carolina Press, 1987), 128–29.
2. Anthony Kohlmann, Letter to Rev. Strickland, September 14, 1810, in *Historical Records and Studies, vol. 1* (New York: United States Catholic Historical Society, 1900), 73–74.
3. William Sampson, *The Catholic Question in America: Whether a Roman Catholic Clergyman Be in Any Case Compellable to Disclose the Secrets of Auricular Confession* (New York, 1813), 6.
4. The Catholic Bar of New York, in *Historical Records and Studies,* vol. 5 (New York: United States Catholic Historical Society, 1909), 416–17.
5. In Sampson, *The Catholic Question in America,* 8–9.
6. Ibid., 9.
7. Ronald Goldfarb, "The History of the Contempt Power," *Washington University Law Quarterly* 1961, no. 1 (February 1961):14.
8. Sampson, *The Catholic Question in America,* 7.
9. In Lance B. Wickman, "In Search of Atticus Finch," *Clark Memorandum* 2, no. 22 (December 2009), 180.
10. Sampson, *The Catholic Question in America,* 7.
11. Ibid.
12. Ibid.

Chapter 5

FROM THE DUNGEONS
OF THE INQUISITION

Life was burying William Sampson with the indifferent repetitiveness of a grave digger. Roughly fifteen years before he sprung to his feet in that New York courtroom, armed guards had escorted him through "dirty streets"[1] to the entrance of a foreboding castle in Lisbon, Portugal. It had been three years since he'd been exiled from his homeland of Ireland. During that time, he had been separated from his wife and children, imprisoned, tried multiple times in England, banished to Portugal, and shipwrecked on the way. Each time he had escaped with his life, and through each experience, he had reason to believe he would one day be free. But on that day in Lisbon, as he approached the looming castle, he noticed pale, blinking faces eyeing him through iron bars on the windows. Prisoners. He appeared to be out of chances.

The irony of his situation was not lost on him. In 1764, Sampson had been born in Londonderry, Ireland, into what was known as the Protestant Ascendancy, the powerful minority who dominated Ireland between the seventeenth and early twentieth centuries. In essence, he had been a prince. The Protestant Ascendancy comprised landowners and members of the Church of Ireland and the Church of England. They controlled nearly every facet of Irish life. Sampson's family belonged. Roman Catholics, Jews, poorer Protestants, and other minority races and religions did not. He had married within the Ascendancy, had trained to be a lawyer knowing he could thrive among the ruling class in Ireland, and had hiked far up the trail to a life of luxury.

Although that prize had been dangled before him, his gaze had never lingered on it long. With every step down that road, he had paused to take in the suffering masses discarded by society on the side of the path. He longed to help them. When nearly seven hundred families had been forced from their homes, without clothes or food in the dead of winter simply for being Roman Catholic, Sampson took up their case.[2] When soldiers burst their way into the home of a printer who had published articles challenging the Ascendency, Sampson rushed in to stop them, a lone figure before all the sheriff's men.[3] He wrote articles defending the Catholics. And when large groups of men were arrested for treason because they tried to overthrow their oppressors, he represented them in court. Like a plant drawn to the sun, Sampson was drawn to those classes of people who could not represent themselves. It was the one compulsion that would define his life. For helping people opposed to their oppressors, he'd been charged with treason. He had given up everything to which his birthright entitled him.

After his banishment to Portugal and a series of sham trials, various Portuguese authorities had encouraged him to travel to Lisbon under armed guard to meet with the English ambassador and Portugal's foreign minister with the promise that they would set him free or allow him to return to England. He had agreed to the trip, thinking he could believe what he'd been told. After all, he wrote years later, "I had committed no murders nor treasons. I had burned no houses, nor tortured no free men. . . . I had legally and loyally defended the acknowledged rights of my countrymen."[4] Now, staring at the faces behind the barred windows of that castle, his sarcasm, as it often did, bubbled inside him to an uncontainable froth, and he asked, "Is this the minister's hotel?"

The guards said no, that the foreign minister was busy but that Sampson would "lodge in a fine apartment, built for kings and queens."[5]

Sampson was not stupid. The building loomed over him, its giant maw ready to swallow him whole. He asked if he was going to jail.

"This is not a jail, but a castle," his escort said, adding that a minister would come to see him in the morning.[6]

As they trudged into the great entrance hall of the Portuguese prison, the trickery of his guards was now evident; no one else knew where he was. Sampson was led to an old man sitting at a table. The man moved with the intentional sluggishness of someone who enjoyed making people wait. He slipped spectacles over his nose and then opened a large tome. He asked Sampson for his name and his country, among other questions.

Sampson asked if the old man knew anything of the English ambassador or the foreign minister coming to see him.

The man did not.

Did he know who Sampson was?

He did not.

"Why then do you detain me in prison, without knowing who I am?"[7]

The old man did not answer. He arose and searched Sampson, taking anything metal or glass. The escorts left shortly after, and Sampson was now alone with the old man and the prison guards in the vast emptiness of the ancient hall. It was apparent to him that this may well be the last time he glimpsed the light of day. He thought quickly and refused to budge. Instead, he asked for an interpreter to come so he could speak with the old man a bit more in-depth. Sampson's Portuguese was almost nonexistent, and the old man clearly spoke only stilted English.

"What language?" the old man asked.

"English or French," Sampson said.

Sampson waited while the old man summoned a French prisoner of war from the bowels of the castle.

While delaying, Sampson surreptitiously tested the guards and learned that none of them spoke French. When the Frenchman arrived, Sampson, while pretending to ask important questions of the jailer, asked the prisoner to watch where they took him because he had been the victim of a horrible deceit and suspected "foul play."[8] He wanted at least one witness who could tell the world where he was.

The Frenchman agreed, and the guards led Sampson out of the room. They took him down a long, filthy passage that stunk with the heavy air of human filth and ran deeper and deeper to a dungeon. Sampson had the ominous sense that the stench was a pungent symptom of what was coming. He was right. They reached a wooden door, which moaned open to reveal a dark cell sealed by a heavy iron gate resembling a cage for a "wild beast."[9] In its bars, there was a slat for thrusting a plate of food in and out. The guards scraped open the gate.

Ordered to enter the chamber beyond, Sampson obeyed. The floor was damp, and the room seemed to swallow all light, just as it would all hope from those locked there. In the peak of the arched ceiling, a square hole offered Sampson some hope that a lick of sunlight or breath of fresh air might penetrate into the gloom every once in a while, just to give him a sense of the outside world, but as he inspected the square more closely, he realized someone had built a wall over the opening.

The guards clanked shut the gate and the wood door. Standing there in the musty, dark chamber, Sampson heard only "the roaring noise of prisoners; the clinking of chains, and the ringing of bars."[10] It would have been easy to abandon hope. No one knew where he was, not his wife or his government. The Portuguese called their dungeons *Inferno*, a reference to Dante's concentric circles of tormenting hell.[11] The name was apt. Sampson's understanding of the Portuguese judicial system was this: that they would thrust people accused of almost any crime into *inferno* until they confessed, whether they were guilty or not. Those who wouldn't break under the constant pressure of rats, bugs, gloom, and moaning men faced an eternity in those dungeons until every ounce of humanity had been leeched from them, drip by lonely drip. Freedom came only when they lost their minds. If they finally did confess, they were shackled with irons and sold as slaves to labor in the plantations of America or Goa, India.[12] When Sampson pointed out to one of the guards that their system would result in innocent people confessing to crimes they hadn't committed, the guard said only, "*Logo confesse.*" They soon confess.[13]

The chamber was not entirely barren. The turnkeys provided Sampson a wooden chair and a small table, along with a thin straw mattress he could place on the stones when he tried to sleep. That first night, he ate dinner—a piece of bread and some butter smeared on a cabbage leaf—under the suspicious gaze of four or five guards. When they finally left him alone, he had nothing to do but inspect the cell and listen to the symphony of other damned prisoners.

He scuttled back into the darkness of his cell, wondering if he would ever again see the light of day. His thoughts lingered on his wife and on what had led him to this moment. He couldn't know it, but some 1,300 miles away, Anthony Kohlmann was ministering to the injured and fevered soldiers in the military hospitals of Pavia, Italy.

———

For the next few years, Sampson would repeat this same mournful dance again and again. His captors would move him from cell to cell, from prison to prison, with few explanations and near silence from his government. Any trials that were held turned into nothing more than kangaroo courts. Sometimes he was locked in chambers with a window and even with other prisoners. Other times, guards would thrust him into dark holes as small as a coach's cabin, with commodes that oozed feces and urine, the surrounding walls smeared with the filth. In at least one of these, the only slit for light and air was a cavity carved into the stone that was so small even a "cat could not creep" through it.[14] A bar blocked its outer end. During the day, it cast a square of light on the wall opposite no larger than a hand, but the rest of the chamber remained in utter blackness. There was no furniture. At night, Sampson and another prisoner struggled to breathe the suffocating air. Bugs and vermin slithered and slunk about them as they tried to sleep on the frigid floor.

It's hard to know why some people's spirits endure in such conditions, while others break. It may have something to do with faith or with having a purpose greater than one's self. Regardless, for some prisoners, the brutal treatment and isolation led to forbidden paths. At one point, when Sampson was in a larger cell that housed four men, one of his cellmates snatched a knife the prisoners had concealed from the guards, locked himself away from the other men, and tried to slit his own neck. Sampson and the others had to slam their bodies into the door, forcing it open, to stop him. The knife was so blunt, he had managed to make only "a long but superficial cut in his neck."[15] For other men, however, no amount of degradation breaks their spirits. One prisoner endured the same treatment as Sampson and had earlier been shot and brutally whipped, leaving his back and shoulders lacerated and mangled.[16] Yet he endured and was even one of the men who helped Sampson prevent the suicide.

As for Sampson, he found triumph in at least two places. The first was inside the fertile fields of his own mind. "I can assure you, with truth," he later wrote, "that often, during my long exile, retiring within myself, in the gloom of solitude, or in the silence of the night, I have passed some of the most delicious moments of my existence."[17] When possible, he would find ways to frolic there, where his guards and the filth on the walls could not touch him. On the rare occasion someone would slip him a pen and paper, he would write to the English ambassador, to his wife, or to anyone else who would listen, and others would help smuggle his letters out of the prisons.[18] He drew pictures, sometimes even of his guards.[19] He played music when possible.[20] In at least one cell, he managed to get his hands on a morsel of charcoal.[21] He used it to draw crude images on the walls and even managed to record, as best he could remember, the lines of a then-popular play, hoping the words would both rebuke his enemies and offer some comfort to prisoners who followed him.[22] These were small victories, but they inspired him nonetheless. He found tremendous comfort in his "unsullied consciousness," calling it a "strong . . . shield against misfortune."[23]

The second was his wife. Perhaps it was his worry for her, more than anything else, that pushed him through those long, dark years. Consumed by what might happen to her, he dwelled less on his own troubles. He knew she had been trying to find him, and he had heard stories of other prisoners' wives sailing into the Portuguese ports only to be immediately imprisoned and accused of the same charges as their husbands. The authorities had secretly imprisoned one British woman until she coughed and spit up blood.[24] They then shipped her to the coast of northern Africa, perhaps as a slave. "What then might be the treatment reserved for my wife, should she arrive?" Sampson wondered as he wasted away lying in his cells. "Such was the consideration which occupied my mind, leaving me otherwise insensible to all the little tricks and vexations I was exposed to."[25]

As Sampson's imprisonment and exile stretched on, his jailers' reasons for detaining him dwindled. Through secret letters and even bribes, he managed to keep just enough contact with the outside world that the jailers couldn't risk simply locking him away and tossing out the key. Eventually, they released him to Hamburg and then France, where he continued to live under guard but where he had considerably more freedom. To see his wife and children, he snuck back into England and reconnected with them briefly only to be captured and exiled again. This time, the English authorities allowed him to choose where he would go, as long as it wasn't England. His options were poor. Every country in Europe was either at war with England or would treat him no better than the Portuguese had or, possibly, far worse. Finally, he decided on the United States, where he was hopeful his wife and children could soon follow.

On May 12, 1806, he set sail on the *Windsor Castle*. A fair wind billowed the masts. The weather started out fine, but soon Sampson was vomiting his way across the Atlantic.[26] The relentless waves toyed with his stomach. Then he developed jaundice.[27] Rheumatism followed, leaving him fatigued, his muscles and joints burning, his limbs aching, and his skin plagued by shivers.

When, at long last, land climbed up over the gray monotony of the sea, the captain told Sampson he could not leave the ship. They had arrived at Halifax, Nova Scotia, but the crew had received strict orders not to let Sampson set foot on ground until that ground was out of English control. They forced him to watch from the harbor. Sick and pale, he did exactly that, still a prisoner.

Finally, some days later, the *Windsor Castle* pierced the outer boundary of New York Harbor and carved toward the Hudson River. It was evening. Sampson was forty-three—penniless, friendless, and country-less.[28] He had no reason to feel optimism, but as the sun escaped behind the waving fields and serene open land of New Jersey to the west, he glimpsed Manhattan island, so alive it might as well have been in the middle of a battle. Bonfires blazed.[29] Cannons exploded over the harbor. Songs wafted from taverns. Drunken men caroused and toasted one another. From the lonely rail of his ship bobbing curmudgeonly in the harbor, Sampson witnessed a celebration so grand and rowdy he wondered why the militia hadn't been called to stamp it out: it was July 4, 1806. Independence Day.

———

In time, Sampson would learn that in early nineteenth-century New York, "liberty" applied only to some, that prosperity was a different matter altogether, and that many of the troubles that plagued Europe still festered in his new home. His family eventually joined him, his freedom was restored, and his desire to help the helpless was about to boil anew.

NOTES

1. William Sampson, *Memoirs of William Sampson: Including Particulars of His Adventures in Various Parts of Europe* . . . (New York, 1807), 105.
2. Ibid., 37.
3. Ibid., 1–2.
4. Ibid., 10.
5. Ibid., 105.

6. Ibid.
7. Ibid., 106.
8. Ibid.
9. Ibid.
10. Ibid., 107
11. Ibid., 132.
12. Ibid.
13. Ibid., 133.
14. Ibid., 138.
15. Ibid., 132.
16. Ibid., 11.
17. Ibid., 264.
18. Ibid., 102.
19. Ibid., 265.
20. Ibid., 264.
21. Ibid., 136.
22. Ibid.
23. Ibid., 264.
24. Ibid., 133.
25. Ibid.
26. Ibid., 265.
27. Ibid., 363.
28. Charles Currier Beale, *Williams Sampson: Lawyer and Stenographer* (Boston, 1907), 16.
29. Sampson, *Memoirs of William Sampson,* 363.

Chapter 6

AN UNLIKELY ALLY

I t's unlikely anyone involved with the case could sleep that weekend. Sampson had three days to prepare for a question that, to his
knowledge, no court in the United States had answered. To win,
he would need to build strong legal arguments and gather persuasive
precedents. And quickly. Kohlmann still had to lie down at night with
the most disruptive bedfellow he could imagine: the knowledge that
in three days, he might be sent to prison, perhaps forever. Sampson
would get a respite. Kohlmann would not. For reasons that are unclear, the case was postponed until the June session of the court, which
meant Sampson would have three months to prepare his arguments.
Kohlmann, on the other hand, had to live with the anxiety for just that
much longer.

While the priest and the lawyer hunkered down for the fight, the
world of politics was turning. Van Wyck would no longer be judge on
the case, replaced instead by Mayor DeWitt Clinton, who had returned
from his travels to Albany.[1] Riker, the district attorney, lost his reelection campaign to Barent Gardenier, a Federalist and wild card.[2] The
War of 1812 raged, pumping pressure into New York City—British
ships blockaded the eastern seaboard and crippled the United States
economy, which likely made nativist Protestants even more skeptical
of immigrant Catholics taking up scarce jobs and their priests seeking
exemptions from laws that generally applied to everyone.

As the new trial date charged closer, Gardenier threw a wrench into the process. At some point in early April, he approached Sampson and offered to drop the case.[3] At least on the surface, his reasoning was fair-minded. He announced publicly that the charges against the criminal defendants weren't important enough to force a Catholic priest into such a difficult position.[4] But things are never so simple. The case had attracted attention like chum in shark-infested water. Protestant ministers and various nativists had been lured to it and were pushing for a ruling against the priest, arguing that Kohlmann's position undermined burgeoning American values. At the same time, the number of New York Catholics was swelling, and they had the right to vote. No matter what Gardenier did, he would upset a large number of voters. But if he could avoid the question altogether, he could escape infuriating either key constituency.

Sampson took the offer to Kohlmann and the trustees of St. Peter's, a group of laymen who managed the temporal affairs for the church. They had much to debate. Though it seemed generous, Gardenier's offer didn't truly free them from their predicament; it simply wedged them into a different corner. If they rejected the offer, Kohlmann was still at tremendous risk of going to jail. If they accepted it, Kohlmann would escape this particular case, but a dark thundercloud would still hover over every Catholic in the city, potentially forever. Every confession to a Catholic priest would come with the shadow that a court might later force the priest to testify. That shroud alone would infringe the free practice of confession. Seemingly generous, Gardenier's deal was actually a prosecutorial move that would creep up often in America in the decades to follow. It continues even today. Prosecutors or regulators drop charges with the hope they can make a plaintiff's case moot and avoid a ruling from a judge. The effects are constitutional violations by government actors that are capable of repetition yet always evading judicial review. This did not sit well with the trustees. Their people would be plagued by doubt.

There was also the question of equality. Protestants in New York were able to live their religion as they saw fit, without government infringement. This wasn't surprising and is the same in almost every case involving government interference with religious free exercise: the majority never pass or enforce laws that inhibit their own practices or beliefs. It is almost always minority religions, views, and practices that come under attack. And the trustees wondered, why shouldn't Catholics enjoy the same privileges as the Protestants? They wanted a judge to say they did.

On April 19, 1813, the board of trustees of St. Peter's Church issued a letter to Gardenier. This is what it said:

> Whereas it has been represented to the board of Trustees of St. Peter's Church . . . that the Reverend Dr. Kohlmann . . . has been called as a witness . . . and that thereupon he declared he knew nothing touching the matter enquire of him, but what had been communicated to him in the administration of the sacrament of penance or confession. . . . That the knowledge thus obtained cannot, be revealed to any person in the world, without the greatest impiety, and a violation of the tenets of his religion. That it would be his duty, according to his religious principles, to suffer death, in preference to making the disclosures. . . .
>
> And whereas the Board of Trustees . . . cannot but feel the deepest solicitude that a doubt should exist upon the subject, they therefore, respectfully request the District Attorney to bring the cause to trial . . . to the end that a judicial determination may be had which shall ensure to all catholics [sic], in common with the rest of mankind, and according to the words of the constitution, "the free exercise and enjoyment of their religious profession and worship."
>
> The Trustees hope that the District Attorney, will be pleased to signify to them, at what time he will probably bring the question to a hearing.[5]

The Catholics would rather risk a loss than continue stumbling forward through a haze of uncertainty. They forced Gardenier's hand. He could have dropped the case on his own without their agreement, but he instead pivoted to preparing his arguments in earnest. The trustees knew Sampson couldn't guarantee a victory, and Kohlmann was being offered up as a sacrificial lamb. Maybe he would lose and rot his days in Bridewell or maybe fate would throw some other unforeseen challenge their way. Regardless, they would stand their ground, take the case to trial with hope steaming inside them, and pray that the promise of the Constitution would be fulfilled.

———————

As the preparation continued, Sampson suffered a devastating discovery. At the original trial, he had told the court he was aware of no case, in any country, where a Catholic priest had been forced to testify of something revealed in confession. He was wrong. There were at least two, and they posed significant problems. When the United States was founded, the obvious question arose regarding what the governing law should be. The Constitution was wonderful, but at the time, it applied only to the newly created federal government and to only a minuscule handful of situations mostly dealing with separation of powers and limitations on government overreach. The colonies, now states, had adopted their own constitutions and statutes, but even those didn't address every legal question percolating in society. For the remaining questions, early American courts turned to the "common law": the body of legal decisions made by judges in England prior to the Founding. Common law was based on customs and precedents when no statutes or codes provided legal authority. A key principle of the common law was that prior decisions were binding on future courts unless the most compelling reasons justified overturning them. The principle provided stability and predictability. For Sampson and Kohlmann, it was a gaping pit as wide as the divide between Protestants and Catholics, unless Sampson could find a way out.

———————

Trial was just a few weeks away. The answer for how Sampson and Kohlmann would give the judge the legal basis he needed to rule in their favor remained elusive. Kohlmann fattened and rehearsed his reasons for why he would not testify; but he and Sampson had already seen that his religious arguments would carry them only so far. They needed more. They found an unlikely ally. Were he still district attorney, Richard Riker's duty would have been to argue against Kohlmann. Riker had signed the indictment in the case—his mandate was to get a conviction. But in the time between issuing that indictment and his lost reelection, Riker had examined the files and the law more closely and had "become convinced" that the exemption Kohlmann sought was legal.[6] He even had arguments against the two cases that said otherwise. Had he still been district attorney, he may have felt compelled not to concede the point and continue with his prosecution. Fresh off his lost bid for reelection, however, he was free to join Kohlmann's legal team.[7] He did, and they began finalizing their arguments and strategy, well aware that Gardenier, the Protestant majority's pressure, the current law, and the political climate in the city were all hefty foes.

NOTES

1. William Sampson, *The Catholic Question in America: Whether a Roman Catholic Clergyman Be in Any Case Compellable to Disclose the Secrets of . . .* (New York, 1813), 7.
2. Ibid.
3. Ibid., 42, 54.
4. Ibid., 42.
5. Ibid., 52–54.
6. Ibid., 13.
7. It is highly unlikely Riker would be allowed to do this today. Modern rules of ethics would have no doubt conflicted him out from representing a party opposed to his former client.

Chapter 7

A BASE AND
UNWORTHY WRETCH

On Tuesday, June 8, 1813, Kohlmann entered the crowded courtroom. As before, reporters and lay people alike packed the galley, but this time the feeling was different. Instead of Van Wyck, a panel of four men now lorded over the room: the mayor, DeWitt Clinton; the city recorder, Josiah Ogden Hoffman; and two aldermen, both attorneys. Together, they would make the decision for the court. Gardenier sat at the prosecutor's table rather than Riker, who now sat on the other side of the aisle alongside Sampson and Kohlmann. Months earlier, Kohlmann had stood alone before a judge; he now had a team of attorneys.

A different jury of twelve Protestant men was called and sworn in.

Gardenier immediately called Kohlmann to the stand. He was sworn in, and Gardenier peppered him with questions. The priest then turned to the panel of judges and pleaded for permission to explain why he was refusing to answer.

The panel acquiesced, allowing Kohlmann to explain.

Kohlmann offered the same reasons he had given Van Wyck, but he expanded on them tremendously. If asked to testify regarding knowledge he obtained outside of confession, he said, he would "deem it a duty of conscience to declare whatever knowledge" he might have.[1] In fact, he had testified in another case not too long before, and he reminded the court of that. "[B]ecause," he explained, "my holy religion

47

teaches and commands me to be subject to the higher powers in civil matters, and to respect and obey them."[2]

He reiterated that he would rather die than give up something he had learned in confession, but he was clearly worried. "Lest this open and free declaration of my religious principles should be construed into the slightest disrespect to this honorable Court, I must beg leave again to be indulged in stating . . . the principles on which this line of conduct is founded."[3]

The panel again gave him permission to proceed. With Gardenier watching, his own arguments prepared, Kohlmann sprang into an impressive explanation of the Catholic doctrine of penance. "For it is, and ever was a tenet of the Catholic Church, that Jesus Christ, the divine Founder of Christianity, has instituted seven sacraments, neither more nor less."[4] Penance, with confession as a crucial part, was one of those sacraments. "It is . . . the doctrine of the Catholic Church that the same divine Author of the sacraments has laid the obligation of a perpetual and inviolable secrecy on the minister."[5]

After explaining the importance of that secrecy—that without it, most parishioners would never be willing to share the darkest weaknesses of their lives to draw closer to God—Kohlmann then explained, "If . . . I or any other Roman Catholic Priest . . . should so far forget my sacred ministry and become so abandoned as to reveal either directly or indirectly, any part of what has been entrusted to me in the sacred tribunal of penance . . . I should forever degrade myself in the eye of the Catholic Church, and I hesitate not to say, in the eye of every man of sound principle: the world would justly esteem me as a base and unworthy wretch. . . . I should be . . . replaced in the condition of a Layman . . . I should deserve to be lodged in close confinement, shut up between four walls to do penance during the remainder of my life . . . I should render myself guilty . . . of everlasting punishment in the life to come."[6]

In that packed courtroom, pulsing with midsummer heat, Kohlmann had placed his feelings upon the altar. His only hope: that the court would not find them "trivial and unsatisfactory."[7]

As heartfelt as Kohlmann's pleas were, they didn't hinder Gardenier. Without waiting for comment from the judges, he tried to regain control of the narrative and the stage of the courtroom. He fired a series of leading questions at Kohlmann and asked if the priest had ever actually had the stolen jewelry in his possession.

Mayor Clinton cut off the questioning. It wasn't because he sided with Kohlmann. It was because Gardenier was abusing the process. The law either allowed Kohlmann the exemption or it did not, Clinton explained, and the court "would not permit that privilege to be frittered away . . . by indirect means, which could not be directly enforced."[8]

In that moment, Kohlmann must have felt an overwhelming sense of gratitude, because the weapons he so sorely lacked his last time on the stand were now ready for battle, and Sampson and Mr. Riker were ready "to argue the point."[9]

Recognizing that the fight ahead was a legal battle only and that there would be nothing for the jury to do until after the court decided the Kohlmann question, Clinton dismissed the jury, ordering them to return the following week. This would give him "time not only to hear the argument, but give an advised judgment."[10] The twelve men trudged from the room.

––––––––

With the jury gone, Kohlmann took his seat. His lawyers would have two chances to make their case. They had agreed that Riker would go first. He rose and stood before the four-judge panel. Peering down his beaked nose, he plunged into the strategy he and Sampson had developed long before that moment. He noted the "novelty" and "magnitude of the case," emphasizing that it was the first time the question had ever been addressed by a court in the United States but also that "every enlightened and pious Catholic" believed the case would directly affect the "free toleration of his religion." Putting the burden on the judges to take the argument seriously, he said, "Under these considerations, we respectfully ask of the Court, a patient and a dispassionate hearing; and, we confidently expect to satisfy your Honors, that the law and the constitution are on our side."[11]

Watching this trained orator, a recent enemy, begin his argument with such confidence must have been comforting to Kohlmann. Riker's discourse was tightly organized. He would prove two points, he said, either of which would justify Kohlmann's request not to testify. The first centered on the 38th Article of New York's Constitution, which, Riker argued, fully protected Kohlmann in the exemption, he claimed. The second involved the known principles of common law. Either point, Riker argued, would demonstrate that the priest should win. These were themes Kohlmann never could have discussed on his own. He needed someone trained in the law.

The former district attorney attacked the common law point first.

He conceded out of the gate that the "general rule is, that every person is bound, when called upon in a court of justice, to testify whatever he may know." But, he pointed out, there were already exceptions to this general rule that Gardenier couldn't deny. "As for example— That no man is bound to accuse himself. That a husband and wife cannot be witnesses against each other. . . . That a Counsel or Attorney can never testify against his client."[12] These exceptions were always applied "whenever it shall be demanded by the suggestions of reason and good sense."[13]

Riker anticipated one of Gardenier's arguments—that none of those exemptions applied to professionals other than attorneys and "therefore a Physician, a Surgeon, or a Priest, is bound to disclose all that has been entrusted to him, no matter under what circumstances it may have been confided."[14] Riker was not impressed. After all, he argued, that "rule" was based on only one case that had been decided in England nearly thirty years earlier.

After explaining the case, where an English Lord had denied a surgeon's request not to testify regarding whether one of his patients was guilty of bigamy, Riker blasted it as being "made on the spur of the occasion—without discussion."[15] But even if the principle were right, he said, "it by no means follows that a clergyman is bound to reveal what a penitent hath confessed to him in the exercise of a religious rite."[16] Even as he made the argument, he felt the vulnerability in it. The same writers who had compiled the various cases on the requirement to testify had also concluded that courts should treat priests the same as physicians. Riker acknowledged his weakness. He dismissed the writers as "elementary," but that wasn't enough, and he knew it.[17]

His Achilles' heel now fully exposed, Riker needed to protect it. He wound up. He knew—and he knew the judges knew—that his arguments against what the legal writers had concluded needed to be as stout as Kohlmann himself. He recognized the moment. He knew he needed to seize it. It was as if he were starting his discourse all over—signaling the judges to perk up. "At the outset I boldly affirm, without fear of contradiction, that the Attorney General can produce but *two* cases, in which the question has ever been raised in relation to a clergyman."[18] These were the two cases Sampson had found. If they were still gnawing a hole in his stomach, Riker was going to try to heal it.

Under the common law, when a legal precedent threatens to trip up a lawyer's case, good advocates have two options: convince a court it should no longer follow the prior case, or explain why the prior decision is different enough that it shouldn't apply to the present case. Riker used both tactics. He first argued that the cases weren't binding in the United States because they had both been decided *after* the Revolution.[19] And he added, "I go farther—I say the cases would not be binding in Great Britain."[20]

It was a bold statement. Riker launched into proving it. The first case, Riker explained, involved a Catholic man slated for execution who confessed his crime to a Protestant minister. A single lower court judge in England ruled that the minister had no choice but to testify about the confession. The prisoner was convicted and executed. Riker labeled the case as inconsequential, saying it was "the decision of a single judge, at the Circuit, which is never considered binding."[21] He also quoted from the chief justice of England, Lord Kenyon, who, when writing about the case, said, "I should have paused before I admitted the evidence there admitted."[22]

"This alone," Riker said, "is sufficient to shake its authority."[23]

But he wasn't finished. That case was clearly different. There, the confession was made by a Catholic to a *Protestant* priest. In that situation, he argued, "It does not appear that the clergyman had any scruples to reveal what had been confessed to him."[24]

The second case hailed from Ireland. It had occurred in 1802. There, Riker explained, a judge had ordered a Catholic priest to reveal something he had learned in confidence from a parishioner outside of confession. Riker noted that key difference, but he blasted the case for something far more nefarious: its country of origin. "It is made in a country more remarkable for nothing, than the religious intolerance and bigotry of its laws."[25] It was true. Despite the population being overwhelmingly Catholic, nearly every law in Ireland was designed to oppress Catholics—anyone not part of the Protestant Ascendency. "Precedents in such a country . . . ought to be admitted by us with the most scrupulous caution," Riker said.[26]

"It may now be demanded," Riker said, "whether the two decisions . . . would be binding, even in Great Britain. They clearly would not be binding. They have not the force of authority."[27] He went on. He spoke of plenty of other cases that seemingly had more weight than those two but that the English courts had overturned. He shifted gears, turning to prominent principles of English common law that United States courts had refused to follow. These were cases, Riker argued, where courts in the new country had wisely "maintained our judicial independence."[28] They had done it before. This court could do it again.

Riker urged the court to "to follow the guidance of liberality and wisdom, unfettered by authority."[29] He then explained that he would demonstrate that even if the common law from England undercut Kohlmann, the New York State Constitution still demanded he be allowed to remain silent, without punishment.

Riker had been on his feet for a long time. He was no doubt getting tired, his mouth pasty from talking so long. Gardenier sat at his own table, certainly taking notes on how he would counter each and every one of Riker's points. Kohlmann must have been watching with gratitude. It is hard to know what the defendants—Bradley, Brinkerhoff, and the Phillipses—thought, except that they knew their freedom hung in the balance.

Riker recited the key language from Article 38 of the New York Constitution:

> [T]he free exercise and enjoyment of religious profession and worship, without discrimination or preference, shall forever hereafter be allowed within this state to all mankind. *Provided*, that the liberty of conscience hereby granted, shall not be so construed, as to excuse acts of licentiousness, or justify practices inconsistent with the peace or safety of this State.[30]

"Now," Riker said, "we cannot conceive of more broad and comprehensive terms. . . . Religious liberty was the great object which they had in view. They felt, that it was the right of every human being, to worship God according to the dictates of his own conscience. They intended to secure, forever, to all mankind, without distinction or preference, the free exercise and enjoyment of religious profession and worship. They employed language commensurate with that object. It is what they have said."[31]

Outside, the day wore on. Across Broadway, St. Paul's chapel baked in the summer sun, and Riker invoked the names of many of the Founders who had sat in its pews. The "Catholic religion is an ancient religion," he told the judges. "It has existed for eighteen centuries. The sacrament of penance has existed with it." It would be foolish, he argued, to think the Founders, "some of the ablest men in this or in any other nation," would have been ignorant of it. "Their names are known to the court. A few still live, and we revere the memories of those who are no more. They all knew the Catholic faith, and that auricular confession was a part of it."[32]

Riker then posed an insightful rhetorical question to the judges: If the Founders had intended the Constitution not to apply to this situation, would they not have made it clear?

He was hitting his stride. The words flowed now, as much passion as legal logic. "Again," he said, "there is no doubt that the [Constitution] intended to secure the liberty of conscience.—Now, where is the liberty of conscience to the Catholic, if the priest and the penitent, be thus exposed? Has the priest, the liberty of conscience, if he be thus coerced? Has the penitent the liberty of conscience, if he is to be dragged into a court of justice, to answer for what has passed in confession? Have either the privilege of auricular confession? Do they freely enjoy the sacrament of penance? If this be the religious liberty, which the constitution intended to secure—it is . . . perplexing."[33]

He mocked English decisions that allowed religious liberty only when it was convenient, noting that it was hardly helpful to tell someone they might exercise their religious freedom from jail or in the face of demoralizing fines. "Is there, in the republic, a man who does not see in this the most scandalous sophistry? Is there, on earth, a man who would not abhor it?"[34]

Riker's speech stretched on. He recognized he had one last weakness. It hung in the air between him and the judges, as distracting as a child's repetitive nagging scream: the Constitution's provision that religious liberty stopped once it resulted in "acts of licentiousness" or if it threatened "the peace or safety" of the State.[35] Riker confronted it head-on.

"Does auricular confession excuse acts of licentiousness?" he asked. The answer was an emphatic no. If anything, the act of confession encouraged "a hearty resolution of turning from . . . evil ways." In fact, Riker said, in this particular case, "It has led to a restoration of the property to the true owner." In that light, if "we could legally and constitutionally compel the clergyman to reveal the name of the penitent, who would afterwards go to confession? What would be gained to the State?"[36]

When answering the question of whether the practice of Catholic confession posed a danger to the peace or safety of the state, Riker was unequivocal. "We know that it exists and is practiced in Russia—In Spain—in France—in Portugal—in Italy—in Germany, and in most of the countries in Europe. Is *their* peace, or *their* safety disturbed by auricular confession?"[37] He left the question dangling. The answer was clear. It would have been a good stopping point, but Riker wasn't finished.

Despite all his experience, Riker began to ramble. Perhaps he was growing fatigued. It's possible his thoughts just weren't as organized as they had appeared when he first started. We don't know if it troubled Kohlmann or not. Riker made key points, but they were disjointed. He quoted Blackstone, a famous legal author who wrote that Catholics should enjoy their practices of confession.[38] He invoked George Washington. "The great body of the American people are protestants [*sic*]," Riker said. "Yet our catholic [*sic*] brethren have never hesitated to take up the sword with us, and to stand by us in the hour of danger. The Father of his country—the illustrious conductor of the Revolution, did not hesitate in the face of the nation to do justice to their revolutionary services—to their good conduct as citizens—and to the aid which they rendered us in the establishment of our free government."[39]

The former district attorney—perhaps again a sign of his wearing out—then declared that he would explain why Kohlmann's request should be granted under the common law. Immediately realizing that he had already argued that point, he said, "I think I can say, with confidence, that I have fully examined all the authorities in relation to it."[40] He then switched direction. He argued that a man should not be forced to disparage himself. That was precisely, Riker said, what would happen if the court forced Kohlmann to testify. He would "be degraded in the Church—he would forfeit his office—he would be stripped of his sacerdotal character—he would lose his clerical rights—he would be disgraced in the eyes of all Catholics—in fine, he would be rendered infamous."[41]

Riker may have been shriveling as his comments dragged on, but he summoned up one last dramatic push. "I confess I feel a deep interest in this cause," he said. "I consider this a contest between toleration and persecution. A contest involving the rights of conscience. . . . To compel the Reverend Pastor to answer, or to be imprisoned, must either force his conscience or lead to persecution. I can conceive of nothing, more barbarous—more cruel—or more unjust than such an alternative." To force Kohlmann to testify, Riker said, "would cast a shade upon the jurisprudence of our country."

He ended by quoting a famous English legal reformer who wrote, "Conscience is not controllable by human laws, nor amenable to human tribunals. Persecution or attempts to force conscience, will never produce conviction, and are only calculated to make hypocrites, or—Martyrs."[42]

Riker, at last, thanked the judges for listening and took his seat.

For their part, the four men on the bench offered absolutely no clue as to whether they believed him.

NOTES

1. William Sampson, *The Catholic Question in America: Whether a Roman Catholic Clergyman Be in Any Case Compellable to Disclose the Secrets of* . . . (New York, 1813), 8.
2. Ibid.
3. Ibid., 9.
4. Ibid., 10.
5. Ibid.
6. Ibid., 11–12.
7. Ibid., 12.
8. Ibid.
9. Ibid.
10. Ibid.
11. Ibid., 13.
12. Ibid., 14.
13. Ibid., 15.
14. Ibid.
15. Ibid., 17.

16. Ibid.
17. Ibid.
18. Ibid.
19. Ibid.
20. Ibid.
21. Ibid., 19.
22. Ibid., 18.
23. Ibid.
24. Ibid., 19.
25. Ibid., 21.
26. Ibid.
27. Ibid., 21–22.
28. Ibid., 21.
29. Ibid., 25.
30. Ibid., 25–26.
31. Ibid., 26.
32. Ibid.
33. Ibid., 27.
34. Ibid., 31.
35. Ibid., 32.
36. Ibid., 32–33.
37. Ibid., 33.
38. Ibid., 34.
39. Ibid., 35.
40. Ibid., 36.
41. Ibid., 39.
42. Ibid., 40.

Chapter 8

A WORTHY OPPONENT

There was a reason Gardenier had won the election for district attorney. He was good on his feet. His speeches evoked strong emotion. Fearless, he had once dueled a man at the Bladensburg Dueling Grounds outside Washington, DC, over a disagreement regarding two opposing speeches the men had given—he had been wounded but survived. Ever the politician, he could command a room, and he knew the power of getting to the point and making a quick exit. After Riker took his seat and a few other matters were resolved, Gardenier entered the fray.

He had offered to let the matter drop, he said, but the Catholics had pushed the question. His "duty now compelled" him "to examine whether the priests of the Roman Church were indeed entitled to a privilege to which no other persons asserted the least pretention: that of concealing their knowledge of matters which . . . concerned the public good and the public safety."[1]

His first argument would look at the common law. Unlike Riker, whose words had started to amass like the clutter in the streets outside, Gardenier wasted no language. It was clear the judges wouldn't need to listen long to understand his message. He readily acknowledged the exceptions for lawyers Riker had mentioned. "But," he said, "the exception only proves the rule." And unless Riker or Sampson could prove

58

an exception for clergymen, "the general rule must prevail, and the priest of course must answer."[2]

Kohlmann's attorneys must have been flabbergasted. They had clearly spent considerable time preparing for the cases out of England, crafting arguments to distinguish and undermine them. Gardenier ignored them as he would an annoying fly. He would not press those cases, he said, because they were not necessary to his argument. "The right to examine this priest in this case, grew out of the general rule that every citizen must answer." Unless there were adjudged cases that said otherwise, he felt it would be of no use to spend any time on the cases Riker had tried to trample.[3] In other words, Riker had just wasted everyone's—and most important, the court's—time.

In Gardenier's view, the case was simple: "*first*; that under the general rule, the priest is obliged, in common with every other member of the community to answer—*secondly*; that there is no case in which he was ever exempted; and *thirdly*, that the decision . . . of every case . . . in relation to this point, is in support of the general rule."[4]

Gardenier concluded with the bluntness of a hammer: "At common law, therefore, the priest has no privilege."[5]

His arguments were so brief they would have made Riker and Sampson feel either supremely confident or extremely foolish. Only the judges knew.

———

Gardenier's pivot to the constitutional argument was just as surgical. Bypassing anything unnecessary, he cut like a scalpel to the provision denying religious liberty to acts that would threaten peace or safety. No one could dispute, he said, "that the people of the state of New York, were at the time of making their constitution, a *Christian, Protestant People*. But aware of the injustice and evils of religious intolerance, they wisely and magnanimously resolved . . . that persons of other religions should also be equal to" Protestants. But, he said, "it was never intended that any one should ever be *superior* to any other."[6]

That was precisely what Kohlmann was asking, Gardenier argued, to be superior, to have different rules apply to him than what governed everyone else. "To tolerate religious profession and worship is one thing; to allow any person whatever, to conceal matters upon the knowledge of which the public safety may depend, is another. . . . If the priest remains silent, crime remains unpunished." This was the crux of Gardenier's argument. "The punishment of crimes is essential to the public safety. That punishment cannot take place, if witnesses are excused from testifying to their knowledge of crimes."[7]

As the afternoon wore on, Gardenier took an interesting tack. He described religious freedom not as an inalienable right but instead as something "granted . . . by a *protestant* [*sic*] people to all *others*."[8] It wasn't inherent. It didn't come from God. The implication was that the Protestants, as the majority, gave religious liberty and could just as easily take it away. He continued: "Yet if the priests of the Roman church are excused from answering, they are permitted to hold the safety of their benefactors in their hands—nay they are bound to disregard it."[9]

His tone turned sarcastic. "A protestant [*sic*] must answer all questions, and by those answers protect all the society," including Catholics. But a Catholic priest "is to be indulged in endangering all the rest. And this is called liberty of conscience!" In essence, Gardenier said, Catholics were asking to be put on a pedestal above the rest of society. "Can society endanger its safety, by yielding to such a claim? . . . It would have been a suicidal act."[10]

What if a Catholic wanted to sacrifice the first born of every family? Gardenier asked. Would that be permitted? What if a priest knew that an invasion of the city by its enemies was imminent—a very real possibility as the War of 1812 continued to rage—but had come by that knowledge through confession? Should he be allowed to stay silent?

With Kohlmann, the defendants, Riker, Sampson, and the crowd in the galley looking on, Gardenier continued to land blow after blow. If the courtroom were a battlefield, he was a blistering cannon. Sampson, no doubt, was frantically taking notes for how to counter

Gardenier's salvos. Quakers, the district attorney pointed out, had been allowed not to fight in every war in United States history, including the Revolution. But they had been forced to pay fines. "Why then, shall the Roman priest be excused from the same great duty? why shall society allow *him* to omit doing that which is essential to safety?"[11]

Gardenier was rolling. The courtroom was hushed. It's likely his next argument had Kohlmann roiling. It wasn't based on law or logic. He attacked the sacrament of confession itself, or at least the way the Catholics interpreted it. In the centuries that would follow, courts and advocates would come to generally avoid embroiling themselves in the merits of people's religious beliefs, recognizing that it is hardly the place of a judge or jury to delve into whether a person's understanding of their duty before the divine is correct.[12] Gardenier didn't hesitate.

Confession may be a sacrament, he said, but how "can secrecy be a *part* of that sacrament? The penitent has a right to confess. Let him confess; he is not punished for *that*, but for his crime. If it be his *duty* to confess, then that duty exists whether the confession be secret or not."[13] But, Gardenier argued, the scriptures didn't support the idea that confession needed to be secret. That was a Catholic concoction. A penitent parishioner could confess whether the priest kept it secret or not, Gardenier concluded. Secrecy, in his view, was not important.

Kohlmann had to have been boiling. Who was this lawyer to tell what was or was not necessary for his religious practices?

Gardenier wasn't finished. The Constitution, he said, protected profession or worship. "Silence on the part of the priest" does not ensure a Catholic layperson will engage in the sacrament of confession.[14] In Gardenier's view, Kohlmann's religious practice of remaining silent was not what mattered, only whether laypeople could engage in confession.

Gardenier's final argument reiterated a point he had already made, but with even more force. It was his strongest argument. The New York Constitution, he argued, protected the free exercise and enjoyment of religious profession and worship "without discrimination or preference."

A rule, Gardenier said, that forced all Protestants to testify but that allowed Catholics to remain silent discriminated against Protestants. The Catholics shouldn't receive special treatment just because they believed they would be punished for testifying. Kohlmann was asking for an unconstitutional preference that put him above his Protestant counterparts, and "society would be false to itself to allow" it.[15]

"Finally," Gardenier said, "the constitution . . . has not granted exemption from previous legal duties. It has expelled the demon of persecution from our land; but it has not . . . yielded" to any sect "any of the rights of a well organized government."[16] With that, he took his seat.

Nightfall was coming. Fatigue was settling over everyone in the room as steadily as a descending mist. Under court procedures, since Kohlmann was the one asking the court for relief, his lawyers would get one more chance to speak and rebut Gardenier's argument. Sampson was ready. The court was not. Given the late hour, Clinton ordered Sampson to make his argument the next morning. Kohlmann faced at least one more night of having to lie awake in the clergy house, the prison doors taunting him with their damning song.

NOTES

1. William Sampson, *The Catholic Question in America: Whether a Roman Catholic Clergyman Be in Any Case Compellable to Disclose the Secrets of . . .* (New York, 1813), 42.
2. Ibid., 43.
3. Ibid.
4. Ibid.
5. Ibid., 44.
6. Ibid.
7. Ibid.
8. Ibid., 45.
9. Ibid.
10. Ibid.
11. Ibid., 47.
12. Thomas v. Review Bd. of Ind. Employment Sec. Div., 450 U.S. 707 (1981).
13. Sampson, *The Catholic Question in America,* 47.
14. Ibid., 48.
15. Ibid., 51.
16. Ibid.

Chapter 9

ALONE IN A CEMETERY

That evening, Sampson took a walk. Although the summer air would have been pleasant, he was restless. His wife and children were now living with him, he had a stellar partner in Riker, and Kohlmann was, in many respects, the perfect client—strident but without a hint of hypocrisy. Still, he felt the weight of his task bearing him down with the pressure of thousands of years of history. If he failed, it wouldn't be just Kohlmann who lost, but all of the Catholics coming to America in the hope of equal treatment under the law. Perhaps even more worrisome to Sampson, it could portend the resurgence of all the same religious oppression that had plagued Europe for more than a quarter of a millennium.

For inspiration, he walked into the hallowed cemetery of St. Paul's chapel. It was just a block away from St. Peter's, and the contrast between the two churches couldn't have provided a more dramatic statement of the challenge he faced. St. Paul's was an extension of the mighty Trinity Church. St. Peter's was the only Catholic church in the city. St. Paul's was the home of presidents—George Washington himself had worshipped there. St. Peter's housed paupers.

From amidst the tombstones, Sampson could see across Broadway to the Commons, with city hall beyond that. The headstones were silent, but they spoke volumes. Nestled among snaking paths, many belonged to babes, aged eleven to nineteen months, and some even seventeen days. Others showed family groupings. There were those who had died before the birth of the nation and many after. Some reflected lives well lived and loves lost. None were Catholic, of course. This was an Anglican cemetery. The "papists," as they were called, had been relegated to the fields on the outskirts of the city.

Looking at these various shrines, Sampson couldn't help but ponder the path he had chosen, that Kohlmann had followed as well, and the differences "between the monument of immortal fame and the monument of immortal life."[1] Gardenier's pointed argument lurked among the shadows in the cemetery. It was always present. Sampson planned how he would slay it, and he ended up pondering auricular confession, its strengths, and the value it brought to society—even if it was something he personally didn't practice.

He had done much good in the world. Even after his exile and journey to the United States, he had salvaged from the darkened alleyways of society cast-off cases other attorneys simply slinked past, their eyes averted. Banned from both the law and life in Ireland, he had managed to convince the courts to admit him to the practice of law in New York. It proved to be a boon for civil rights.

This case was different. The enemies were intelligent and ideological. The consequences of failure would land on tens of thousands. The Catholics in the city were gambling a great deal on him, trusting he could secure a ruling that would place them on equal footing with their Protestant neighbors. It must have been a tremendous burden to contemplate in that graveyard. As the night thickened, silence crept across the city. Sampson steeled himself for the morning.

NOTE

1. William Sampson to Gulian Verplanck, April 17, 1827, New York Historical Society.

Chapter 10

A BUDDING TREE IN THE RAVAGES OF A BURNED WORLD

The next morning, Sampson stood alone. The judges, Kohlmann, the other attorneys, the crowd, the reporters—they all watched him. This was his moment. The judges had slept with Gardenier's arguments whispering in their dreams. He had to silence them.

Sampson's character was one of integrity, compassion, and a desire to help the less fortunate, but he lacked his opponent's ability to strike at the heart of a matter. If tangents were his friends, his home would have been packed with guests. In a thick Irish accent, he thanked Gardenier for bringing the question to the court and for his able arguments.[1] This took minutes when it should have taken seconds.

When he finally began his argument, he emphasized that "if a victory is sought it is of that blessed kind, where every virtuous citizen is to share in the triumph, and none to suffer by the defeat."[2]

He then said, "I shall avoid repeating what my learned colleague has so ably urged. We have already agreed that each should take his part, as well as to share the burden of the argument, as to spare the Court the pain of a story twice told."[3]

It was a nice promise. Sampson couldn't keep it, at least not entirely. At first he seemed on track. He summarized Riker's arguments just enough to throw a javelin at Gardenier: Riker "shewed the current of authority to be so strong, that our ingenious adversary was compelled to evade it, and driven to maneuver with what dexterity he could, in the counter current and eddy of popular prejudices."[4] But then he devolved into trying to dismantle the various cases Riker had already argued, except from a different perspective.

After what must have seemed to the gallery like hours, it was as if all Sampson's pent-up emotions from his exile and time in the dungeons came blasting from him with the ferocity of steam and metal exploding from the overheated belly of an engine. He bounced from one atrocity in Ireland to another. He cited cases of bigotry. He launched into a series of rhetorical questions. He berated Irish statutes.

At one point, it was clear the judges were starting to get impatient. Sampson had ranted about a case in Ireland only to get sidetracked on some other point. One of the judges interrupted him and asked how the case was ultimately decided. "I will conceal nothing of it from the court," Sampson said. "I wish the case to be understood and fully weighted." But he followed yet another confusing path in the jungle of his mind, only to be interrupted by the judges again to try to get him back on track.[5]

He quoted at length from Edmund Burke, who had lambasted an Irish statute related to Catholics.[6] He compared the history of Europe to the smoldering remains of a great civilization, "the ravages of a convulsed world . . . under which lie buried and incrusted the treasures of civilization."[7] The toleration of the United States was a glorious tree, vibrant and green, "whose spreading branches stretch towards the heavens—in which the native eagle builds his nest."[8]

Buried within his arguments were salient gems, to be sure. Religious persecution had been rampant for centuries, he said. "Were there rebellions? Were there massacres? Aye, to be sure, there were! They were the natural crop. For he that sows must reap! Away then with Irish cases and Irish authorities: for to adopt them here would be as mad as wicked."[9] To Sampson, "providence had decreed this land, to be the grave of persecution, and the cradle of tolerance."[10]

The points he was trying to make were actually quite simple. First, despite all the persecution Catholics had faced in Ireland, no one had ever tried something as egregious as committing a Catholic priest "to prison till he answered, or in other words till he died."[11] Second, "that we should never look to Ireland for a precedent, where the rights of catholics [*sic*] were concerned."[12] And finally, that English law was no better than Irish and should also be ignored.

Though they did nothing to rebut Gardenier's arguments, they were fair themes. The judges, however, didn't have Sampson's statements in writing. Everything was oral. It would have been easy to get lost or distracted. Whether they would be able to pinch the pearls from the thousands of grains of sand Sampson had piled before them remained an open question—one Kohlmann no doubt couldn't answer. Gardenier, it seemed, was winning.

The day dragged on. The district attorney sat unscathed and most likely unworried.

Mayor Clinton interrupted Sampson, who had been droning on about the writings of William Pitt. "From what book do you take those queries of Mr. Pitt?" the mayor asked.

"I read them," Sampson said, "if it please the court, as general history, from Mr. Plowden's historical survey of the state of Ireland. They are I presume, upon the journals of parliament."[13]

It was a low point in Sampson's argument, in part because it showed just how far off topic he had gotten but also because it suggested, perhaps, a hint of distrust from Mayor Clinton in what Sampson was presenting. It was also a turning point. From rock bottom, Sampson had nowhere to go but up.

"It is time now," he said, "to take leave of foreign history. . . . for our own constitution is so explicit."[14] It appeared as though he had received the hint Clinton had lobbied.

If Gardenier recognized in that moment that Sampson's focus was shifting, we have no record of it. He should have.

"The constitution is . . . simple, and precise, and unequivocal," Sampson said. "It may like other human institutions be perverted, but it cannot be easily mistaken." He then turned his focus directly at Gardenier. "The people whose will it speaks, were not of any one church, as the learned attorney has said; but of many and various sects, all of whom had suffered more or less in Europe for their religious tenets, and many of whom had unrelentingly persecuted each other."[15] It was a direct assault on Gardenier's claim that the United States—and New York in particular—was a Protestant country that had merely gifted tolerance to Catholics and could just as easily take it away.

At the time of the Constitution's drafting, Sampson said, "the catholic [*sic*] religion was surely as well known as the that of the quaker [*sic*]. No Christian could be ignorant of it: . . . All catholics [*sic*] knew it because it was their religion. All protestants [*sic*], because they must know that against which they protested. . . . [T]hree fourths of the whole christian [*sic*] world are catholics [*sic*]. . . . It was with full knowledge of all this, and to close the door forever against religious contention, that the 38th article of our constitution was framed, by which all religions are put upon the very same footing, without preference or discrimination."[16]

Sampson then made a key argument: "If there be any, who does not see the wisdom of this enactment, let him open the page of history, and read of the bloody religious wars of Europe, of which the wounds are still fresh and bleeding."[17] It would have been a poignant image. Still alive in the minds of Clinton and other educated people of the day were images of immeasurable human suffering that is impossible to list completely: a religious war lasting three decades that cost the lives of approximately twenty percent of Germany's population; Catholics and Protestants sent to prison, denied voting rights, stripped of land, and brutally imprisoned; hundreds of Protestants executed; people fined and imprisoned for not attending the right church services; converts to Catholicism executed; an attempt to blow up the English House of Parliament; an English civil war; beheadings; the massacring of two entire cities; witch hunts; the imprisonment of scores of nonconformists.[18] The list was endless.

Sampson had hit his stride. He again turned on Gardenier. "The District Attorney has laid it down, as though it were conceded, that the general principle of law is with him, and that we who claim an exception, must shew ourselves entitled to it. I explicitly deny that proposition. The constitution here lays down the general rule, that all mankind shall be tolerated, without preference or discrimination, and we claim no exception from that rule." Gardenier, Sampson said, was the one trying to shoehorn Kohlmann into the licentiousness and danger or safety exceptions to the general rule, "and it was for him to shew how we fell within it. It was for him to shew in what our acts were licentious, or our practices dangerous."[19]

He couldn't, Sampson argued. Kohlmann was a man of "modest worth and unambitious courses" who was "often to be found by the bed of sickness, or in the abode of sorrow." His very lifestyle "repels all idea of licentiousness."[20]

Gardenier, Sampson said, then had no choice "but to fall back upon the subject of danger. And truly, Mr. Attorney with all his invention, was much put to it to imagine a case of danger."[21] The only threat the district attorney had suggested prowled in the forests of his mind alone—the possibility that a priest might be aware of some impending Catholic invasion and wouldn't tell anyone. It was nonsense, Sampson argued. If imaginary dangers could be used to remove constitutional protections from Catholics, then the "38th article of the constitution is a dead letter."[22]

The longer he stood before the judges, the stronger Sampson grew. His voice now commanded the room. Gardenier's fear was not just imagined, he said; it was as unrealistic as a child's dread over the boogeyman. "I maintain in the presence of my clients, and in their name, that doctrine boldly and firmly. That though the catholics [*sic*] must acknowledge the pope [*sic*] as supreme head of their church, yet they know, their duty as citizens would oblige them to resist him . . . if . . . he should make war upon that country, which is theirs, and theirs by choice. . . . and if the government was too slow in providing them with arms, they would with their pickaxe, or their spade, or their cart-rung . . . drive the enemy from his cannon, as it has happened before."[23]

There was only one way, Sampson said, to make the Catholics the enemy of the United States. And that was "to put their clergyman in prison for not betraying the most holy of all engagements towards God or man."[24]

For Kohlmann, Sampson's rebound must have answered a desperate prayer. His attorney had been faltering. The judges had been wandering. Now, the four men were no longer interrupting. They, like everyone else in the room, were enraptured.

"But let no man be alarmed," Sampson said, now going after Gardenier's contention that the Catholics were seeking favoritism. "We claim no supremacy. We seek nothing but pure and perfect equality. From the bottom of our hearts we sincerely tolerate you all. We will lay hands on none of you, for your worship or profession; and for ourselves, we claim neither more nor less. Hands off on all sides. And if any of you are aggrieved we will invoke the constitution in your favor, as we do in our own. We will join with all good citizens in loving, respecting, and defending it. For it is our own."[25]

At the prosecutor's table, Gardenier waited in forced silence, unable to defend himself. Sampson's arguments shook his own. All he could do was hope that Sampson didn't land a killing blow.

For his sake, Sampson reiterated that there was absolutely no danger in allowing Kohlmann to remain silent. He explained the benefits of confession. "If it led to licentiousness or danger," he said, it "would have come to light" long before then, given how many Catholics practiced it in so many countries.[26] More important, it provided a path for those who were a danger to society to "turn aside and escape the throng that hurries him along."[27]

As he pushed toward the end of his argument, Sampson turned personal. Was there any reason, he asked, to begrudge someone else for living their religion? "It is not . . . nor never shall be, an offence to me, that the pious catholic glories in his faith. . . . It is enough for me, that amongst the friends I have had, none have been more true, more loyal, or more noble hearted, than catholics [*sic*] have proved."[28] Whatever dangers or licentiousness the drafters of the Constitution had feared, it was not Catholic confession.

"But I have been too long," Sampson said. The putrid dungeons, the filth in which he'd been forced to sleep, the years in exile—it bubbled to the surface. "The peculiar reasons I have had to dread and abhor every colour and shade of religious persecution, has communicated to my argument, perhaps, an over earnestness. Those who have not seen and felt as I have done, may think it common place. . . . In that case, I am more beholden to the patience of the court."[29]

It was a heartfelt apology, made all the more so by what he had suffered.

"To sum all of this," Sampson said. "The constitution has spoken plain, the gospel plainer to our purpose." As Christ commanded, "THOU SHALT LOVE THY NEIGHBOUR AS THY SELF."[30]

With that, Sampson stepped down. Everything was now in the judges' hands. All eyes turned to Mayor Clinton. If the judges had already made up their minds, they could have issued an order right then. They could have done it even if they needed just a few minutes to deliberate. Instead, Clinton ruled that everyone should come back the following Monday. Kohlmann stared at five more days of boiling uncertainty.

Notes

1. William Sampson, *The Catholic Question in America: Whether a Roman Catholic Clergyman Be in Any Case Compellable to Disclose the Secrets of . . .* (New York, 1813), 52–54.
2. Ibid., 54.
3. Ibid.
4. Ibid., 55.
5. Ibid., 62–63.
6. Ibid., 68–70.
7. Ibid., 72.
8. Ibid., 91.

9. Ibid., 71.
10. Ibid., 65.
11. Ibid., 58.
12. Ibid., 68.
13. Ibid., 76.
14. Ibid.
15. Ibid., 77.
16. Ibid., 79–80.
17. Ibid., 81.
18. Douglas Laycock, "Continuity and Change in the Threat to Religious Liberty: The Reformation Era and the Late Twentieth Century," *Minnesota Law Review* 80 (1996):1047, 1049–66.
19. Sampson, *The Catholic Question in America,* 81.
20. Ibid., 81–82.
21. Ibid., 82.
22. Ibid.
23. Ibid., 83.
24. Ibid.
25. Ibid., 85.
26. Ibid., 89.
27. Ibid., 89.
28. Ibid., 92–93.
29. Ibid., 94.
30. Ibid., 95.

Chapter 11

THE MOST
PROFOUND WISDOM

On June 14, 1813, Kohlmann took his seat in the steamy
courtroom, wondering what would happen. The jury had
been called and seated—they were necessary only if the case
were going to proceed to trial, which would happen only if Kohlmann
were forced to testify. His word was, after all, the lone evidence.

Mayor DeWitt Clinton sat at the judges' bench. He began by announcing that the judges were unanimous in their decision but had
left it to him to offer their reasoning. "In order to criminate the defendants," he said, "the reverend Anthony Kohlmann, a minister of
the Roman catholic [*sic*] church of this city, has been called upon as a
witness, to declare what he knows on the subject of this prosecution.
. . . The question . . . is, whether a Roman catholic [*sic*] priest shall be
compelled to disclose what he has received in confession—in violation
of his conscience, of his clerical engagements, and of the canons of his
church, and with certainty of being stripped of his sacred functions,
and cut off from religious communion and social intercourse with the
denomination to which he belongs."[1]

To Kohlmann, it must have been a relief to know that, at a mini-
mum, the judges understood what was at stake.

Unfortunately for the priest, Clinton was in no hurry to get to his
conclusion. "This is an important enquiry," the judge said. "It is important to the church upon which it has a particular bearing. It is important

73

to all religious denominations, because it involves a principle which may in its practical operation affect them all."[2] But, Clinton said, before he answered it, he wanted to thank everyone involved in the case, which he did for a laboriously long time.

When he finally turned to the substance, he still refused to reveal the answer. "It is a general rule, that every man when legally called upon to testify as a witness, must relate all he knows. This is essential to the administration of civil and criminal justice."[3] On some level, this was bad news for Kohlmann. It implied that Mayor Clinton saw the case the same way Gardenier did: that it was Kohlmann seeking the exception to a general rule, not the state, and so it was Kohlmann's burden to prove the exception was justified.

Whether Clinton believed that or not, he wouldn't say. Instead, he embarked on a journey of legal exploration that spanned hundreds of years and multiple precedents. For Kohlmann, it must have been a painful experience listening to Clinton give the background on a series of cases that seemingly had nothing to do with his own.

Clinton had his reasons. At long last, he said, "We have gone more particularly into this branch of the subject, because it has a very intimate connexion [sic] with the point in question." All of the cases "touch upon it, in a greater or less degree." Clinton then provided what he thought was the most important aspect of Kohlmann's case: "[I]f we decide that the witness shall testify, we prescribe a course of conduct by which he will violate his spiritual duties. . . . If he commits an offense against religion . . . we must consider that this cannot be done without our participation and coercion."

"There can be no doubt," Clinton said, "but that the witness does consider, that his answering on this occasion, would be such a high handed offence against religion, that it would expose him to punishment in a future state—and it must be conceded by all, that it would subject him to privations and disgrace in this world. It is true . . . he would not confess a crime, or acknowledge his infamy, yet he would act an offence against high heaven, and seal his disgrace in the presence of his assembled friends, and to the affliction of a bereaved church and a weeping congregation."[4]

The crowd was silent. Clinton was building to something, but he had not yet tipped his hand. The wait was no doubt agonizing for Kohlmann and the defendants. Newspaper reporters furiously scribbled notes so they could accurately report the story.[5] Years earlier, Sampson had mastered his own form of shorthand, which allowed him to transcribe trial proceedings in real time and report on key cases.[6] He had used the skill to advance civil rights, publishing his reports so the public could see injustice or justice occurring in the courtrooms of both Ireland and the United States. His efforts were part of the reason he had been banned from England. As Clinton spoke, the Irishman scratched the judge's words into history.

"It cannot therefore," Clinton continued, "for a moment be believed, that the mild and just principles of the common Law would place the witness in such a dreadful predicament; in such a horrible dilemma . . . : If he tells the truth he violates his ecclesiastical oath—If he prevaricates he violates his judicial oath. . . . The only course, is for the court to declare that he shall not testify or act at all."[7]

The sentence slipped into the decision almost like a jewel thief in the night. Its wake soaked every word and sentence that followed with a different sensation.

Kohlmann may have jerked in his chair, sensing victory. Sampson wouldn't have been so quick. The judge was talking only about the common law—he had yet to discuss the Constitution and its question of dangers to society. As Sampson well knew, anything could happen in a courtroom.

Any "court prescribing a different course," Clinton said, "must be governed by feelings and views different from those . . . of a just and enlightened tribunal."[8]

Even if Sampson couldn't guarantee a victory at that point, Clinton's tone seemed to create an irresistible sensation that their horse held a dramatic lead well past the halfway point in the race.

Clinton turned to the two key cases the parties had argued. He dismissed them as simply and quickly as he would annoying gnats. Their facts were either too different, he said, or for "those who have turned their attention to the history of Ireland, the decisions of Irish courts, respecting Roman Catholics, can have little or no weight."[9]

Then, for perhaps the first time in Sampson's life, a sitting judge acknowledged the injustices in Ireland that had become the crusade of the lawyer's life and that had sent him to dungeons, exiled him from his family, cost him his country, and forced him to trudge through humanity's depths. In every other courtroom where Sampson had railed against the barbaric treatment of Irish Catholics, the only result had been his own punishment. Clinton was different.

"That unfortunate country," he said, "has been divided into two great parties, the oppressors and oppressed. That Catholic has been disenfranchised of his civil rights, deprived of his inheritance, and excluded from the common rights of man; statute has been passed upon statute, and adjudication has been piled upon adjudication in prejudice of his religious freedom."[10]

In his argument, Sampson had rambled. He had known it. He had apologized for it. But in that moment, his hard-tested faith that all of his suffering was not in vain had paid off.

An instant later, Clinton changed course. "[L]et us now look at it upon more elevated ground; upon the ground of the constitution, of the social compact, and of civil and religious liberty."[11]

If Gardenier still clung to any hope that he might win, the judge ripped it from his grasp. "Although no human legislator has a right to meddle with religion," Clinton said, "yet the history of the world, is a history of oppression and tyranny over the consciences of men. And the sages who formed our constitution" sought to prevent the "introduction of calamities, that have deluged the world with tears and blood."[12]

Perhaps it came from his firsthand views of the blood and destruction of the Christmas riots in Irishtown seven years earlier, or maybe it stemmed from studious learning, but Clinton held an appreciation for the value of religious liberty that most then, and even many today, fail to appreciate. The "framers of our constitution," he explained to the raptured courtroom, were among "the first legislators who had just views of the nature of religious liberty, and who established it upon the broad and imperishable basis of justice, truth, and charity."[13]

The judge seemed to understand that there was an inherent value to society—in avoiding the wars and oppression of the past—in recognizing the religious freedom of others, even when their beliefs or practices were offensive to us. Not everyone in that courtroom grasped the concepts. Clinton comprehend two truths, explained well by preeminent legal scholar Douglas Laycock: first, "beliefs about religion are often of extraordinary importance to the individual—important enough to die for, to suffer for, to rebel for, to emigrate for, to fight to control the government for";[14] second, although it can require tremendous self-confidence to allow all people with whom we disagree the right to believe, disbelieve, or practice as they deem fit, "[o]nce it is understood that government efforts to control religious belief create conflict and suffering, that they cannot succeed without the most extraordinary tyranny (and often not even then), any government will abandon such attempts if it is committed to liberty or even if it is committed only to utilitarian avoidance of human suffering."[15]

Clinton's teaching wasn't finished. "It is essential to the free exercise of a religion," he said, "that its ordinances should be administered—that its ceremonies as well as its essentials should be protected. The sacraments of a religion are its most important elements."[16]

He noted that in his own Protestant tradition, there were only two sacraments: "Baptism and the Lord's Supper." If any law were passed that prevented either of those sacraments, every "man who hears me will answer" that the freedom of religion is infringed. "Will not the same result follow, if we deprive the Roman Catholic [sic] of one of his ordinances?"[17]

Clinton challenged Gardenier's arguments regarding dangers to society as nothing more than "hypothetical" and based on "false reasoning, if not false assumptions."[18] To try to establish a threat from "extreme cases, which may sometimes happen in the infinite variety of human actions, is totally repugnant to the rules of logic and the maxims of law."[19] The exception language in the Constitution required an immediate threat to safety. "[U]ntil men under pretense of religion, act counter to the fundamental principles of morality, and endanger the well being of the state, they are to be protected in the free exercise of their religion. If they are in error, or if they are wicked, they are to answer to the *Supreme Being*, not to the unhallowed intrusion of frail fallible mortals."[20]

With that, Clinton announced that the court would never force Kohlmann to testify.

Clinton's last act was to acquit all four defendants. There was simply no evidence against them. Bradley, Brinkerhoff, and the Phillipses walked free and quietly slipped from history's grasp. It's safe to assume that whatever happened to them, Bradley and Brinkerhoff didn't have easy lives as America struggled through the horrors of slavery and the Civil War.

There is a record around the same time of a Mary Phillips being indicted for disturbing the peace. Whether it is the same Mary Phillips is not known.

To this day, no one knows who confessed to Kohlmann.

———

Riker and Gardenier led remarkably similar lives. After the gavel fell, they bounced from various positions in government and private practice, succeeding just enough to live on in the history books.

Gardenier lasted as district attorney for only two years and died young, at age forty-five.

Riker lived to be sixty-nine, but rumors surfaced over time that he used his later years to help convict free blacks and ship them to the South as slaves. Historians continue to debate the veracity of those claims.[21]

As he placed his pen to the side, his hand likely strained from note-taking, Sampson undoubtedly felt a wave of vindication cloak him with the comforting salve of a warm blanket. His afflictions had been turned to serve a greater good. Outside, the maturing of a grand constitutional experiment was still taking shape.

He didn't stop writing or lawyering. He carried his pen almost like part of his hand. It never stopped working. As the United States stumbled on the path to realizing the promise of the Constitution, he wrote and published a history of Kohlmann's case. He drafted letters to friends and acquaintances across the globe. He published his memoirs. New religions formed. Followers of others immigrated to the new and expanding country. Sampson enjoyed his place as one of the world's first civil-rights lawyers.

He lived the same number of years before the turn of the century as after. The thirty-six years after 1800 were definitely better than those before.

For the first time in nearly six months, Kohlmann was able to breathe a sigh of relief. He exited the courthouse to a nation still in the throes of war and a congregation not yet accepted. He set back to his work of tending to the sick and dying. He pushed for the growth of his beloved literary school. He remained dedicated to the Jesuits and their mission. The case spurred a huge debate between himself and Protestant ministers across the United States regarding the scriptural basis for secrecy in confession.

In a relatively short time, he would be transferred back to George-town, where he would serve as one of the university's first presidents. Eventually, he was summoned to Rome, where, as a professor of the-ology, his students included a future pope and archbishop of Dublin.

His work in New York would survive in still-standing churches, books, and names etched in stone on various parish walls, but much would fade underneath a city quickly gobbling the rural island he had known. Historians, scholars, and judges debate the long-term importance of his case, but its reasoning and history provide profound lessons: a lack of religious freedom prior to the founding of the United States led to immeasurable human suffering, and Clinton recognized that. As Kohlmann's life faded into relative obscurity behind larger historical wars and migrations and civil-rights battles, many Americans came to enjoy the absence of religious conflict, largely because of cases like Kohlmann's. Many now take for granted just how crucial true religious liberty is and how it has eradicated religious warfare in the United States. Without it, government could force people to issue abortifacients against their religion. It could force an atheist to go to church. It could ban Muslims based on their religion. It could force a Catholic priest to testify. Enough of that, and religious warfare could very well return.

In 1836, Kohlmann contracted pneumonia while filling an assignment in the Church of Gesu in Rome.

He died the same year as William Sampson.

NOTES

1. William Sampson, *The Catholic Question in America: Whether a Roman Catholic Clergyman Be in Any Case Compellable to Disclose the Secrets of . . .* (New York, 1813), 95–97.
2. Ibid., 97.
3. Ibid.
4. Ibid., 102–3.
5. *Commercial Advertiser,* June 19, 1813, 2.
6. Charles Currier Beale, *Williams Sampson, Lawyer and Stenographer* (Boston, 1907).
7. Sampson, *The Catholic Question in America,* 103.
8. Ibid.
9. Ibid., 107.
10. Ibid., 107–8.
11. Ibid., 109.
12. Ibid.
13. Ibid., 110.
14. Douglas Laycock, *Religious Liberty, Volume 1, Overview and History* (Grand Rapids, Michigan: Wm. B. Eerdmans Publishing, 2010), 59.

15. Ibid., 61.
16. Sampson, *The Catholic Question in America,* 111.
17. Ibid.
18. Ibid., 112.
19. Ibid.
20. Ibid, 114.
21. Leslie M. Harris, *In the Shadow of Slavery: African Americans in New York City, 1626–1863* (Chicago: University of Chicago Press, 2003), 208.

PART 2

SIGN ON THE LINE

Much changed in the United States from the time of Anthony Kohlmann. Manhattan grew into a metropolis of subways and skyscrapers. The Civil War freed millions. The country expanded westward, gobbling up much of North America. With all that change came an explosion that perhaps even the Founders couldn't have anticipated: an unprecedented flowering of religious diversity. New religious groups formed. Others grew as immigrants struggled to reach America's shores in search of prosperity and freedom.

In many respects, the waves and waves of immigrants reflected the unique genius of the United States and the Constitution's protections for, among other things, religious freedom. No country in history had provided such a robust promise. So the number of belief systems grew, and that growth tested the nation's commitment to liberty for all. Members of The Church of Jesus Christ of Latter-day Saints, Jehovah's Witnesses, Muslims, Jews, atheists, agnostics, Seventh-Day Adventists, and dozens of other creeds—all either were formed or came to the United States in the century after the Anthony Kohlmann case.

This forced courts around the United States to explore, truly and for the first time, what religious liberty actually meant. Would it protect belief systems foreign to the judges reviewing them? How should the courts even define "religion"? And which religious groups or practices deserved protection over others? Over time, courts would need to grapple with these and other questions. As the United States transitioned from a mostly Christian country—largely divided between Catholics and Protestants—to a nation representing hundreds of different religious beliefs, the question loomed: Would these other religions receive the same treatment as the religious majority?

Chapter 12

A LEAP OF FAITH

M ore than a century and a half after Anthony Kohlmann walked free from that New York courtroom, in the summer of 1959, long after the development of Manhattan and the bloody battles of the Civil War, a middle-aged office manager at a Bethesda, Maryland, construction company slogged up the steps of another courthouse. His name was Roy Torcaso. To those who knew him, he mirrored the monuments on the National Mall: he loved freedom, and he wouldn't be moved.[1] Once people toured his mind, they knew where he stood on a given matter.[2] He was a short man with a crisp part in his hair and an even crisper logic to his thoughts. He lived in a small home, loved his budding family, and toiled in anonymity to provide for them. So it wasn't his physical bearing or societal stature that made his positions clear. Nor was it how he spoke, for he could be content not arguing his views.[3] There was something else, something indefinable. Those who knew him say it came from his conviction. It emanated from him like sunlight reflecting off white marble. His beliefs—about life, reason, science, and humanity's place in the universe—were as deeply and sincerely held as any principles could be. There was a certain sense of strength from Roy Torcaso, a firmness that no matter how torrential the floods around him, his foundation would not wash away.

On that hot, muggy day, Roy began for the first time to truly test that footing, driven by nothing more than his conviction and his desire to provide for his family. His boss had asked him to become a notary public, saying it would help the business. Torcaso had submitted the paperwork. His state senator had approved it.[4] The governor as well. The secretary of state had sent it to the county and with it an assignment for Roy to appear before the county clerk to be sworn in. It seemed a simple enough task. Roy didn't anticipate any problems.

At the appointed time, on June 22, 1959, he trudged up the gray steps of the Montgomery County Court House in Rockville, Maryland, just north of Washington, DC. The sun beat down. It would push the thermometer into the nineties that day.[5] Wrinkles shown around Roy's eyes. Sweat likely built up along his forehead. A tinge of gray laced the sides of his hair.

He was a man with a strong inner sense of both discipline and duty. Years in the military had taught him that. He had a daughter and son, and his wife was swelling with another girl. He knew he needed to provide for them. He was intelligent, but his job didn't pay well. He welcomed any chance to make himself more valuable to his employer. As he climbed the steps, the American flag hung from a pole next to the stairs. A little farther away, a bronze statue of a young confederate soldier, his arms crossed defiantly, stood atop a pedestal honoring the "The Thin Gray Line" of the Confederacy. Roy would have understood the soldier's defiance. His cause, not at all.

He passed under the six English-Georgian columns supporting the grand portico and through the heavy doors that led to the clerk's chambers. Among the bustling busyness of the courthouse, Roy's presence would largely have gone unnoticed, one ant marching about his business among dozens of others. The judges held their hearings, clerks would have scurried about on assignments, litigants likely whispered with their lawyers in dark corners of the courthouse's entry hallway, and criminal defendants waited to hear what hand fate would deal them.

Roy found the clerk's office and stepped through the door. In some respects, the setting couldn't have been more mundane, perhaps just one step above registering a car at the Department of Motor Vehicles.

To receive his commission as a notary, he needed to fill out some traditional paperwork and take a simple oath.

The desk clerk handed him a sheet of paper. This is what it read, exactly as written:

> State of Maryland, Montgomery County ss:
>
> In the presence of Almighty God, I, Roy R. Torcaso, do solemnly promise and declare that I will support the Constitution of the United States; and that I will be faithful and bear true allegiance to the State of Maryland, and support the Constitution and Laws thereof; and that I will, to the best of my skill and judgment, diligently and faithfully without partiality or prejudice execute the office of
>
> Notary Public of the State of Maryland
>
> In and For
>
> Montgomery County according to the Constitution and Laws of this State.
>
> I, Roy R. Torcaso, do declare that I believe in the existence of God.
>
> _____
>
> Sworn to and subscribed before me, Clerk of the Circuit Court for Montgomery County, at Rockville, Maryland, this _____ day of _____ AD, 19_____.
>
> Test:
>
> _____ Clerk

Roy was stunned. He had long known that he would have to sign an oath of some sort to become a notary public. That didn't concern him. He was comfortable affirming his support of the Constitution and of declaring allegiance to the state of Maryland. As a soldier in two wars, he had already served his country faithfully. He was willing to do so again. But the last sentence left him aghast.

Roy was many things: a veteran of two wars, a family man, a dedicated father, a devoted husband, a complicated son, a handyman, a lover of chess, and a thoughtful philosopher. He was also an atheist. He refused to sign the statement. There were many sacrifices he would make for his family, but signing a document saying he believed something he didn't was too much. In fact, he believed it would harm his family. He set the pen on the paper and informed the clerk that he would be happy to sign the oath without the declaration that he believed in the existence of God.

The head clerk in Montgomery County at the time was a man named Clayton K. Watkins. He informed Torcaso that unless he was willing to sign the oath as written, he could not receive his commission.

If he did sign it, he later told reporters, "I would be making a false statement."[6]

They argued. Roy was, if anything, not afraid to stand for his opinions. How could the government force him to say he believed something he didn't? Why would they want to? Couldn't he do just as good a job regardless of his religious beliefs?

Watkins would not be moved. Roy needed to sign or be on his way.

Roy emerged from the courthouse, his anger building.[7] He had been rejected not because of his skills or his dedication or his work ethic. He had been rejected solely because of his religious beliefs, and from a position that was largely available to anyone. He marched down the steps of the courthouse.

That afternoon, he drove from Rockville to his home in Wheaton, his hands likely stiff on the steering wheel.[8] He eased his car to a stop in front of his home and killed the engine. The house was modest: a one-story brick Cape Cod style, not more than 850-square feet, typical of what had been popping up all across the suburbs outside the Eastern United States' largest cities. It reflected Roy's financial status. The truth was, he and his wife could barely make ends meet. And the tiny house, with its few rooms and partially finished basement, reflected that.

Roy lumbered from the car to the short steps leading to the front door. Inside, the smell of dinner wafted through the living room. He traipsed into the kitchen. Everything in the room spoke to the family's precarious financial situation. It was tiny. Standing in the middle of it, he could touch the stove, the refrigerator, the counter, and the kitchen cabinets simply by reaching out.[9] They couldn't afford an air conditioner. Eileen, his wife, was cooking over the stove, the summer and culinary heat, turning the room into a boiler. Her rounded stomach hinted at the additional expenses that would come with another child.

Roy's seven-year-old son, Bill, sat at the kitchen table, which was crammed into a small nook next to a desk with a typewriter, a checkbook, and an address book.[10]

Roy was clearly tense, and Bill immediately knew something was wrong. Roy generally walked into the house with a casual and relaxed step. This time, his face was long, his demeanor solemn, his muscles tight.

What Bill didn't know was that, despite everything—the financial struggles of the family, the impending birth of a new child, the complete lack of means to fight against the power of the state, the knowledge that he would likely face fierce retribution—Roy Torcaso had made a life-altering decision, one whose outcome he couldn't possibly predict. For a man who prided himself on basing his decisions on reason and logic, he was about to make a remarkable leap of faith.

He looked to his wife and said, "I'm gonna sue."[11]

Eileen, of course, had no idea what he was talking about. "What!?"

NOTES

1. Donald Torcaso, Linda Bernstein, and Bill Torcaso, in discussion with author, July 28, 2017, and August 9, 2017.
2. Ibid.
3. Donald Torcaso, in discussion with author, August 9, 2017.
4. "Legal Vow Challenged: Aspiring Notary Public to Fight Pledge to God," *Baltimore Sun*, July 12, 1959, 38.
5. "The Weather," *Baltimore Sun*, June 22, 1959, 12.
6. "Maryland Constitution Bars Atheist from Office," *Washington Post*, July 24, 1959, B9.
7. Bill and Linda Torcaso, in discussion with author, July 28, 2017.
8. Ibid.
9. Ibid.
10. Ibid.
11. Bill Torcaso, in discussion with author, July 28, 2017.

Chapter 13

THE SHADOW
OF MOUNT RAINIER

Two things were obvious: Roy wanted to stand up for his beliefs, and he didn't have the money to do it. This wasn't surprising. Perhaps every moment of his life to that point had been building, brick upon brick, to those two conclusions. Three thousand miles away, forty-nine years earlier, in 1910, he had been born to an American mother and an Italian immigrant father, who'd literally hacked out a living in King County, Washington, lumberjacking and farming a modest plot of land. They had little to give their children, financially or emotionally. From the time he was old enough to feed himself, Roy had been forced to embrace the reality that life wasn't going to give him anything.

If anything, it was going to beat him down. His childhood bore an uncanny resemblance to a tree hardening itself with each unrelenting storm. His father, Frank Torcaso, came from a different world—a destitute region of nineteenth-century Italy—and was a lapsed Catholic jack-of-all-trades: he'd been a coal miner, a farmer, a lumberjack, a mechanic, and a powder monkey—someone who used blasting skills for mining, clearing land, and speedy justice.[1] Torcaso lore tells of a time when the family's personal firewood was being stolen; Frank bored holes into some of that wood and inserted blasting caps, hoping the thief would take those logs. A few days later, the neighbor's stove exploded and burned down his house.[2] Roy's mother, Cathryn (whom everyone called Katie), was a Protestant American with a frontier plainswoman's can-do toughness. The history of their marriage has the unsatisfying and incomplete quality of unconnected dots on a partially drawn map: they were married somewhere in Kiowa, in what would become Oklahoma; lived in Ohio; saw a daughter born in Kansas City only to see her die there as well; worked in Chico, California, around the turn of the twentieth century; moved to Auburn, Washington, by 1906; and eventually settled in a small town fifteen miles away called Enumclaw. It appears that more than anything else, necessity was what drove them across the landscape.

By the time Roy was born, they had been married for more than twenty years and had given much to simply trying to keep themselves and their children alive. They weren't always successful. Three of their first six children died of natural causes before they were even two years old. Roy was the seventh. He survived, but his life was unquestionably hard. In the shadow of Mount Rainier, amidst the lush fields and thick fir forests, he knew only the rigors of a farmer's life. He passed his days working the land, chopping down trees, sawing trunks on the gasoline log splitter outside the family farmhouse,[3] or stacking wood into cords for sale. He helped feed the family by hunting for deer and elk. The Torcasos heated their home with the very wood they cut from the forest with their own hands.

Roy's father was a taskmaster. Disobedience or failure to show proper deference often resulted in quick beatings. Sometimes the disciplinary episodes were even more random than that. They would, in fact, become the dominant memory of Roy's childhood. With each one, he grew stronger, taller, more able to stand on his own without the winds of life moving him. The need to both defend himself and to fend for himself was instilled in him from almost the day he was born.

Perhaps nowhere was this more true than with his education. In rural Washington State in the early 1900s, school was seen as more of a luxury than a necessity. Roy's father treated his son's education the way modern families treat youth sports today. If you had the money and resources to do it, wonderful; if not, it placed a distant second behind survival. At one point, Frank pulled Roy from school, demanding instead that he help with the family's work. For a time, Roy's older sister Jennie, who was eighteen years his senior and already married, gave Frank a modest amount of money every week to let her younger brother continue his schooling, but when she fell on hard times, even that dried up. Throughout his life, Roy was uniformly described as intelligent and a sound thinker who was adept at using reason to reach conclusions, but his chances of developing that natural gift seemed all but gone.

We don't know the source of Frank's tyrannical discipline. It may have been driven by his own upbringing in a poor region of Italy or perhaps simply out of an immigrant's sense that the world was harsh and unforgiving and his children needed to understand that. There may have been no rational reason. Regardless, the day came when Roy would no longer take it. He had branched beyond the confines of his own familial forest. As much as he loved and revered his mother (decades later, his children recalled, he would tear up anytime he spoke of her), he didn't need his parents. He ran away.

Frank tried to force him back, even summoned the police and local authorities, demanding they force him to stay and help the family with the work. The police sided with Roy. Though not yet a man, he was on his own.

As he bounced around the state trying to make ends meet, change was coming. Larger cities and complex financial systems continued to expand. Many people from rural America flocked to urban centers and the industrial opportunities they provided. The roaring twenties made young Americans like Roy feel as though nothing could cut them down. Then, just before Roy's nineteenth birthday, the stock market crashed. The Great Depression fell across the Western world like a menacing shadow.

Agricultural industries, including lumber, were hit hard. Finding a job proved nearly impossible. A few years later, when Roy was in his midtwenties and with no work, he felt inspired to return to school. He had moved to Wenatchee, a town on the other side of the mountains, along the Columbia River, where his older sister Rose had settled years before. There, he decided to finish high school. Though four years older than his younger brother Jesse and eight years older than the last Torcaso brother, Don, Roy graduated high school the same year as both of them. In was 1936.[4] He was twenty-six years old.

Along the way, he learned how to type. When he finally took a civil service test, his typing skills provided a path out of his troubled childhood. He was offered a job as a typist with the federal government in Washington, DC. He hopped aboard a car on the Northern Pacific and never looked back.

As Roy's train snaked its way out of the shadowy forests of Washington and across the continent, the rest of the world was rumbling. Japan had withdrawn from various international treaties, conquered parts of China, continued its colonial conquest of the Far East, and prepared for what it saw as a war mandated by destiny. Meanwhile, in Europe, a frenzied mustached man and his band of nationalist socialists were tightening their grip on Germany.

Free from the shackles of his childhood, Roy spent the next few years developing his skills at whatever jobs he could find. He dutifully did his work for the government. His eyes were open to a world outside the shade of the conifers of his home state, and he waited for what life would bring his way.

He didn't have to wait long. He was aware of the political happenings of DC,[5] and as he strove to make a living, he would have seen the headlines oozing out of Europe:

Hitler Is Given Sudetenland; Accord Averts World War;[6]

Nazis Loot Jews' Shops, Burn City's Biggest Synagogue to Avenge Paris Embassy Aide;[7]

U.S. Denounces Nazi Invasion of Czecho-Slovakia as 'Wanton' and Abrogates Trade Treaty for All of the Area Annexed;[8]

Reich Is Closing in: . . . Cities Are Bombed; Troops Enter from East Prussia, Pomerania, Slovakia, Silesia;[9]

Britain and France in War at 6 A.M.; Hitler Won't Halt Attack on Poles; Chamberlain Calls Empire to Fight;[10]

Germany and Norway at War; Nazi Army Invades Denmark;[11]

Nazis Invade Holland, Belgium, Luxembourg; Widespread Land and Air Battles Raging; Planes Bomb Brussels;[12]

Italy Invades Greece, Starting Balkan Drive, As Athens Rejects a Three-Hour Ultimatum; Metaxas asks Greeks to Fight to the Death;[13]

Hitler Declares War on Russia: Nazis, Fins and Rumanians March Against Soviets.[14]

Many in the United States, including Roy most likely, had taken a passing interest in the war in Europe. It was distant. It had little effect on day-to-day life. The notion of American isolationism ruled the day. Then Japan changed everything. As the Land of the Rising Sun continued its domination of the Far East, the United States responded mostly with economic sanctions. Top Japanese military officials, however, knew that approach would not last forever; once Japan conquered the Philippines, the Americans would no longer stand idly by. They decided that a preemptive attack, annihilating the American fleet and rendering it useless, would be their best approach. Preparations began.

On the morning of December 7, 1941, there would have been little in the DC newspapers to get Roy excited. In fact, the headlines that morning in *The Washington Post* and other papers focused merely on continued negotiations with Japan and hopes for peace. Citizens in the nation's capital gobbled their breakfasts, donned their clothes, and ventured about their days as they would any other Sunday. Hours later, roughly five thousand miles to the west, 183 Japanese planes would plunge toward Oahu, Hawaii, in the first wave of the attack. By mid- to late afternoon, every radio station in the nation's capital would have interrupted its normal broadcast with a message similar to what NBC injected: "We interrupt this program to bring you this special news bulletin. The Japanese have attacked Pearl Harbor."[15]

After the attack, Roy, like many men, decided to serve his country. At thirty-one, he was also older than nearly all soldiers sent to combat, with considerably more experience in an office. He was assigned to serve near Lakenheath, England, as a member of the quartermaster corps. He was made an officer. At the time, the Nazis had invaded and conquered most of Europe. Their bombs and planes now targeted Roy's station.

———

As he went about doing his duties, Roy seemed likely to navigate the river of life solo.[16] It was as inevitable as the pending Nazi invasion. But war has a knack for being unpredictable—in all sorts of ways. Roy was charged with ensuring the troops had all the supplies they would need and that those defending the British coast would have everything necessary for building defenses along the beaches.

One day, as the war raged on, "a work item passed over" his desk. He "made two phone calls, and that was the end of it."[17] Or so he thought. One of those calls was inconsequential. The other would change his life. It was to a man named William Lusher, a builder who'd helped construct British defenses along the country's eastern seaboard. Something about Roy's demeanor must have caught the builder's attention, because he eventually invited the American officer to his home for a dinner party. There, he met Eileen Ruth Lusher, William's beautiful daughter.

For the rest of the war, Roy courted Eileen. In between the anxiety brought by the sputter of airplanes soaring overhead and the threat of Nazi bombs, they found time to waltz, to talk, and to fall in love.

When the war ended, England was largely ravished. Luxuries took a back seat to necessities, but Roy was determined to marry his sweetheart. Leaving his love behind, he traveled to the United States and, as his daughter retells, "amassed the necessary fabric . . . for the wedding dress and the bridesmaid's dresses."[18] After sailing back across the Atlantic, he married Eileen in January 1946. Their faces beaming, they trotted down the steps of Eileen's family church, Roy in his full army captain's uniform, she in her flowing white wedding gown. The war over, their lives were as free and open as the ocean horizon.

After the wedding, Roy and Eileen settled in Washington, DC, and began the arduous process of building a life. Their first daughter, Linda, was born the next year. With no formal college education, Roy did his best to make ends meet while Eileen set about the challenging task of raising the family. Roy remained in the National Guard, and when the conflict in Korea broke out in 1950, the army shipped the entire family to Monterrey, California. There, at the Army Language School, he learned Korean so he could help interrogate prisoners of war. He and Eileen also had a second child, Bill. Through all of this, Roy earned enough money to provide for the family, but little more. Eventually, they moved back to Maryland and bought a quaint brick home in Wheaton. Roy was shipped to Korea.

As he put his language skills to use in the Land of the Morning Calm, the family kept a black-and-white photo of him in his army uniform on a frame above the television. The headlines out of Korea conveyed dismay. Initially the war went well. But the United States suffered heavy losses, especially after China injected itself into the conflict. The photo above the TV begged the unspoken question of whether Roy would ever return.

While he was away, just shortly before his return, on October 5, 1953, he and Eileen had another baby, a little girl. They named her Diana. She died the next day.

His service to his country complete, Roy continued the struggle of providing for the family. Times were tough. Whatever jobs he could find were enough to put food on the table and a roof over the heads of his wife and children, but he was in his midforties and, between his tumultuous childhood and two wars, had missed the opportunity for college. He wasn't a quitter—he tried to go to night school at George Washington University. In the end, balancing that with a family, the death of a baby, and a full-time job proved too challenging. He never graduated.

That was a minor problem compared to his religious views. Although his path to atheism is as hazy as the Washington coast obscured by a summer fog, one thing is for certain: Roy did not embrace his religious views to be popular. He learned through sad experience what every other atheist throughout American history has come to know long since. In the mid-twentieth century, to be an atheist in the United States was to be an outcast.

In American history, few groups have been more maligned than atheists. From the early days of the republic, the public and even the courts were skeptical that they could be trustworthy witnesses in court.[19] The vast majority of atheists and agnostics faced severe discrimination nearly everywhere they went, including in their homes, at school, and in the workplace.[20] Many parents would rather their children died alone and penniless than marry an atheist.[21] And during Roy's formative years in DC and the wars, one prominent lawyer noted that to most people, an atheist was "but a monster, in human form."[22]

By the 1950s, fear of the godless communism seeping out of the Soviet Union had forced atheists so far into the shadows it appeared they might never see sunlight again. In the eyes of many Americans, atheists and Soviet communists were indistinguishable. This is not entirely surprising, since the Soviet Union had declared atheism its state religion. As the Cold War raged, to ensure the United States stood in stark contrast to the USSR, Congress in 1954 added the phrase "under God" to the Pledge of Allegiance. In 1956, they adopted "In God We Trust" as the national motto. This was—and remains—a cause for rejoicing for many Americans, but for people like Roy, it would likely have been further evidence that his country, which he had served faithfully in two wars, didn't want him.

The culture became so toxic that atheists like Roy had two choices: they could "keep still"[23] and pretend to believe something they didn't, or they could make their beliefs known and risk losing their jobs, their livelihood, and any social standing they enjoyed. So for Roy, the choice to believe in the absence of divinity carried absolutely no worldly benefit. His reasons for embracing it came from elsewhere.

It may have had something to do with his parents. Family lore suggests they were hardly devout—one story whispers that his father even sent a letter to the pope denouncing Catholicism.[24] But given Roy's seeming desire to escape his childhood, it appears unlikely that he would have been following in his father's footsteps. One theory is that he was contrarian in nature, and atheism was a way to rebel against the dominant religious culture of his day. It's possible but unlikely. Roy was not a caricature and can't be reduced so easily. Like all people, he was complex, a bundle of contradictions. It is true that he learned to stand up for himself during his youth, but he also had little trouble with authority—he served honorably in two wars and in the National Guard. He was not, by any stretch, an anarchist. We know it wasn't Eileen—she was a Methodist and played piano at church most Sundays. And Roy even allowed his children to attend the Methodist church for much of their upbringing even as he explained to them that they would one day need to make their own choices regarding religion.[25]

Most faith journeys are akin to a seed growing and maturing over time as it is nourished through pondering, prayer, study, and action. Roy's was likely no different. Those who knew him best say one of his most distinguishing characteristics was his logical mind. He valued evidence, reason, and rational thinking. For that reason as much as any other, he enjoyed chess with the same fervor most men enjoy team sports; he founded and served in leadership positions on the Suburban Chess Club of Wheaton[26] and even retiled the floor of his partially finished basement to resemble a chess board.[27] It may have simply been that he couldn't believe in something for which he perceived no physical evidence. Roy had seen a world of abuse, privation, war, death, and hardship—one that had given him very little.

We know he contemplated the question deeply and for a long period of time. Just like millions of others, he pondered, he studied, and he may have even prayed—but without direct, concrete evidence, his journey led him to the conclusion that there was no one in the heavens watching over the affairs of humanity or of the earth. Whatever path he followed, by the time he reached adulthood, he believed in the absence of a divine being with the same sincerity and passion that had boiled in Anthony Kohlmann's heart when he took the stand in New York City nearly 150 years earlier.

Roy would not be forced into confessing something he didn't believe. If he was going to change his mind about God, eternity, or things of a spiritual nature, it would be on his own terms, on his personal timeline, as a result of his own spiritual journey, not because the government had forced a false profession of belief upon him.

He also had few resources. Chance, he believed, had not placed him the same economic pedestal it had some others. But that didn't mean he couldn't stand up for himself and anyone who didn't want the government telling them how to believe. In late summer of 1959, he set out to do exactly that.

Notes

1. Donald Torcaso, Jr., in discussion with author, August 9, 2017.
2. Ibid.
3. Bill Torcaso, in discussion with author, July 28, 2017.
4. Wenatchee High School Commencement Program, 1935–36 school year.
5. Donald Torcaso, Jr., discussion with author.
6. *Atlanta Constitution,* September 30, 1938, 1.
7. *New York Times,* November 10, 1938, 1.
8. *Washington Post,* March 18, 1939, 1.
9. *New York Times,* September 2, 1939, 1.
10. *New York Times,* September 3, 1939, 1.
11. *Washington Post,* April 9, 1940, 1.
12. *Washington Post,* May 10, 1940, 1.
13. *New York Times,* October 28, 1940, 1.
14. *Washington Post,* June 22, 1941, 1.
15. NBC Radio Broadcast, December 7, 1941.
16. Bill Torcaso and Linda Bernstein, in discussion with author, July 28, 2017.
17. Bill Torcaso in ibid., discussion with author.
18. Linda Bernstein in ibid., discussion with author.

19. Leigh Eric Schmidt, *Village Atheists: How America's Unbelievers Made Their Way in a Godly Nation* (New Jersey: Princeton University Press, 2016), 276.
20. Ibid., 20.
21. Ibid., 20.
22. Frank Swancara, in Schmidt, *Village Atheists*, 24.
23. Ibid.
24. Donald Torcaso, Jr., discussion with author.
25. Linda Bernstein, in discussion with author, July 10, 2017.
26. "Officers Elected by Chess Club," *Washington D.C. Evening Star*, D6, October 25, 1964.
27. Torcaso and Bernstein, discussion with author.

Chapter 14

INSURMOUNTABLE ODDS

I f his crusade was a chess match, Roy's first step was as unprovocative as pondering the risks and strategy of which pawn he should move first: he visited the library. He needed research. Something about the state's position struck him as obviously unfair, but he wasn't a lawyer. He wanted to know if the law matched his gut.

We don't know precisely what he found. Most likely he realized he was in over his head. For most lay people, understanding a new area of the law is nearly impossible. More important, even if Roy had been able to locate the right books and in them the correct content, what he found would have been disheartening. The odds were stacked against him.

By 1959, religious liberty in the United States was a house of cards. It survived mostly because there were few religious minorities who stressed it. The ones who did often faced violence, dispossession of their property, imprisonment, and even murder—the very things DeWitt Clinton had foreseen. Despite the victorious moment Anthony Kohlmann had enjoyed and the clarity with which Clinton had seen the issue, in the decades since, the United States Supreme Court, federal agencies, and many state governments had essentially sucked all meaning out of the constitutional protections for religious minorities.

Maryland, along with many other states, had put explicit text in its constitution that allowed government officials to require a belief in some form of God for anyone who wanted to hold public office.[1] So under the state constitution, the clerk's refusal to give Roy a job because of his religious beliefs was completely legal. That meant Roy had only one desperate move to avoid checkmate. He had to show that the United States Constitution trumped the Maryland Constitution. Unfortunately for him, the Supreme Court had made that strategy nearly impossible.

Throughout the latter half of the nineteenth century, as more and more religious minorities—including atheists—began migrating to or forming in the United States, the more the majority culture pushed against them. The results were appalling. In 1838, the governor of Missouri issued an order against members of The Church of Jesus Christ of Latter-day Saints, which, at the time, were often referred to by the nickname "Mormons," that read, "the Mormons must be treated as enemies, and must be exterminated or driven from the State if necessary for the public peace—their outrages are beyond all description."[2] In 1831, a court in Pennsylvania forced a Jew to violate his Sabbath to appear for trial.[3] In 1859, a public school master in Massachusetts whipped a Catholic boy's hands with a rattan stick until he agreed to recite Protestant sayings in class.[4] The children of Jehovah's Witnesses were expelled from schools because they wouldn't salute the American flag.[5] In 1886, in Boston, an atheist was convicted of committing the "crime" of blasphemy, resulting in fines simply for professing his unpopular beliefs.[6] The list goes on.

The outcome was exactly what history had taught would happen when religious liberty is suppressed. Violent skirmishes bubbled up throughout the United States. *The New York Times* reported on an angry mob in Boston that had pelted the aforementioned atheist with "ancient eggs and vegetables" when he set up a tent for preaching. "They chopped away the guy ropes of the tent and slashed the canvas with their knives," according to the article. "When the tent collapsed, the crowd rushed for the speaker to inflict further punishment."[7] Catholics formed their own private schools to escape persecution in public schools. In the 1940s, a group of public officials and American Legionnaires imprisoned several Jehovah's Witnesses, forced them to drink large amounts of castor oil, and then dragged them by rope through the streets of Richwood, West Virginia, all in an attempt to prevent them from preaching in the town.[8]

Some of these matters went to the courts; many have been lost to history. The cases that affected the law the most involved the members of the Church of Jesus Christ. In Missouri, hundreds were shot, killed, or otherwise assaulted.[9] Approximately eight thousand fled their homes while mobs burned them to the ground and stole their property.[10] They later trudged out of the United States, setting up refugee camps on the plains of Nebraska and Iowa. One in twelve died.[11] Though they eventually arrived in what is today Utah, the violence didn't stop. Some members of the Church of Jesus Christ wrongly retaliated against what they perceived as external threats, slaughtering nearly 120 emigrants passing through the desert territory.[12] In 1857, the federal government sent an entire army to Utah to suppress a perceived uprising against the United States.[13] Tensions were so great, the so-called "Mormon struggle"—stemming from a lack of religious liberty—became, as one scholar put it, "one of the all-consuming conflicts of the second half of the nineteenth century" for almost all Americans.[14] Newspapers followed it. Cartoonists and satirists invoked it frequently.[15] Novelists—including Harriet Beecher Stowe—monitored it with great interest.[16]

For Roy, huddled alone in a library, poring over books, the state of American religious liberty would have been demoralizing. When the "Mormon question" had raged near the end of the previous century, a series of cases had bubbled up to the Supreme Court. The last of these gutted Roy's arguments. It was known as *Davis v. Beason*[17] and had involved the religious practice of plural marriage and an Idaho statute that prohibited anyone from voting in that state if they engaged in plural marriage.[18] If that had been the end of it, the case would not have affected Roy at all. But the Idaho statute went further, much further. It prohibited from voting anyone who even *encouraged* the practice of plural marriage. It banned those who did nothing more than teach the doctrine. It blocked people for simply being members of The Church of Jesus Christ of Latter-day Saints, even if they didn't engage in that practice. In fact, the law was so extensive it could have been interpreted to bar even those who did nothing more than *believe* in the Church of Jesus Christ.[19] And it required all voters to sign an oath signifying that they weren't in the prohibited groups.[20]

The Supreme Court upheld the statute.[21] For casual observers, the case likely stood only for the proposition that states could ban the practice of polygamy. For careful readers, however, it stood for much more: the idea that government could regulate people even for their beliefs. Thomas Jefferson would have turned in his grave. More than one hundred years prior, he had developed a list of religious behavior to include:

> religious conduct
> worship
> religious speech
> membership in a religious group
> belief

The further down the list you went, he believed, the less the government should regulate. For conduct, Jefferson had acknowledged that "legitimate powers of government extend to such acts only as are injurious to others."[22] Once you got to belief, however, Jefferson had been adamant that government simply didn't belong. He said, "[I]t does me no injury for my neighbor to say there are twenty gods, or no god. It neither picks my pocket nor breaks my leg."[23]

In *Davis v. Beason*, the Supreme Court obliterated that understanding. Government could regulate any belief or practice that was simply unpopular in the majority culture.

If Roy was going to win, he needed to defeat not only the Maryland Constitution but a binding precedent of the United States Supreme Court. It was like beating a queen with nothing but a pawn. He was outmatched, and he needed help.

NOTES

1. Leigh Eric Schmidt, *Village Atheists: How America's Unbelievers Made Their Way in a Godly Nation* (New Jersey: Princeton University Press, 2016), 276.
2. Lilburn W. Boggs, Letter to General John B. Clark, October 27, 1838, as cited in

T. Ward Frampton, "'Some Savage Tribe': Race, Legal Violence, and the Mormon War of 1838," *Journal of Mormon History* 40, no. 1 (2014): 176.

3. *Phillips et al. (Simon's Executors) v. Gratz*, 2 Pen & W. 412 (Pa. 1831).

4. *Commonwealth v. Cooke*, 7 Am. L. Reg. 417 (Boston, Police Ct. 1859).

5. Shawn F. Peters, *Judging Jehovah's Witnesses: Religious Persecution and the Dawn of the Rights Revolution* (Lawrence: University of Kansas Press, 2000).

6. Schmidt, *Village Atheists*, 171–72.

7. "At 1886 Trial, An Atheist Paid a Price," *New York Times*, January 26, 1997.

8. *Catlette v. United States*, 132 F.2d 902, 903–05 (1943).

9. Joseph Young, Affidavit, Adams Co., IL, June 4, 1839, L. Tom Perry Special Collections, Brigham Young University, Provo, Utah; Beth Shumway Moore, *Bones in the Well: The Haun's Mill Massacre, 1838, A Documentary History* (Norman, OK: Arthur H. Clark Company, 2006).

10. Clark V. Johnson, ed., *Mormon Redress Petitions: Documents of the 1833–1838 Missouri Conflict* (Provo, UT: Brigham Young University Religious Studies Center, 1992), 18.

11. Richard E. Bennett, *Mormons at the Missouri, 1846–1852: "And Should We Die . . ."* (Norman: University of Oklahoma Press, 1987), 141.

12. Ronald W. Walker, Richard E. Turley, Jr., and Glen M. Leonard, *Massacre at Mountain Meadows: An American Tragedy* (New York: Oxford University Press, 2008).

13. William P. MacKinnon, ed., *At Sword's Point, Part 1: A Documentary History of the Utah War to 1858* (Norman, OK: Arthur H. Clark Company, 2008).

14. Schmidt, *Village Atheists*, 144.

15. Ibid., 141–52.

16. Preface by Harriett Beecher Stowe, *Tell It All*, Fanny Stenhouse (Hartford: A. D. Worthington & Co., 1875).

17. *Davis v. Beason*, 133 U.S. 333 (1890).

18. The vast majority of members of The Church of Jesus Christ of Latter-day Saints did not engage in the practice of plural marriage, so a law banning all such members from voting would have swept up thousands of people who had nothing to do with the practice.

19. *Davis*, 133 U.S. at 346–47. The statute at issue in *Davis v. Beason* read, in part, as follows: "[No] person who is a bigamist or polygamist or who teaches, advises, counsels, or encourages any person or persons to become biga mists [*sic*] or polygamists, or to commit any other crime defined by law, or to enter into what is known as plural or celestial marriage, or who is a member of any order, organization or association which teaches, advises, counsels, or encourages its members or devotees or any other persons to commit the crime of bigamy or polygamy, or any other crime defined by law, either as a rite or ceremony of such order, organization, or association or otherwise, is permitted to vote at any election, or to hold any position or office of honor, trust."

20. Ibid., at 347.

21. Ibid., at 347–48.

22. Thomas Jefferson, "Notes on the State of Virginia," Query 17, 157–61 (1784); accessible online at http://press-pubs.uchicago.edu/founders/documents/amendI _religions40.html.

23. Ibid.

Chapter 15

A GLIMMER OF HOPE
IN THE DARKNESS

With no money, Roy explored the jungle of DC attorneys, looking for someone to help him. In the midst of the Cold War, there were few takers. As an atheist, Roy was a second-class citizen. But he had no choice. "I absolutely cannot take the oath," he told reporters. "I would be making a false statement if I did say that I believed in God. My only religious guide is a profound respect for the Golden Rule."[1]

He finally approached the Washington office of the American Civil Liberties Union, who referred him to two attorneys, brothers, who, based on their political aspirations, were both hungry for prominence and willing to fight lost causes: Joseph A. and Carlton R. Sickles, of the law firm Sickles & Sickles. Both men wore warm smiles and kind eyes. They were politically connected and had their eyes set on higher offices. Neither knew anything about religious-liberty law.

Joseph agreed to take the case for free. His strategy was simple. They would first petition the governor, whose office had already approved Roy's commission, and argue that the state could not require a religious oath for someone to hold office. His hope was that they could resolve the problem through political channels.

The governor, however, did what politicians do best and deflected the problem away from his office. He referred it to the state attorney general to render an opinion. His administration would force the county to change its practice only if the attorney general concluded Roy was correct.

Sickles submitted arguments to the state's legal department. He argued that it violated certain provisions of the state constitution and the federal Constitution. He and Roy then waited for an opinion.

The petition landed on the desk of an aspiring thirty-nine-year-old lawyer named Stedman Prescott, Jr. A former collegiate athlete at the University of Maryland who enjoyed boating, he was a deputy attorney general for the state.[2] He was an experienced and capable man with a keen legal mind whose father was a former state senator. He was heavier now than in his basketball days,[3] but his mental abilities were in peak form.

In less than two weeks, he issued the opinion.

It was a slap in Roy's face. Prescott wrote that his office had "held in many opinions that the office of notary public is an office of profit and trust under the State Constitution. The declaration of belief in the existence of God is not an oath of office as such, but is merely a declaration prescribed by the Constitution which must be made to qualify the official to take the oath of office."[4] He concluded that the Maryland Constitution allowed it, and the United States Constitution did not prohibit it. The attorney general would not help Roy against the county. In fact, they would now be Roy's greatest enemy. They would defend Watkins if Roy sued.

Roy was irate. Sickles declared they would fight. He announced it the next day.

"The point at issue," Roy told reporters, "is not whether I believe in a Supreme Being, but whether the State has a right to inquire into my beliefs."[5] Despite his determination, he must have felt a sense of foreboding. He was taking this to court with a lawyer who was officially outside his comfort zone. Sickles was a talented attorney, but he knew little about this kind of fight.

And until that point, Roy had largely been operating in obscurity. His boss, neighbors, friends, coworkers, the state, his opponents—none of them truly knew what he was up to or what he believed. That was about to change.

———————

Far away, sitting in his office in New York City, a bald lawyer named Leo Pfeffer noticed something interesting that had just crossed his desk. Pfeffer was slender, with the kind of pointed gaze that projected intelligence and demanded people take him seriously. His eyes were intimidating, as if they could see right through you. He was both demanding and savvy, the kind of man who could drive his agenda through a bureaucratic organization with the same skill as a general leading an army.[6]

He had been searching for something for a long time. In many respects, he had been alone in that search, even derided.

Through full-rimmed glasses, he scoured the Religious News Service wire. Roy's situation was listed. It popped off the page like a gun shot.

Unbeknownst to Roy and Sickles, Pfeffer started scrambling.

———————

Still reeling from the defeat with the attorney general's office, Sickles decided he would file a petition for writ of mandamus, which is essentially a request for an order from a court mandating that the county clerk swear Roy in as a notary public.

Roy agreed.

The petition would argue two points: that the First Amendment of the United States Constitution, and specifically its clauses related to religion, banned the religious test, and that the Maryland Constitution should not be interpreted the way the attorney general had read it. The case would be titled *Roy R. Torcaso v. Clayton K. Watkins, Clerk of the Circuit Court for Montgomery County, Maryland.* Joseph prepared the paper work. They filed it on August 13, 1959.

To a newspaper reporter following the case, Roy said, "God means many things to many people. I don't believe the state has any right to inquire into my beliefs."[7]

The petition would have reached Prescott at the attorney general's office at roughly the same time. His role had officially changed. He was no longer simply giving an opinion. His job now was to represent Clayton Watkins. He had plans to run for Montgomery County circuit court judge. That meant this was a case he needed to win.

He carefully read Roy's petition. Then he started preparing for battle.

———

Back at home, even at work, Roy languished in the gut-wrenching position of a person whose destiny rested in someone else's hands. The petition had been filed, and that meant there was little for him to do but wait on his lawyers and the court. Like most people, he no doubt wanted instant justice. But the legal system moves like Congress.

As the days crawled by, Roy and Eileen kept their chins up, wondering how the lawsuit would affect them, unsure if the goodwill of the attorneys—or Roy's boss—would last forever. As was common in their home, to pass the time, Roy worked on the car or the house, fixing electrical or plumbing problems, his seven-year-old son, Bill, at his side holding the flashlight.[8] Occasionally Roy would go play chess in the cafeteria of the Wheaton nursing home, or he would teach the game to Bill. Sometimes they would wrestle on the living room rug after dinner.[9] Roy built a model railroad in the basement.[10] On Saturdays, he would ease himself down on the back porch, lay out his Kiwi shoe polish, and buff his shoes.

Eileen, increasingly uncomfortable as her pregnancy progressed, worked with Linda to prepare for the coming baby. Around the dinner table, Roy would grill Bill and Linda on what they had learned each day. Given the lack of educational opportunities he had received as a child, he was devoted to schooling for them.[11]

Fall eventually skulked in and stole away some of summer's heat. As the leaves began to drop, Roy and Bill put in the winter storm windows and prepared the house for the blister of the coming months. It's possible that even then, during the earliest days of the case, as newspapers began running more and more articles about Roy, rumors swirled among neighbors and colleagues about his case and his religious beliefs. Prejudices began to crawl from their holes.

In New York, Leo Pfeffer rejoiced. In Roy's case, he had finally found what he was looking for. The intellectual attorney, whom Roy likely didn't even know existed, hastily put together a memorandum to a colleague of his in which he wrote, "I strongly recommend that we pursue this matter further."[12] He emphasized that the DC area office of his organization should investigate, look into Roy, scrutinize his attorneys, and report back.[13] Time was of the essence.

At the attorney general's office, Prescott began drafting a document known as a demurrer. It would allow him to argue that no matter what Roy put in his petition, he should still lose. In other words, there was absolutely no set of facts under which Roy could win his case, so the judge should simply rule in favor of the clerk immediately and not let the case proceed any further.

His argument was simple. Article 37 of the Declaration of Rights of the Maryland Constitution provided that "no religious test ought ever be required as a qualification for any office of profit or trust in this state, other than a declaration of belief in the existence of God." Under that provision, Watkins was perfectly entitled to require that Roy declare he believe in God.

As Prescott crafted his arguments, he had every reason to be confident.

Joseph Sickles did not. He would have been searching for a silver bullet that simply didn't exist. And he wasn't having any luck.[14] He knew the demurrer from the state was coming. Like Roy, something in his gut told him that the state's position was just wrong, but the law he could find wasn't helpful. The First Amendment to the Constitution includes two clauses relating to religious liberty. They are inextricably connected:

"Congress shall make no law respecting an establishment of religion, or prohibiting the free exercise thereof . . ."

The Establishment Clause had been read to mean largely that government could not establish a formal, national religion. Sickles likely had no idea how far it went beyond that. The Free Exercise Clause seemed to mean that government could make no law restricting the exercise of religion. *Davis v. Beason* and the other cases involving The Church of Jesus Christ of Latter-day Saints had largely obliterated that concept. For Sickles, neither clause gave him the ammunition he needed. And he apparently didn't find anything else that would be helpful either.

As he started the arduous process of putting together the brief that would support Roy's petition, he had to come up with something. The best he could think of was to argue that the Establishment Clause forbade the use of religious tests to determine if someone could hold public office, even one like Maryland's, which required a declaration of belief in God.[15] No court had ever held that, but Sickles felt he could make the argument in good faith.[16]

He had no idea if the judge over Roy's case would take the leap. Judges were assigned to cases randomly, and the judge they drew, a church-going conservative named Ralph Shure, was unlikely to jump. He was newly appointed. He had been on the bench only a couple of months, and his appointment was only interim, lasting just until the upcoming election the following year. That meant Judge Shure was going to run to try to get enough votes to earn the actual fifteen-year seat. When votes counted, controversial rulings could be devastating—the chances of success seemed slim.

If that weren't bad enough, Joseph Sickles also had to deal with the costs of the case if it escalated. His client didn't have the money to pay him. He had agreed to handle it *pro bono*, but with the state adamantly defending its position, who knew how long the battle would rage? He was going to war with a skeletal strategy and no armory.

As Sickles did his best on his own to slog through the murky jungle of an area of law he'd never before navigated in depth, at least one worry had to have nagged him. One thing that plagues trial lawyers perhaps more than anything else is the fear that they may be missing an argument. This is more than a minor concern. The rules of appellate litigation do not allow someone to raise an argument for the first time on appeal, which means if a party fails to bring an argument before the trial court, they waive that argument forever. Unfortunately for Sickles, he didn't know what he didn't know. He likely hoped he had researched the issues thoroughly, but if he was missing a key case or point, he might not realize it until after Roy's case was lost.

In New York, Leo Pfeffer had seen enough. His team had reported back. They had investigated the case. They had researched Roy and Sickles. The ruling from the attorney general's office had reached Pfeffer's desk, along with Sickles's arguments. It was time to reveal himself before it was too late.

Pfeffer was born in Austria-Hungary in 1910 but immigrated to the United States when he was two. He graduated from New York University Law School in 1933, dabbled in private practice for a time, and then became staff counsel for the American Jewish Congress (AJC). Formed in 1918, the group originally had only two goals: provide aid to Jews in Europe who had suffered during World War I and restore the State of Israel in the Holy Land. Over time, its mission had morphed. Spurred by the horrors of the Holocaust during World War II, by the 1950s, the AJC had gotten involved in litigation to protect the rights of Jews. Along the way, Pfeffer had climbed the ladder to become the organization's lead counsel. He and his team realized "perhaps more than any other group that a legal principle established by one minority group will often accrue to the benefit of others."[17] The AJC had begun to take action for minorities beyond just Jews, including for black Americans.[18] They also realized that a victory for Roy Torcaso, this maligned atheist in Maryland, would be a victory for the religious liberty of everyone. Pfeffer, especially, knew that if a state could prevent people from holding jobs simply because they were atheists, it could one day do the same to a Jew, a Christian, a Muslim, a Catholic—anyone.

By the time he decided to help Roy, Pfeffer was already a gravitational force in the world of religious liberty litigation. Every case of any significance seemed to be in his orbit. He had the strategic mind of a politician. He knew which battles to avoid and which ones to fight. For some time, he had been looking for the right case to champion.

In the fall of 1959, after thoroughly vetting Roy's case, he knew he had found it.

———

Sickles's phone rang in mid-September 1959. It was Pfeffer. The call would have materialized like manna from heaven. Pfeffer offered to have the AJC assume chief responsibility for the legal strategy of the case and to cover the costs from trial and on through appeal. The more Pfeffer talked, the more Sickles must have realized that the AJC had the expertise he was sorely lacking. Pfeffer knew of cases and laws that would help. He knew the best strategy to reach a victory. With Roy's permission, Sickles agreed.[19]

Pfeffer wanted Sickles to remain on the case, but he suggested serious additions to the arguments Sickles had developed. To that point, Sickles had really only fleshed out one point: that the federal Constitution's Establishment Clause did not allow the state to exclude people from public office based solely on their religious beliefs. Pfeffer believed they could add so much more. First, because the state was trying to favor theistic religious belief over nontheistic religious belief, Roy could also make an argument based on the Constitution's Equal Protection Clause—that is, government must treat everyone equally. Second, the federal Constitution contained a provision that prohibited the federal government from refusing public office to anyone based on a religious test. It was unclear whether that provision applied to state governments. But the reasoning for it certainly did, in Pfeffer's view. Untold human suffering had resulted from government's attempts to give positions of power only to certain sects.[20]

Finally, Pfeffer knew that changes were occurring in the field of religious liberty. Despite the sandy foundation the cases involving the Church of Jesus Christ had created, the Supreme Court in recent years had been showing signs of a new willingness to protect religious minorities. In 1940, it had ruled that Jehovah's Witnesses had the right to preach their faith openly in the streets without first getting a license from the state and without being guilty of disturbing the peace.[21] A series of similar cases protecting other Jehovah's Witnesses bubbled up at the same time. Because almost all of them involved both speech and religion, there was some question of how strongly they actually protected religious liberty by itself. Even so, Pfeffer saw the ice beginning to thaw. He knew what arguments to make. He knew what cases to invoke and how to get around *Davis v. Beason*.[22]

Not everyone was willing to help. An endless stream of bad news about the Soviet Union's attempt to force atheism on its people made atheists in the United States feel like lepers. No one wanted to be associated with them. Though the ACLU was willing to file an amicus brief on Roy's behalf and the American Jewish Congress had thrown its weight behind him, other groups remained distant. The Anti-Defamation League, another Jewish advocacy group, refused to support Roy. One influential member of the group penned a letter to a colleague, reflecting the thinking of the time: "In my opinion the situation is so obviously unjust and unconstitutional that there is no doubt that [Roy] will succeed in establishing the point without the assistance of the ADL. On the other hand, an interference in the case might be construed as an ungodly attitude and, therefore, be inadvisable."[23]

Simply being associated with Roy was toxic. For a case as high profile as his, he had surprisingly little support. Only a few individuals, like Pfeffer, who truly understood that religious liberty for one was a liberty for all, were willing to publicly align with Roy. They prepared for court.

Notes

1. "Legal Vow Challenged: Aspiring Notary Public to Fight Pledge to God," *Baltimore Sun*, July 12, 1959, 38.
2. "Former Md. Official, Lawyer Stedman Prescott Jr. Dies," *Washington Post*, February 10, 1989, C4.
3. "Prescott Jr. to Seek Montgomery Judgeship," *Washington Post*, February 11, 1960, B5.
4. "Maryland Constitution Bars Atheist from Office," *Washington Post*, July 24, 1959, B9.
5. "Torcaso Set to Fight for Notary Post," *Washington Post*, July 25, 1959, D1.
6. Roger K. Newmann, ed., *The Yale Biographical Dictionary of American Law*, "Pfeffer, Leo" (New Haven, CT: Yale University Press, 2009), 425–26.
7. "Atheist Files Suit for Notary Post," *Washington Post*, August 14, 1959, B8.
8. Bill Torcaso and Linda Bernstein, in discussion with author, July 28, 2017.
9. Ibid.
10. Ibid.
11. Ibid.
12. Leo Pfeffer, memorandum to Shad Polier, July 30, 1959, Leo Pfeffer Papers, box 13, Special Collections Research Center, Syracuse University Libraries.
13. Leo Pfeffer, letter to Mannes F. Greenberg, Esq., July 30, 1959, Leo Pfeffer Papers, box 13, Special Collections Research Center, Syracuse University Libraries.
14. Joseph A. Sickles, letter to Leo Pfeffer, September 16, 1959, Leo Pfeffer Papers, box 13, Special Collections Research Center, Syracuse University Libraries.
15. Gregg Ivers, *To Build a Wall: American Jews and the Separation of Church and State* (Charlottesville: University Press of Virginia, 1995), 107–8.
16. Joseph A. Sickles, letter to Leo Pfeffer, September 16, 1959, Leo Pfeffer Papers, box 13, Special Collections Research Center, Syracuse University Libraries.
17. "Private Attorneys-General: Group Action in the Fight for Civil Liberties," *Yale Law Journal* 58, issue 4 (1949), 590.
18. Ivers, *To Build a Wall: American Jews and the Separation of Church and State*, 54.
19. Joseph A. Sickles, letter to Leo Pfeffer, September 16, 1959, Leo Pfeffer Papers, box 13, Special Collections Research Center, Syracuse University Libraries; Sandy Bolz, letter to Leo Pfeffer, September 21, 1959, Leo Pfeffer Papers, box 13, Special Collections Research Center, Syracuse University Libraries.
20. Leo Pfeffer, letter to Joseph A. Sickles, October 28, 1959, Leo Pfeffer Papers, box 13, Special Collections Research Center, Syracuse University Libraries.
21. *Cantwell v. Connecticut*, 310 U.S. 296 (1940).
22. *Davis v. Beason*, 133 U.S. 333 (1890).
23. Ben Strouse, memorandum to regional board, Anti-Defamation League, December 8, 1959, Leo Pfeffer Papers, box 13, Special Collections Research Center, Syracuse University Libraries.

Chapter 16

PRIVILEGE

On November 3, 1959, Roy stepped into the courtroom. Joseph Sickles, as well as lawyers for the ACLU and the American Jewish Congress were at his side. Reporters filled in the galley. Judge Shure likely entered the room shortly after. Mustached, with neatly combed hair, Shure was the same age as Roy; he had practiced law in the county for more than twenty-three years before the governor had given him this interim position.[1]

Because the demurrer had been filed by the attorney general's office, Prescott would have argued first. Tall and thick, with a commanding voice, he stepped to the podium. Given the very early stage of the case and the purely legal questions at issue, there would have been no jury. The argument was to the judge alone. Prescott largely stuck to what was already in his written briefs. With Roy looking on, he added that a "non-believer in God has the right to be a non-believer," but "he does not have the right to hold public office."[2] Holding such a position "is not just a right but a privilege, and the State must set up qualifications. One of those qualifications is the belief in God," as are "age, residence, experience, etc."[3]

When Sickles arose, he too stuck to the arguments in his written documents, but he disagreed vehemently with Prescott, saying that the state "is without authority to ask anyone what his views are for any position of trust. . . . Man is granted the right to worship as he pleases and the State does not have the authority to question his belief."[4]

"To try to set forth orthodoxy in religion," Sickles argued, "and thereby punish the nonorthodox is an attempted discouragement of religious creed."[5]

Whatever the judge was thinking, he remained stoic. He did point out that, in Maryland courts, a witness had to affirm belief in a Supreme Being before being allowed to testify.[6]

That rule was "equally unconstitutional," Sickles argued.[7] He added, "It cannot be contended that this religious freedom applies up to, and only up to, the door of government employment."

After he finished, Pfeffer and the lawyers for the ACLU asked for permission to make arguments as well. Judge Shure gave them each ten days to file written briefs as friends of the court. He would review them and then rule.

As Roy and his team left the courthouse, reporters bombarded them with questions. Roy refused to answer even one about something as simple as his age. "My religion, my beliefs and my age are my secret," he said. His legal team did provide some comments, although it appears they may have been directed more at the judge than anyone else. The spokesperson for the American Jewish Congress told reporters that his group would take the case to the United States Supreme Court if necessary.[8] If there is one thing trial court judges fear, it is being overruled by an appellate court. Roy's team wanted the judge to know that he would be facing an immediate appeal if Roy lost. The message was clear: he better be thorough in his ruling.

No one could blame Roy for feeling optimistic. He now had a powerhouse legal team behind him, and in Pfeffer, a lawyer with the expertise to explain his case. He returned home. Eileen was on the verge of giving birth. The shadow of the death of their previous child, sweet little Diana, no doubt lingered in the air.

In every area of his life, all Roy could do now was wait. There was the rush of the hearing, the click of reporters' cameras, the filing of the briefs by the ACLU and AJC, followed by the excruciating lull that always trails arguments on important motions. By November 13, 1959, Judge Shure had everything he needed. He ruled five days later.

Roy lost.

Becoming a notary was a privilege, not a right, the judge reasoned. For that privilege, the "people of Maryland have imposed a qualification of belief in the existence of God as a condition."[9] He agreed with the state that the Maryland Constitution allowed the requirement and the federal Constitution did not prohibit that practice. "Just as the state can set qualification for entrance to its university, or for the practice of a profession, by the same token it can set this qualification for would-be notaries."[10] And he saw "no conflict with the traditional guarantees of religious liberty."[11] In other words, Roy couldn't be a notary public simply because of his religious beliefs. When word reached Roy, he was perplexed a judge could rule that way. It wasn't as if the job would bring him acclaim or praise or even, necessarily, a raise in pay. It was the insult of it—the notion that his heartfelt beliefs were somehow inferior to those of others in the eyes of the law. It was one thing for a private individual to disagree with him, to debate the existence of God or the morality of religion. It was entirely different when the government injected itself into the debate.

Still reeling, Roy met with his legal team. Leo Pfeffer, his eyes steeled against defeat, likely saw this coming. He knew the road to success would be long. They put together a hasty news conference and provided Roy a prepared statement. It read in part, "It is incomprehensible to suggest that one's ability to perform the duties of a public office is dependent upon his belief in the Christian or Jewish religion."

They would appeal by early December.[12]

NOTES

1. "Judge Ralph Shure Dies at 89," *Washington Post,* September 23, 1999; "Judge Shure to Seek Full 15-year Term," *Washington Post,* February 13, 1960, A20.

2. "Belief-in-God Requirement for Office Argued in Court," *Baltimore Sun,* November 4, 1959, 21.

3. Ibid.; see also "Notary Post Sought in Religion Case," *Washington Post*, November 4, 1959, B1.

4. "Belief-in-God Requirement for Office Argued in Court," *Baltimore Sun*, November 4, 1959, 21.

5. "Notary Post Is Sought in Religion Case," *Washington Post*, November 4, 1959, B1.

6. "Atheist Plans to Fight Ruling on Notary Job," *Washington Post*, November 22, 1959, D18.

7. Ibid. It is important to note that the quoted language was actually something Sickles told reporters after the ruling came down, but it is highly likely that Sickles made the same or similar argument to the judge himself.

8. Ibid.

9. "Court Denies Notary Post to Atheist," *Washington Post*, November 19, 1959, A1.

10. Ibid.

11. "Test Oath," *Washington Post*, November 25, 1959, A18.

12. "Atheist Plans to Fight Ruling on Notary Job," *Washington Post*, November 22, 1959, D18.

Chapter 17

INCOMPETENT

A welcome distraction tempered the loss. Five days after the judge's ruling, Eileen and Roy welcomed their fourth child into the world. They named her Susan Elizabeth. She was healthy and strong.

————

In the Torcaso home, during the days and weeks after the defeat, as Roy and Eileen slogged through late nights and soiled diapers, their eleven-year-old daughter, Linda, watched as lawyers regularly scuffled into her living room, authoritative in their suits and ties. The feeling was not one of despair but of resoluteness. In the nighttime hours, Linda would stand in the doorway between the kitchen and the front room, silent but observant, as Pfeffer and Sickles, and perhaps others, would visit the Torcaso home. Bill was likely downstairs playing with the model railroad Roy had built for him or watching the new hit show *I Love Lucy*.

The men would unfold a square card table in front of the sofa and drag chairs to it from the kitchen. There they discussed strategy. Pfeffer, especially, knew that this case was not going to be won before the trial judge. The defeat was irrelevant. In his mind, everything pointed to the appellate courts. In fact, that was his goal. Trial court rulings largely apply only to the locale in which they're located. Appellate court decisions apply to far more people. For a state supreme court, the decision governs everyone in the state. For the United States Supreme Court, rulings apply to the entire country. The key was to hone their arguments and stay the course. Their next move: file an appeal to the Maryland Court of Appeals, the highest court in the state.[1]

Pfeffer's determination, his understanding that Roy's case was destined to go beyond the tiny courtroom of Ralph Shure, permeated the conversations. Linda felt confidence swell within her. Her dad was going to win.

Thanksgiving followed. Winter descended. They filed the appeal. The next step was to prepare their brief in support, which was due in the spring. As Pfeffer and Sickles worked on that, Roy worried about how to feed yet another mouth. In addition to his normal job at the construction company, he spent his evenings working at a hardware store. At some point, he took an additional job selling encyclopedias and whatever else he could do to provide for the family.[2] Eileen nursed the baby. When possible, she played the organ and piano at local churches.[3]

Roy had become front-page news. Editorials across the nation started to chime in, either for or against him. *The Washington Post* editorial board, in particular, took a strong stance on his case. They weren't sure, they wrote, that he should win on the law, but they would leave those "constitutional questions to the courts." Instead, they took the position that Maryland's "religious test is poor public policy." They continued:

> The men who wrote the United States Constitution . . . showed rather more wisdom than the men who wrote the Maryland constitution. For they remembered what the long and tragic experience of their forebears had taught them—that persecution, or disqualification, on grounds of belief, no matter how mistaken the belief may seem to be, gives rise to more dangers than it averts and that the only real safety lies in absolute toleration so far as conscience is concerned. They remembered, too, that to compel a profession of faith is to invade the shrine of conscience in a most odious way.

Who will define the God in whom a Maryland notary public is required to profess belief? Innumerable men have died in religious wars and crusades, in massacres and pogroms, at the stake and the scaffold, because their concepts of God were deemed mistaken by their fellow men. The men who established the American Republic sought forever to bar that kind of bitterness and strife by forbidding the Government to fix any kind of official orthodoxy in religion—by excluding the Government from any manner of influence whatever in matters of worship. Maryland would do well to follow their lead.[4]

The support from one of America's leading and most influential newspapers must have been validating for Roy. He needn't feel alone. At the same time, other editorials weren't nearly as supportive. Readers submitted letters both blasting and supporting *The Washington Post's* position. One, taking the former stance, emphasized that it "was inconceivable that integrity, responsibility, morality, justice and free social order could exist without recourse to a cosmic law higher than the laws of state."[5] This must have been especially galling to Roy, who prided himself for having the very traits the reader described.

Holmes Alexander, a columnist whose writings appeared in newspapers across the nation, wrote in the *Los Angeles Times* that Roy didn't have a right to public office. It was merely something he wanted, and the state could therefore require him to profess certain religious beliefs to get it.[6]

As the media continued to focus on Roy's case, so did his neighbors and even his boss. While the attention may have helped his cause in some ways; in others, it simply heated the waters. It would boil soon. The pressure was building.

———

On the first day of March 1960, the temperature barely rose above freezing.[7] The nation was gripped by a bitter cold spell. A courier navigated the icy roads of Annapolis, Maryland, and delivered several copies of a brief to the court of appeals. It was Roy's first salvo in his appeal.

The brief was straightforward and made the same key points Roy had made to Judge Shure, although more refined. Pfeffer's influence permeated it. It quoted Jefferson and invoked Madison. It summoned, once again, the notion that government has absolutely no right to touch on a person's belief.

The brief slammed Judge Shure's reliance on the idea that becoming a notary public was a "privilege." The bottom line, it argued, was that the state could not give or take away privileges based on someone's religious beliefs. It didn't matter if the state wanted to call something a privilege or a right. Under the Fourteenth Amendment's guarantee of equal treatment under the law, a state could not deny privileges based on discriminatory reasons. In fact, the United States Supreme Court had already held that, and in numerous settings: school attendance, taxation, and becoming a lawyer. Religion simply was not a valid basis for determining who would receive favorable treatment from government.

The state had several weeks to file a response. After it did, Roy's team would have filed one more brief. The ACLU filed a brief on his behalf as well. Everything was now before the judges.

The court held oral arguments on April 8, 1960. It was a Friday. Though the day was cool, the rising sun tempered the effects of the morning breeze.[8] Reporters milled about the courthouse grounds. Roy must have felt a tremendous knot in his stomach. In many respects, this was his last chance. It was true that his team could still appeal to the United States Supreme Court if he lost, but that court didn't have to take the case. In fact, the number of cases the Supreme Court had agreed to hear had been declining for decades. Despite their bluster in the press, for Roy and his team, getting a victory in front of Maryland's highest court was crucial.

Inside the courtroom, five justices sat behind a raised mahogany bench with intricately carved panels made from the same wood behind them. Each was an elderly man in a black robe.[9] One was Prescott's father.[10] The chief justice sat in the center. The American and Maryland flags hung from standing flagpoles behind him, framing his figure as he called the session to order.

Roy would have been at the table with Pfeffer and Sickles. Prescott sat at the other table. Roy's attorneys had agreed ahead of time to split the argument. Sickles dealt with the state constitution, repeating the argument that it did not allow for the oath without an act by the state legislature. To Pfeffer, the justices seemed, at best, hostile.[11]

When Sickles finished, Pfeffer rose to the podium. In his thick New York City accent,[12] he reiterated the arguments from the written briefs. The judges peppered him with questions, but not as many as he expected. Pfeffer spoke quickly and succinctly. On his feet, he was unflappable. He could verbally construct complicated sentences filled with complex ideas as efficiently as construction crews built houses in the nearby suburbs. Generally, he hesitated for dramatic effect only.

His most poignant point during the oral argument was that there was a clause in the federal Constitution that prohibited any religious oath for anyone holding a position in the United States government. This meant that under the state's position, Roy could serve as president of the United States, but he could not be a notary public in Maryland.[13] It didn't make any sense.

Prescott stood next. He reiterated the arguments that had been so successful with Judge Shure. Surprisingly to Pfeffer, the justices seemed just as skeptical of Prescott's position. After all the lawyers had finished, the chief judge allowed everyone involved in the case to exit the courtroom. Roy was, once again, waiting. Pfeffer and Sickles felt optimistic. It seemed to them that the judges had understood the arguments and might rule in Roy's favor.[14] Roy passed the time as he had before. He worked ceaselessly to put food on the table. When he wasn't grinding at two jobs, he worked on the house and played chess.

All the while, we don't know precisely what the judges were doing. They no doubt deliberated. They perhaps debated with each other over how they should rule. As far as Roy knew, they were arguing bitterly with each other. Judge William Henderson took a stab at drafting the opinion. The other judges critiqued it and offered revisions. They did it all in judicial secrecy. Roy, Pfeffer, Sickles, and so many others woke up each morning wondering if that day was the one the ruling would come.

———————

In his office, trying to stay cool from the scorching heat and humidity, Sickles would have received a larger-than-average envelope. He would have known what it was. He tore it open. Inside, a copy of the opinion from the court of appeals awaited. The same opinion would have been arriving at the attorney general's office and at Pfeffer's office as well. It was dated June 30, 1960. The court had issued it almost exactly one year from the day Roy's ordeal had begun.

The opinion was striking, both for its unanimity and for the power and strength of its language.

It was not lengthy, just five pages. The court of appeals quickly dismissed the technical argument regarding the question of whether the Maryland Constitution allowed the oath. "We entertain no doubt on that score," Justice Henderson wrote for the court. The provision of the state constitution allowing the oath did not require the legislature to do anything, which meant the county clerk could include it if he wanted to.[15]

"We come, then," the justices wrote, "to the question whether the declaration in question violates the Federal Constitution. It is well settled that the provisions of the Federal Constitution are supreme, even over a provision of the State Constitution."[16] But there were certain provisions that clearly didn't apply to the states. The federal Constitution's ban on a religious test oath for *federal offices* clearly didn't apply to Maryland. Otherwise, the federal government could dictate to the states the qualifications for state officers. That could not be, "at least not so long as we retain a Federal form of government."[17]

Sickles was likely skimming now, trying to get to the meat of the ruling. The justices acknowledged that the religion and speech clauses of the First Amendment did apply to the states, not just to the federal government. The start to their analysis was encouraging: "We are referred to no case directly in [*sic*] point," they said. "In general, the cases distinguish between a right to believe, and a right to act on one's belief. The first is absolute, the second is not."[18] It was a strong opening, and Sickles may have felt excitement starting to build.

But the justices' pivot was immediate. Roy was "not compelled to believe or disbelieve, under threat of punishment or other compulsion" they wrote. "True, unless he makes the declaration of belief he cannot hold public office in Maryland, but he is not compelled to hold office." The federal Constitution "does not prevent the states from establishing qualifications for office, at least where the qualifications are not based on such an unreasonable and improper classification as to be discriminatory."[19]

They then reached the crux of their conclusion. "[W]e find it difficult to believe that the Supreme Court will hold that a declaration of belief in the existence of God . . . as a qualification for State office, is discriminatory and invalid." After all, the Maryland justices reasoned, one of the Supreme Court justices had recently written for a majority of the court that "[w]e are a religious people whose institutions presuppose a Supreme Being."[20] The state court felt that it was in good company.

To drive home their point, the justices invoked the history of Maryland's 1867 constitutional convention. "To the members of the Convention . . . belief in God was equated with a belief in moral accountability and the sanctity of an oath. We may assume that there may be permissible differences in the individual's conception of God. But it seems clear that under our Constitution disbelief in a Supreme Being, and the denial of any moral accountability for conduct, not only renders a person incompetent to hold public office, but to give testimony, or serve as a juror. The historical record makes it clear that religious toleration, in which this State has taken pride, was never thought to encompass the ungodly."[21]

They finished with one last paragraph, arguing that requiring belief in God was an appropriate means for ensuring good conduct and so didn't violate the Constitution, but it's unlikely Sickles, and later Roy when he read it, would have cared about that last paragraph. Roy's mind would have been stuck on those previous words—that because of his beliefs, he was not competent to testify, even to serve as a juror. His conviction, his heartfelt position on the divine, and his refusal to compromise his beliefs made him not a model of integrity but a reject. As the justices had said, he was unworthy of protection. And he may have been out of options.

NOTES

1. At the time, Maryland did not have an intermediate appellate court, so any case that was appealed went directly to the Maryland Court of Appeals, which is the state's supreme court.
2. Bill Torcaso and Linda Bernstein, in discussion with author, July 28, 2017.
3. Ibid.
4. "Test Oath," *Washington Post*, November 23, 1959, A14.
5. "Test Oath," *Washington Post*, November 25, 1959, A18. (Note that this article, though it carries the same title as the article cited above, is actually a letter of opinion disputing the first article.)
6. Holmes, Alexander, "The Religious Test for Public Office," *Los Angeles Times*, December 2, 1959, 52.
7. "The Weather," *Baltimore Sun*, March 1, 1960, 20.
8. "Torcaso Appeal Slated on Friday," *Washington Post, Times Herald*, April 6, 1960, B2; see also "The Weather," *Baltimore Sun*, April 8, 1960, 18.
9. Some years later, the Maryland Court of Appeals justices would wear scarlet robes. Today, they are the only court in the country to do so.
10. Leo Pfeffer, Letter to Shad Polier, April 14, 1960, Leo Pfeffer Papers, box 13, Special Collections Research Center, Syracuse University Libraries.
11. Ibid.
12. Oral argument, April 24, 1961 (part 1), at *Torcaso v. Watkins*, Oyez, https://www.oyez.org/cases/1960/373.
13. "Atheism Case Is Heard Before Appeals Court," *Washington Post, Times Herald*, April 9, 1960, A3.
14. Ibid.
15. *Torcaso v. Watkins*, 162 A.2d 442 (Md. 1960).
16. Ibid.
17. Ibid.
18. Ibid.
19. Ibid.
20. Ibid., at 443; the latter half of this is quoting from *Zorach v. Clauson*, 343 U.S. 306, 313.
21. Ibid.

Chapter 18

STRANGERS IN THE NIGHT

The opinion from the court of appeals may have begun the darkest period of Roy's life. For Prescott, it was no doubt one of the greatest. He had won at trial. He had a unanimous victory in Maryland's highest court. For the upcoming election, he really couldn't have been better positioned. Judge Shure was probably feeling the same. The high court had vindicated him.

For Roy, the court had gone even further than it needed. He was not only denied the right to hold certain jobs because of his religion, but the court had also declared he couldn't testify or serve on a jury. He was less than the dust of the earth.

The attorney general of Maryland, C. Ferdinand Sybert, who had really done nothing on the case to that point, was also reveling in the victory. And pressing salt into Roy's wounds. On the night the opinion came down, like any good politician, he stood front and center and fielded calls from reporters. He called the decision "deeply rooted in the Maryland Constitution."[1] With a thick head of neatly combed hair and lips that seemed permanently pursed, Sybert told reporters, "I cannot believe that the Supreme Court would say that Maryland cannot set the qualifications for those who serve in public office." Maryland had always "had a deep religious foundation," he said.[2]

In what must have been especially galling to Roy, Sybert said,

"Perhaps the founders believed that those without a belief in a Supreme Being and sanctions hereafter could not always be believed."[3]

Still stinging with disappointment, Roy tried to pick himself up and continue about his daily life. He pursued his work. He continued to lead the local chess club. The evenings were once again filled with lawyers surrounding a card table in his house, talking strategy, young Linda looking on. The case had progressed to the point that everything was now out of Roy's hands. He had sailed completely out of his element.

Pfeffer had charged into his. This was his time. Supreme Court litigation had become his professional home over the previous decade, and he had a plan for how they would convince the United States Supreme Court to take the case. In his fast-paced but soft-spoken way, he likely explained to Roy the difficulties ahead of them. The Supreme Court is unique. It doesn't have to hear every appeal. By and large, it takes only those cases where at least four of the nine justices agree it should get involved.[4] The dollar value or complexity of a case is largely irrelevant. The justices won't take a case simply because a lower court judge or jury understood the facts wrong or because one party or other feels there has been a massive injustice. The Supreme Court's role is limited. Its resources even more so. Because of that, the justices have to be careful about which cases they agree to review. They focus on ensuring lower courts have properly applied the federal Constitution and on resolving disagreements among lower judges to ensure consistency. Sometimes, though, even if some of the justices feel a lower court has made a wrong decision, the justices might let a case bake for a while. If one state supreme court or one federal appellate court decides something, the United States Supreme Court may wait for other courts to weigh in before agreeing to take a case. If all the lower courts agree, the Supremes are less likely to get involved.

It all must have been very daunting for Roy. If he were playing the percentages, the chances of the Supreme Court taking his case were less than one percent. It was highly likely that Maryland's decision would stand. The key, Pfeffer would have emphasized, was to help the justices understand the importance of the issues. They needed to convince the justices that the questions in Roy's case deserved answering, that they affected more than just one man in Maryland, and that allowing the state's interpretation of the Constitution to stand would wreak havoc for religious freedom and from there for the stability of the country.

The process for doing that was relatively straightforward. For a case like Roy's, they simply filed a direct appeal. The court, if it determined the questions raised were not "substantial" enough, could simply declare that it lacked jurisdiction. The state of Maryland, of course, would file their own legal paper in opposition. Pfeffer, Sickles, and the rest of the team set to work.

———

The American Jewish Congress sent the announcement of the appeal to all the major newspapers. In New York, Pfeffer hosted a news conference, announcing that the "same Bill of Rights that protects Catholics, Jews and other religious minorities from discrimination in the holding of public office by reason of their beliefs also protects the non-theist and the non-believer. . . . Our Constitution does not have two First Amendments, one for those who believe in God and one for those who do not."[5]

The papers picked up the stories. Roy's plight danced among front pages across the nation. For good or ill, his name now carried the strange gravity that comes with press. And nearly every newspaper that ran his story printed his and Eileen's home address.

———

In the summer of 1960, Roy's seven-year-old son, Bill, roamed his neighborhood with his friends like a pack of puppies. No yard was off-limits. Brightview Street wound like a narrow jungle river through the shadows of weeping willows and maples. A lone, slender sidewalk meandered on just one side of the road. Gravel driveways spilled onto the asphalt. Nooks and hiding places abounded. For a horde of boys and girls, there were no boundaries.

They flitted across property lines. They sprinted between and around the tiny brick homes. They cowered in the tendrils of willows, fearful their enemies would capture them in a battle royale of hide-and-seek. Muggy days morphed into pleasant evenings. And the games raged on. They lunged at each other in an effort to survive the challenge of ultimate tag in one yard only to pick up the same game in a neighbor's grass just a few minutes later, likely with different rules. They screamed. They fought. They made up and started it all over again—endless summer days.

One day, as Bill engaged in this mindless euphoria, not a care in the world, he and his mob stumbled into the yard of some neighbors down the street. Bill didn't know them. With the kids darting about in the grass, the door to the house flung open.

A man, heavy set and older than Roy, stood at the door.

"Hey, you!" he hollered.

Bill and his friends stopped playing. The man's gaze searched through the throng until it landed directly on Bill.

When Bill made eye contact, the man yelled, "Is your dad the one doing that court case?"

Bill nodded.

"Get outta here and don't come back!" the man screamed.[6]

Bill obeyed. He didn't understand it. What did he do? Scuffling back to his own house, one thought lingered in his mind: there were some who felt his dad was doing a bad thing, and Bill's family wasn't welcome there.

Around that same time, one evening after dinner, a rapping lured Roy to his front door. He had taken off his tie to start relaxing for the evening but still wore his customary button-down dress shirt. He slogged to the front of the house, Bill on his heels, curious. The lingering smell of dinner wafted through the house.

When Roy opened the door, two strangers loomed there in business clothes. Both were white, middle-aged men. They asked if he was Roy Torcaso.

Roy confirmed he was.

They immediately began berating him for his case and his beliefs.

Roy, never one to back down when attacked, probably surprised the men. Instead of slamming the door on them, he invited them into the living room.

By then, Eileen had ambled up behind him. If he had started dancing with the men right there in the living room, she wouldn't have been more surprised. She pulled Roy to the side. Straining his neck, Bill goggled up at his parents as they debated in hushed tones the appropriateness of allowing the men inside. The look on Eileen's face told Bill she was not happy. And she didn't want her little boy in there, either. Roy insisted. Eileen pushed back. Roy eventually won.

With Bill looking on, Roy eased onto his sofa. Behind him, photos of Mount Rainer and Norwich, England, hung on the wall. The two men took seats opposite Roy. It wasn't clear who they were or what organization they represented.

They debated atheism and the legitimacy of Roy's case. At one point, one of the men said, "You're a communist. You should go back to Moscow."[7]

"I'm not a communist," Roy said. "I'm an atheist. I'm not a communist." He pushed off the sofa and walked to a nearby pile of books. From it, he hefted a thick tome. It was a dictionary. With it in his lap, he whipped through page after page until he found what he wanted: the definition of "communist."

He read it to the men. "An adherent or advocate of communism," he said. "Communism" meant "a theory advocating elimination of private property; a system in which goods are owned in common and available to all as needed."

"That's not me," Roy said, setting the book aside.[8]

The men didn't buy it, Roy didn't back down, the men eventually left, and Eileen went to bed that night with the realization that her husband's enemies knew where they lived.

———

Disaster struck Roy at work. In all those days on the farm as a child splitting logs, tilling the land, and avoiding his father's explosions, Roy had developed a lot of skills. One that evaded him was the subtle art of navigating a business setting through political maneuvering. But the time had come when he needed that skill more than ever.[9]

The newspapers had been relentless. Americans feared the spread of Soviet Russia—its communism and established atheism—the way they feared a deadly virus. On the pages of the nation's broadsheets, every time a column about Roy appeared, there lingered somewhere else on the page another article or commentary about the threat of the Red Menace. The press didn't do it deliberately. There were always articles about the threat of Soviet Russia. But in time, it became impossible for Roy's coworkers not to at least subconsciously connect the two. In many people's minds, Roy was the precise threat America was fighting.

His boss lost his patience. Perhaps it was the bad publicity, or Roy's firmness in his opinions, or perhaps it was just plain old discrimination against someone with different beliefs. Whatever the reason, Roy's boss fired him. And Roy didn't have the political savvy to keep it from happening.

Tensions at home would have escalated. The family had always struggled for money. Eileen, now at home with another baby swaddled in her arms, had to have wondered if this fight was worth it. She agreed with Roy, if not theologically, then at least on the fairness of it. But in her mind, it was probably not worth the attention, the toll on her children, strangers at her home in the night, the insecurity of wondering how they would generate their next paycheck.[10] They didn't need to be the ones charging on the front lines of this fight.

For Roy, his integrity was everything. He had come too far,

endured too much, to give up his case now. And so he went searching for more work, hoping his lawyers could pull off a miracle.

———

On September 30, 1960, the state pounced. Pfeffer's team had already filed the appeal. In response, Maryland's attorney general told the Supreme Court that it should "dismiss . . . the appeal on the ground that the question is so unsubstantial as not to warrant further argument."[11] In truth, the state used the phrase "unsubstantial" because that was the precise legal term required. The court took only those cases it believed dealt with a "substantial" question of federal law. To Roy, unversed in the technicalities of Supreme Court litigation, it simply would have read that his appeal wasn't worth the court's time. After all, the state argued, the Declaration of Independence, the Maryland Constitution, the National Anthem, even the oath taken by the Supreme Court justices themselves—all of them cited God. The state's message was simple: this inconsequential man in Maryland is raising a ruckus about nothing; his little complaints don't deserve getting the Constitution involved.

The Supreme Court disagreed. On November 7, 1960, they issued a one-sentence order. It read only, "In this case probable jurisdiction is noted."[12] To the uninitiated, it was a meaningless sentence. It seemed nothing more than technical babble. To Pfeffer, it meant they were taking the case.

———

NOTES

1. "Oath Roots Seen Deep: Sybert Calls Ruling in Line with View of Constitution," *Baltimore Sun*, July 1, 1960, 46.
2. Ibid.
3. Ibid.
4. There are some cases over which the Supreme Court has original jurisdiction and must take the case, such as when one state sues another, when a state sues the federal government, or when a case affects an ambassador or similar official. All of these types of cases were rare and did not affect Roy.

5. "Jewish Congress Backing Torcaso: To Take Oath-For-Notary Case To Supreme Court," *Baltimore Sun*, July 11, 1960, 20.
6. Bill Torcaso and Linda Bernstein, in discussion with author, July 28, 2017
7. Ibid.
8. Ibid.
9. Ibid.
10. Ibid.
11. "State Asks Supreme Court To Back Oath Citing Deity," *Baltimore Sun*, October 1, 1960, 26.
12. *Torcaso v. Watkins*, 81 S. Ct. 171 (1960).

Chapter 19

DEFINING RELIGION

On Tuesday, April 24, 1961, Bill Torcaso hung close to his mother. They walked past columns so thick they looked like the legs of giants. Linda trailed as well, her nerves tingling in her stomach. The room had such an air of authority and solemnity she felt if she even breathed wrong, some stern, tyrannical usher would whack her on the hand or drag her from the place. She was certain her family was breaking all sorts of rules just by bringing children into this space.

It's not surprising. For those seeing the Supreme Court building's courtroom for the first time, it's nothing short of breathtaking. Twenty-four ionic columns made of veined Italian and Spanish marble surround the galley. Red-and-gold drapes hanging from the windows make the room feel like something from the *Wizard of Oz*. The chamber and the building it's housed in—modeled after a neoclassic temple—is so ostentatious that when it was built, Associate Justice Harland Fiske Stone described it as "almost bombastically pretentious . . . wholly inappropriate."[1] Another snarked that the room was so grand the justices ought to enter it riding on elephants.[2]

Roy and his family found their seats. The attorneys found theirs. At the front of the room, nine empty black chairs faced them, as if they held secrets all their own. High in the air, etched into the recessed frieze of the hall's ceiling, mythical figures loomed over them. One portion of

136

the frieze told the allegorical story of the battle of good versus evil—in the center was the mythical figure of Justice leaning on her sheathed sword and ready to protect the forces of virtue, charity, and peace from the powers of despotism, slander, and corruption. Behind Justice was a figure of divine inspiration. It held the scales of justice in its hand. How Roy felt about that notion of divinity is hard to say.

For a little family with no money, despised by the culture they were in, it must have been astonishing to find themselves sitting in the highest court of the land. As the time approached for the justices to enter, a hush fell over the room. Linda watched the marshals pacing the space between the rows.

A gavel echoed throughout the chamber.

Everyone stood.

A man to the side of the justices' bench arose and yelled, "The Honorable, the Chief Justice and the Associate Justices of the Supreme Court of the United States."

At that, the nine justices emerged from behind the immense red drapes. They were majestic in their black robes flowing about them like magicians' cloaks. All were aged, with graying hair or balding scalps. Their collective eyes hinted at hundreds of years of legal wisdom, although Roy was seasoned enough in life to know that all the legal experience in history might not overcome the prejudices he was facing. The Maryland justices had been wizened as well.

As they shuffled to their seats, the marshal continued his chant, "Oyez![3] Oyez! Oyez! All persons having business before the Honorable, the Supreme Court of the United States, are admonished to draw near and give their attention, for the Court is now sitting. God save the United States and this Honorable Court!" The justices eased into their chairs. The audience did the same. For Roy, the invocation of God must have been a bad omen. For Linda, the anticipation of what was about to happen was intoxicating.

Bill was almost immediately bored out of his mind. To his nine-year-old brain, the justices were just babbling about one pointless topic after another. He found himself staring at whatever he could to distract him. Counting the decorative notches in the marble above the pillars was particularly helpful.

Pfeffer, on the other hand, was watching a potential nightmare unfold.

The 1960–1961 term for the Supreme Court was particularly grueling. *The Washington Post* called it "one of the busiest and most important terms in the Court's history."[4] The justices had agreed to hear 148 cases. It was a high number. The decisions would touch "many aspects of American life."[5] And the ideological gap between some of the justices might as well have been the Grand Canyon.

They announced six decisions before calling up Roy's case for argument. Of those, the justices had decided four of them with a five-to-four split.[6]

With the Torcasos looking on, Justice Hugo Black announced the court's decision to grant a new trial to a man convicted of murder some eight years earlier.

Seventy-eight-year-old Justice Felix Frankfurter didn't respond well. Peering down the bench at his colleagues through wire-rimmed glasses, he launched into his dissent. Traditional practice in the court is to read a dissent if a justice wants to draw particular attention to it. And justices rarely do anything but stick to their written opinions. Justice Frankfurter didn't read a thing. Instead, he launched into a lengthy tirade of his fellow jurists, accusing them of all sorts of judicial overreach.

When he finished, Chief Justice Warren leaned forward. He said, "I must say that although I did not file an opinion in this case, that was not the dissenting opinion that was filed. This is a lecture. . . . It is properly made, perhaps, in the conference room but not in a courtroom. As I understand it, the purpose of reporting an opinion in the Court is to inform the public and not for the purpose of degrading this Court."

The two justices continued to snap at each other. The tension was palpable. It was the third time that year they had engaged in this verbal warfare. The next day, *The Washington Post* would report that "Chief Justice Earl Warren ripped into Justice Felix Frankfurter . . . in the sharpest exchange of public remarks between Supreme Court Justices in years."[7]

The two men were fuming. The other justices weren't happy either. Roy likely worried that the divide between them did not bode well for him. The fault line that split the court was a "fundamental ideological" difference between two blocs of jurists that was all the more volatile that year "because of the divisive and controversial cases" the court had to decide.[8] Those cases touched on everything from "the role the Court should play in the Nation, to the approach judges should take to cases, and to the meaning of the Bill of Rights."[9]

In other words, Roy's case was one highly likely to trigger the divide. It was entirely possible a large bloc of the court would rule against him simply because they disagreed with the broader judicial philosophy espoused by the other side. Pfeffer watched as the justices snapped at one another. Tempers rose. By the time Chief Justice Warren was ready to announce Roy's case, every single judge on the bench appeared angry. The two factions eyed each other warily.

In a monotone voice, no doubt made even more stilted from trying to rein in his irritation, seventy-year-old Chief Justice Warren read into the microphone, "Number 373, Roy R. Torcaso, Appellant, versus Clayton K. Watkins, Clerk of the Circuit Court for Montgomery County, Maryland."

With hair so white it could have been bleached, he peered through his rounded glasses at Roy's table. "Mr. Pfeffer," he said.

Pfeffer arose. He likely vibrated with pent-up energy, just waiting for this opportunity to release it. If he was like almost all Supreme Court advocates, he had been preparing for this for months. He had spent late nights perfecting every turn of phrase. He knew his arguments backward and forward. He knew the relevant historical cases.

During the months prior, the parties had already submitted their written briefs to the justices. Those were iterations of what they had argued in the lower courts, only more robust and precise. A few *amici* had filed friend-of-the-court briefs as well. Pfeffer knew the state's arguments as well as anyone. They were etched in his mind. They were simple:

1. The oath doesn't violate the Free Exercise or Establishment Clauses because it doesn't establish an official religion, it doesn't restrict Roy's exercise of his religion, and it simply "recognizes and reaffirms the organic utterances of the people that this is a religious nation."[10]

2. The oath doesn't prefer one religion over another. It only places a reasonable qualification on holding public office.

3. Holding public office in Maryland is a privilege, not a right, and withdrawing that privilege does not violate the Equal Protection Clause of the Constitution.

4. The constitutional provision forbidding oaths for federal officers doesn't apply to Maryland.

Lodged in Pfeffer's brain were ready counterarguments to each of the state's points. As he maneuvered from his seat to the lectern, *what he didn't know* was what would have worried him. He didn't know what the justices would ask him. What about the briefing had piqued their interests? What about it had troubled them? Which of the state's arguments did they find persuasive? Which of the justices were on Roy's side? How divided were they, really?

He stood at the podium. It was surprisingly close to the justices, so tight, in fact, that he couldn't see them all at once. If he looked to his right, the justices to his left fell completely out of view. Five of the justices sat on tall, high-backed chairs that allowed them to tower over the courtroom. The four others used "smaller swivel chairs taken from their offices."[11] They were so low their heads were only "half visible to the audience."[12]

Pfeffer settled in. The room was hushed. He cleared his throat. "Mr. Chief Justice," he finally said, "if the Court pleases. The—this case presents one single issue. It is whether a state may, consistently with the federal Constitution, bar from public office a person who cannot conscientiously declare that he believes in the existence of God. We contend that a state cannot do so on four separate grounds. We believe such a requirement constitutes a law respecting an establishment of religion within the prohibition of the First Amendment. . . . We believe that it constitutes a law prohibiting the free exercise of religion. . . . We suggest that it constitutes a denial of the equal protection of the laws and the deprivation of liberty without due process and finally, . . . we suggest that the ban . . . with respect to religious test for office, may be applicable to the States as well as to the Federal Government."[13]

Pfeffer gestured to a man joining him at counsel's table. "I shall undertake to discuss the first two contentions and I shall leave it to my colleague Mr. Speiser to discuss the latter two." The man was Lawrence Speiser. He was the head of the Washington office of the ACLU. The justices knew him. A World War II veteran, several years prior he had argued on his own behalf that forcing veterans to sign loyalty oaths to receive special tax exemptions for veterans violated the Constitution. The justices had voted for him seven to one.[14]

"In respect to the ban on establishment of religion," Pfeffer continued, "what exactly that means has been subject to interpretation by this Court in several cases. And at the very least, I think there is no dispute. That means Government, federal or states, may not prefer one or more religion over other religions. It's our contention that a law which requires an expression of belief in the existence of God prefers . . . theistic religions over non-theistic religions."

Pfeffer then explained that there were hundreds of millions of people around the world who were very religious but who did not believe in a God. "For example," he said, "the Buddhist religion, the Confucian religion." That may have been irrelevant to the United States prior to World War II, Pfeffer explained, but with the "admission of a state like Hawaii to the Union, which there are a substantial number of Buddhists . . . I think this is a factor which must always be considered in defining religion."[15]

It was a salient point. It also tickled Justice Potter Stewart's curiosity. Oral argument before the justices of the Supreme Court can be as helter-skelter as trying to have a conversation with a toddler. You never know when you'll get interrupted. The justices can, and do, ask questions whenever they want.

"Mr. Pfeffer," Stewart said, cutting Pfeffer off. "I'm asking out of ignorance, really, but . . . doesn't religion involve a belief in a supernatural being or more than one supernatural being?"

"I don't think so," Pfeffer said. "I think that's a common impression. But if we were to accept that, we would have to exclude from the compass of religion, the literally hundreds of millions of persons who are of the Buddhist faith or the Confucius faiths, as well as the hundreds of thousands who are members of the Ethical Culture Society in the United States."

Justice Stewart didn't challenge him on that. Several other justices made comments. Pfeffer tried to stay on point. "But I think there are many humanists . . . who would insist that they are a religious group and to them the supreme obligation of religion is the ethics of man's relationship to man rather a man's relationship to a god or gods."[16]

Pfeffer continued, "Now, if . . . the First Amendment bars a state from preferring a particular religion over other religions, even if it's an orthodox, a generally accepted religion, and if, as I suggest, the concept of the term 'religion,' as used in the First Amendment, does not exclude non-theistic religions, then I think it follows clearly that this particular requirement of the State of Maryland, as well as other States, is a preference of certain religions over others. I think it is quite clear that this is so."[17]

As the arguments continued, Pfeffer explained the history of Maryland's law. He noted that it originally allowed only Christians to hold public office. Then it allowed Jews as well. It finally expanded to everyone who believed in God. "[N]ow, I am suggesting . . . that within the Constitution, it must include all those who are of a religion whether or not that religion encompasses or requires a belief in the existence of God."[18]

Pfeffer then switched gears. He reiterated that some of the court's prior history ensured that certain religions not receive government aid over others. He then said, "I think that a statutory requirement excluding from public office, all those except in the preferred groups, constitutes preferential aid to religion within the compass and meaning of the First Amendment's No Establishment Clause."

Again Justice Stewart interrupted him. "You talk in terms of groups, how about an individual who wasn't associated with any organized group at all?"

On some level, Justice Stewart's questions had to have troubled Pfeffer. Justice Stewart was a swing vote. Roy needed him. Where he voted could be how the case would get decided. His questions suggested he was struggling with something.

Pfeffer stuttered, "I wouldn't—I would contend that the—this would apply equally to individuals."

"How about an individual atheist?" Justice Stewart asked.

Pfeffer tried to respond, but Justice Stewart cut him off again. "I'm associated with nobody else. This is just my individual active non-belief. Now . . . would that non-belief be a religion?"[19]

"That non-belief would not be a religion, in the sense of preferential aid to a particular religion over other religions," Pfeffer said.

"I'm talking about the free exercise," Stewart said.

"Well," Pfeffer said, "surprisingly enough, I think the Free Exercise Clause, as it was understood by the Fathers of our Constitution, would encompass those without religion."[20] He then provided a lengthy history of various quotes from some of the Founders showing that they believed even those without religion should have been able to hold public office.

"Well that's a different argument, isn't it?" This came from Justice Hugo Black. He should have been one of the justices squarely in Roy's camp. He hailed from the University of Alabama Law School. Like the other justices, he was getting on in years. What hair he had left was as white as paper. His voice sounded aged but forceful. Though he had spent much of his career in DC, his Alabama accent still lingered in his speech. Like his intellectual rival Justice Frankfurter, he had chosen one of the shorter chairs, so his head had a tendency to appear and disappear behind the mahogany, his eyes peeking out from behind the bench like, as one reporter described it, an "alert and sagacious" otter, "floating on the constitutional water."[21]

"I understood," Justice Black continued, "you were claiming . . . maybe you aren't, that atheism itself is a religion. Quite different to say that the idea of religious freedom would leave a man the right . . . not to be religious at all?"[22]

"I do not contend that atheism is a religion," Pfeffer said. It was an interesting choice. He was trying to navigate his ship through a very narrow opening, one that may not have even existed, and his strategy could very well backfire. To this point, he had argued that atheists should receive all the protections of the religion clauses but none of the burdens. He had claimed that atheists should be protected as if they were part of a religion, but by claiming that atheism was not a religion, he was leaving open the possibility that the government could establish atheism as the official religion of the state and the Establishment Clause would not prevent that. Whether he realized the logic of his arguments extended that far remains unclear. But at that moment, the risk was very real that his attempt to have it both ways may well have sunk Roy's case.

Justice Frankfurter, perhaps sensing the problem, asked Pfeffer if the justices really needed to decide what "religion" meant. Wouldn't it be enough simply to rule on the legality of the oath in Maryland in this particular case and not try to get into defining the word *religion*? The implication was clear. If they had to do something grand like define the scope of religion, they might not ever agree on anything, and Roy would most likely lose.

Unfortunately, Justices Frankfurter and Black began bickering with each other across the bench. It wasn't surprising. They sat on polar opposites of the judicial divide. Justice Black argued that he wanted "religion" defined even if Justice Frankfurter didn't. Chief Justice Warren interrupted with a different point, and the argument faded away unanswered.

Eventually, Pfeffer pivoted to the Maryland Court of Appeals' reliance on the Supreme Court's language that the United States is a religious country that presupposes a "Supreme Being." Maryland had relied heavily on that statement in its brief. "This language," Pfeffer said, "whatever it means . . . cannot be interpreted to mean to authorize Government, federal or state, to compel a belief in a Supreme Being as a prerequisite for Government office."[23]

The justices didn't argue with him. That meant they either all agreed with him or all disagreed. He couldn't know which. Pfeffer then launched into a lengthy discourse regarding government having no jurisdiction over religious belief and the historical facts supporting his position. The justices again didn't say a thing.

Throughout history, the "inescapable stamp of establishment of religion," Pfeffer said, was government forcing people to believe certain things before allowing them to hold public office. He was right. And that applied to jobs in the private sector as well. Throughout history, excluding people of certain religions from various jobs was a telltale sign of a society that didn't respect religious freedom.

Without interruption from the justices, Pfeffer was now on a roll. "I think it's important also to note that we are concerned here not with action, but with belief. The State of Maryland . . . demands that you believe in the existence of God and if you don't believe in the existence of God, you are barred from serving. For the first time, a state has imposed a test in respect to religious belief."[24]

This was partially true. The cases involving The Church of Jesus Christ of Latter-day Saints had certainly come close. Justice Black, perhaps perceiving this, finally interrupted Pfeffer. "Are—are you correct in that statement that it's the first time that's occurred and is to be considered?"

"That's the first time before this Court, as—as far as I know," Pfeffer said. "[R]eligious belief is and must be absolute. . . . Nothing I think could be more fundamental than that in our democratic system."[25]

Pfeffer's time was running out. Unlike in days gone by, when lawyers could blather on forever with their arguments, the Supreme Court had implemented strict time restrictions. If Pfeffer had a key point to make, this was his chance. He needed to sit down to make sure he didn't eat up all of Speiser's time.

Instead, Potter Stewart interrupted him, asking simple questions about the duties of notaries and whether the oath requirement applied to all officers in Maryland. The answer was yes.

After that exchange of questions, as Pfeffer was trying to take his seat, Justice Warren wouldn't let him. He asked even more questions. Justice Frankfurter then chimed in as well. Most of the inquiries seemed born of curiosity more than anything. They were simple historical questions about various statutes.

Speiser's time was vanishing. Pfeffer could feel the pressure to sit. In a matter of moments, he was able to do just that.

Speiser stepped up to the podium. "Mr. Chief Justice," he said. The timidity of his voice didn't match his frame. A former navigator on B-29 heavy bombers on raids against Japan during World War II, he still looked like a hulking military figure.[26] His hair was still in a crew cut. Where Pfeffer was skinny and lithe, Speiser looked as if he would have been just as comfortable on the football field as in the courtroom. Where Pfeffer spoke quickly and with a booming confidence, Speiser, at least starting out, seemed hesitant. It was almost as if he were afraid of what would happen if he started out too aggressive. He was an experienced Supreme Court advocate and had spent significant time lobbying Congress, so he was in his element and likely wasn't nearly as shy as he first sounded. Given his experience, it is clear that somewhere along the way, Roy's legal team felt Speiser would be better than Sickles at this stage to help argue to the court.

It didn't necessarily start out well. After a few preliminaries, Speiser said, "I'm going to discuss the question of the reasonableness of the classification that's been made by this position of the Maryland Constitution." He launched into summarizing his arguments, but Justice Black cut him off.

"May I ask, what is the basis of that argument you're making now?" the justice said in his soft, Southern drawl.

It's never a good sign when the justices don't know why a lawyer is making an argument.

Speiser didn't even hesitate. "Our basis is the Equal Protection Clause . . . and the Due Process Clause," he said. In other words, Roy was protected not just under the religion clauses but also by the other clauses. His argument was that government couldn't treat people differently or fail to give them proper process if it didn't have a good reason. It had to show that its purposes for acting the way it did were reasonable. Maryland couldn't, Speiser said. "[T]he broad sweep of history is very much against the fact that we cannot trust in public office, nonbelievers or we cannot believe nonbelievers in office, who take an oath that they will support and defend the Constitution or to perform the functions of their task."[27] Speiser pointed out that every federal officer, including the president of the United States, takes an oath without declaring a belief in God. If we can trust them, Maryland's requirement was clearly unreasonable.

He reminded the justices that England, "which even now has an established church, doesn't require such a statement as this of a belief in God."

Chief Justice Warren interrupted. "What do they permit in England as the equivalent of the oath?"

"There's nothing that I know of that's the equivalent of requiring a belief in a Supreme Being," Speiser said. "They do promise to . . . perform their task, but they—they have nothing beyond that that I know of, Your Honor."

"And just to say that they will tell the truth or they will do so and so," the chief justice said.

"Or they will perform their office, that's correct," Speiser said.

The exchange continued, but Justice Black interjected with an entirely different question. "If you . . . get away from the protection you claimed under the First Amendment, how can you say it might not be reasonable . . . for a state to say that a Notary Public, whose business is to administer the oath which contained statements, 'So help me God,' that an atheist would not be the right man to do that . . . ?"

Speiser stumbled. He and Justice Black talked over each other. Speiser never addressed the question but instead tried to provide another reason why Maryland's oath wasn't reasonable.

Justice Black refused to let him off the hook. "Do I understand that the only . . . duty on this man is to administer oaths?" Justice Black was known as a champion of civil liberties. He should have been squarely in Roy's camp. Yet the tone of his voice sounded skeptical.

"He has some other duties, but—but the duties are ministerial," Speiser said. "Uh . . . There's—"

"And does the oath contain the statement 'So help me God'?" Justice Black asked.

"Which oath are you referring to, Mr. Justice Black?"

"The oath that he would have to administer in Maryland."

Speiser finally locked into Justice Black's concern. His question was simple: if someone were giving an oath that included the words "so help me God," wasn't it reasonable to require him to at least believe in some form of God? Rather than tackling that question directly, Speiser danced around it. He argued that the words "so help me God" were really just a procedural device—they didn't require someone to say they believed in God.

Another of the justices asked if there was a statute in Maryland that required all state officers to say something like "so help me God."

Speiser hesitated. He ruffled through his notes. He didn't know the answer off the top of his head.

Chief Justice Warren answered for him. "It says, 'In the presence of God.'"

Speiser found what he was looking for. "Yes," he said. "It starts out 'In the presence of Almighty God' and then it does not set out 'So help me God' at the end of it."

Justice Black pounced. His question still hadn't been answered. With irritation lingering in his voice, he said, "Well, might that not . . . operate as grounds for a state to say, 'We do not want a man to be an official when his duty is to impose an oath that says *in the presence of God* when he doesn't believe in God'?"

For some reason, Speiser simply didn't want to say "no." Instead, he stumbled. "Well," he said, "it's not up to him to determine whether the individuals before him do or don't believe in God." His stumbling led to panic. His speech intensified. His tone was more emphatic. It appeared to those outside his mind that he feared he was losing the court. He had prepared a series of arguments. Rather than providing any more direct answers to Justice Black, he fired them off one at a time.

They were persuasive. But it appears his nerves had caught up with him. He stuttered through them. "How do you know that a person doesn't believe in God?" he asked rhetorically. "Because he says so, because he says so. So you believe him when he says he doesn't believe in God, but then . . . you refuse to believe him when he says he's going to perform his office in a true and diligent fashion or when he says he's going to support the Constitution."[28]

After pausing, he continued. "There's a good argument also as to why you should believe a nonbeliever even more than a believer . . . because the nonbeliever is suffering disadvantages. He suffers public opprobrium. He's barred from public office." In this context, Speiser argued, the words "I believe in God" are often being offered simply because the state is bribing the speaker to say them. "If he says these words, he gets the public office, if he doesn't, he doesn't get the public office. So what good are the words when it's to his advantage to say them?"

Speiser then looked directly at Justice Black. "I think that at one time, Mr. Justice Black, you yourself said that words . . . uttered under compulsion are proof of nothing but loyalty to self-interest. And I think the same thing would apply here that where a person says words under compulsion, 'I believe in God,' . . . it proves nothing other than his own self-interest is . . . at stake. This is not a reasonable classification, it seems to me."[29]

The justices didn't say a word. But Speiser also never directly answered Justice Black's question.

He had run out of time.

At the table, Roy looked on, no doubt wondering what the justices' questions and demeanor meant.

NOTES

1. "Homes of the Court," The Supreme Court Historical Society, http://www.supremecourthistory.org/history-of-the-court/home-of-the-court/.
2. Ibid.
3. For those not familiar with the tradition, this is pronounced "Oh yay." Until the eighteenth century, speaking English in an English court of law was not required and participants could instead use a form of French that evolved after the Norman Conquest when Anglo-Norman became the language of the upper classes in England. *Oyez* descends from the French word *ouïr*, meaning "to hear"; thus *oyez* means "hear ye" and was used as a call for silence and attention.
4. "High Court Resumes Work on Vital Cases," *Washington Post, Times Herald,* April 17, 1961, 13.
5. Ibid.
6. "Court Deeply Divided on Controversial Cases: Justice Warren Chides Frankfurter for 'Lecture' on Decision in Murder," *Washington Post,* April 25, 1961, 1.
7. Ibid.
8. Ibid.
9. Ibid.
10. "Brief of Appellee," *Torcaso v. Watkins,* 367 U.S. 488 (1961) (No. 373), 1961 WL 102253, at *4–5.
11. "Drama Builds in High Court," *Christian Science Monitor,* June 20, 1961, 1.
12. Ibid.
13. *Torcaso v. Watkins* (part 1), Oyez, accessed October 10, 2018, https://www.oyez.org/cases/1960/373.

14. "Lawrence Speiser, 68, a Civil Liberties Lawyer," *The New York Times*, September 1, 1991.
15. *Torcaso v. Watkins* (part 1), Oyez.
16. Ibid.
17. Ibid.
18. *Torcaso v. Watkins* (part 2), Oyez, https://www.oyez.org/cases/1960/373.
19. Ibid.
20. Ibid.
21. "Drama Builds in High Court," *Christian Science Monitor*, June 20, 1961, 1.
22. *Torcaso v. Watkins* (part 2), Oyez.
23. Ibid.
24. Ibid.
25. Ibid.
26. "Lawrence Speiser Dies," *Washington Post*, August 31, 1991; "Civil Liberties Union Director Named Here," *Washington Post, Times Herald*, September 2, 1959, 18.
27. *Torcaso v. Watkins* (part 2), Oyez.
28. Ibid.
29. Ibid.

Chapter 20

UNIVERSAL PHILOSOPHIES
OF THE PEOPLE

"Attorney General Finan," Chief Justice Warren said.

At the other table, a bald man with a serious but kind expression rose from his chair and approached the podium. Like so many others in the courtroom, he had also served in World War II. In the European theater, he had been held as a prisoner of war. Because of his exceptional service, he had been awarded the Legion of Merit.

This was likely the first time Roy had seen him. The previous attorney general, C. Ferdinand Sybert, had accepted a position as a justice on the Maryland Court of Appeals just after that court had ruled against Roy. Finan had replaced him. He was a devout Catholic and had spent most of his life in public service. Something about his face and the thickness of his eyebrows made him look younger than he was.

"Mr. Justice," he began. Then he corrected himself. "Chief Justice, members of the Court." He offered a short summary of Maryland's arguments before starting more in depth at the beginning. His first volley had to have felt like a sucker punch to Roy. "A declaration of a belief in the existence of God as set forth in our Constitution in Maryland is something which we feel is more or less an important parcel to what has been recognized as the universal philosophy of this nation that we are a religious people."[1] For Roy, who had served the country in two wars, it must have been hard to see himself dismissed so cavalierly. It was as if his beliefs—and the beliefs of anyone else who didn't subscribe to the majority's viewpoint—were invalid and therefore not part of the "universal philosophy" of the nation.

Finan supported his statement by citing a number of documents from the time of the Founding that mention some form of creator or supreme being.

Justice Black, however, changed the direction of the conversation. "Do I understand from your argument that you think it would be all right [for] a Federal Government to impose a test of this kind?"

"Mr. Justice Black, I uh . . . let me state this. We are primarily concerned here with a question of a right which we feel has been reserved to a state. I wouldn't go that far, no sir."

"But you couldn't really, could you?" Justice Black said, emphasizing that the Constitution explicitly forbade it.

"That's right," Finan said.

After a brief exchange on that point, Finan dove for the crux of the case. "I think this question resolves itself into this premise: can a state constitutionally exclude an atheist from public office?" He pointed out that Roy had relied heavily on the notion that the First Amendment applied to atheists as much as it did to anyone else. "We feel that religion as . . . mentioned in the First Amendment to the Constitution of the United States . . . does not include the atheist."

To support his argument, Finan needed a Supreme Court precedent defining "religion." Almost nothing existed. He invoked the cases involving The Church of Jesus Christ of Latter-day Saints, *Davis v. Beason*, in particular, because the court there had said that the term "religion" referred to "one's views of his relations to his creator."[2] In another case, one of the justices had said, "[T]he essence of religion is belief in the relation to God, involving duties superior to those arising from any human relation."

None of these quotes were binding on the court. They were only examples.

Justice Black seemed uninterested. "Have you indicated just when this statute originated?"

"It was in the Constitution of 1867," Finan said.

"Was it in the law of Maryland before that, when it became a state?" Justice Black asked.

"In various forms, Mr. Justice," Finan said.

"What people did it bar from holding office then?" Justice Black said.

Finan stumbled. "At the time of the . . ." he began but paused. Perhaps he understood the implications of Justice Black's question. And the answer wasn't good for him. He finally admitted that originally, immediately after the Revolutionary War, only Christians could hold public office. Jews were banned. As he spoke, he paused and cleared his throat several times. "I think it was 1854 that it was amended to embrace not only Christians but Jews as well."

"Am I wrong in thinking . . ." Justice Black said. "I thought I read somewhere, when Mr. Carroll was representing Maryland, he was disqualified from holding public office?"

"Who?" Finan asked.

"Mr. Carroll," Justice Black said. "The great Carroll, who—" He was referring to Charles Carroll, who had been the only Catholic to sign the Declaration of Independence and who had represented Maryland as a senator to the newly formed United States Congress for several years.

He "was not allowed to hold public office the first 20 years of . . . what might be termed his public life," Finan said.

"Why?" Justice Black asked.

"Because they barred Catholics in Maryland at that time," Finan said.[3] He continued to talk. He hopped from one historical fact to another, trying to navigate the river of Maryland's history.

As he did so, the implications of Justice Black's questions couldn't have been lost on Roy. One of the major problems with Maryland's constitutional provision was that it could be applied to anyone. If a state could ban one person from public office simply because of their religious beliefs, it could ban anyone. What applied to atheists in one instance could apply to Catholics, Christians, Muslims, Jews, and Buddhists in the next. It all depended on who was in power. And that led various religious groups to fight for that power, to try to control the government. As one scholar explained,

> If the government is permitted to attempt to influence religious beliefs and commitments, each religious faction must necessarily seek to control or at least influence the government so the faction's members will be more benefited than harmed. Even if government is permitted only to express views about religion, religious factions will seek to control or influence the government so that they can control or influence the religious views that it expresses.[4]

As religious factions battled to control the government, it was only a matter of time before those battles became violent.

Justice Black didn't press the point. He and Finan discussed for a time how Carroll felt about Catholics being excluded in Maryland, never really coming to a resolution.

Finally, Chief Justice Warren said, "Could a Buddhist become a notary public in Maryland?"

Finan didn't answer. It was odd, but for some reason the silence lingered.

"A Buddhist?" the chief justice asked again. "As I understand, Buddhists do not believe . . . in a god. Yet there are many . . . in this country, particularly in Hawaii . . . and I know in other States they have many Buddhist temples of which citizens are members."

Finan couldn't lie. There was a hesitancy in his tone, but he said, "Well, Mr. Chief Justice, if they did not believe in some sort of a . . . deity or a Supreme Being, in all honestly, I would have to state that according to the interpretation of the laws, as we have it, they could not become a notary."

"Yet it is recognized as one of the religions of the world, is it not?" Warren asked.

"Yes, it is," Finan said.

"Then . . . what basis in the Constitution is there for excluding those people, if they have a religious belief and want to practice it . . . in this country?"

Roy had to have felt that Finan was on the ropes. These were powerful intellectual body blows. He was staggering. But like most fighters, he still had some energy for a counter. The attorney general hurled himself at the chief justice's question. "[A]s the appellants have set forth in their brief, you cannot have any discussion of this question without some discussion of . . . the separation of church and the state."[5]

"Yes," Warren said.

The message was clear. Finan had considered this question. He was ready to answer it. He fired off a series of cases he felt were similar to Roy's, where the courts had allowed states or universities to require people to take certain oaths. Those cases all dealt with situations where what the person wanted was "a matter of privilege," Finan pointed out, then continued, "just as in this case, there's no compulsion for Mr. Torcaso to become a notary public. He has suffered no penalty. He suffers no punishment. There's no abridgment of his own belief as an atheist to luxury in that belief as long as he wants. If he seeks public office, which is a privilege, then the State places that sanction on him."[6] These were the arguments that had persuaded Ralph Shure, the trial court judge. They were enticing.

"If you had been barred from running for attorney general on the ground of your religion, would you consider that abridged *your* rights?" Justice Black asked.

"Uh," Finan began, "Mr. Justice, the courts have almost universally held that there is no property right in public office, that . . . public office is merely a matter of privilege, it's not a matter of right."

"Would you accept that in your belief that you had been barred because of your religion?" Justice Black asked.

"I probably would not like it, Mr. Justice, but I would be compelled to accept it." Finan explained that the oath was designed to ensure that public officials believed in moral accountability. It was a reasonable safeguard, he argued.

After a brief exchange, Justice Black followed up on that point. "I understood you to say that on balance here, you insisted that the interest of the State in having Notary Publics who might do no wrong outweighed the interest of . . . this man and the public and leaving him complete freedom to believe or not to believe what he saw fit. Is that about the way you had weighed the scale?"

"That's correct, Mr. Justice," Finan said.[7]

It seemed everyone in the room was taking one thing for granted: that Roy's religious beliefs guaranteed that he lacked moral accountability. It's a common accusation. People of one religious belief—including atheists and agnostics—tend to be skeptical of people of any different tradition. It must have eaten at Roy, given his dedication to his family and country.

After a series of minor follow-up questions and repeated points, Finan's argument fizzled. One question lingered. Did the justices agree with how Maryland had weighed the scale?

And something else was odd. Finan still had time left, yet he stepped away from the podium. There didn't seem to be any additional arguments, but another attorney from the state's table stood in his place.

Roy looked on, likely curious about what this newcomer would bring.

The youthful lawyer approached the podium. His name was Joseph S. Kaufman. Just over thirty, he was by far the youngest advocate in the room. He was one of Finan's deputy attorneys general.

With the entire court looking on, he reminded the justices of the actual nature of the case—that Roy was seeking an order to the court clerk commanding him to give Roy his commission. It seemed an odd path. Surely the justices knew what type of case it was. He then explained how notary public commissions work in Maryland. By law, a person must receive a recommendation from the state senator who represents the county where the person resides. The governor then must sign off. After that, the clerk of the court had to issue the commission. All commissions expired by law two years after the senator had given a recommendation, and they must be renewed. Roy's commission, Kaufmann explained, would expire on May 1, 1961, just one week after oral argument.

"I point that out because I think it was overlooked and we think that the Court should be advised of that fact," Kauffman said in a voice far less gravely than anyone else who had spoken that day.

"You mean nobody pleaded this?" Justice Frankfurter called out, his tone incredulous.

Pfeffer undoubtedly knew why. This was a new argument, but it potentially gave the state a silver bullet. If Roy understood the significance of this, panic would have swelled within him. What Kaufmann was telling the justices was that Roy's case was moot. Even if the court ruled in Roy's favor that very day, he wouldn't be able to serve more than a week.

A lengthy discussion ensued between several of the justices and Kaufman, all focused on the timing and logistics of becoming a notary. At one point, even, Justice Frankfurter chuckled a little about the "arbitrariness" of the whole process.

The chief justice finally brought the discussion back to the real issue at hand. "Suppose," he said, the court ruled "after Monday, under Maryland law?"

"Well, his term has expired," Kaufman said. "There's no office to fill at that time." In other words, even if the Supreme Court ordered the clerk of Montgomery County to issue the commission, which was all Roy was asking, he couldn't do so because it would no longer exist.

"It seems strange," Chief Justice Warren said, "you wouldn't present that to the Court before this." The annoyance in his voice reverberated throughout the grand chamber.

"Well," Kaufman said in a diminutive tenor, "if Your Honor please, I think where everybody was directing their attention to the main issues and it was overlooked. We've had all new counsel in this case also since the trial in the lower court and in the Court of Appeals, because we've had a change in stewardship in the Attorney General's Office, Attorney General Sybert having been elevated to the Court of Appeals while this case was pending and we have a complete new stewardship here."[8]

The justices were clearly intrigued. Nearly all of them asked some question or another on the issue.

The argument dragged on. Kaufman discussed why Maryland should win based on some of the other legal doctrines. He reiterated that the Supreme Court in *Davis v. Beason* had already approved government regulating belief that is "inimicable to our society." But it was largely a rehash of what the justices had already heard.

Roy's and Pfeffer's minds would have lingered on the mootness question. Kaufman had just given the justices an easy out. Ordinarily, the court didn't rule on dead issues. If its ruling here would have no effect on the outcome of Roy's case, it made no sense for it to wade into such thorny issues as the meaning of "religion" and the scope of the Religion Clauses.

The justices didn't give Roy any hope either. As Kaufman's time ticked to a close, Chief Justice Warren demanded that both sides submit supplemental briefs before Friday of that week to flesh out the issues related to the mootness question. He was taking it seriously. For this cause, Roy had given up his job, sacrificed his social standing, suffered tension in his home, subjected his children to rejection, endured strangers in his house, and faced assaults in the press. Now, it appeared, the justices might not even rule on it.

NOTES

1. *Torcaso v. Watkins* (part 2), Oyez, https://www.oyez.org/cases/1960/373.
2. Ibid.
3. Ibid.
4. Douglas Laycock, "Religious Liberty as Liberty," *Journal of Contemporary Legal Issues* 7, no. 2 (1996): 321.
5. *Torcaso v. Watkins* (part 2), Oyez.
6. Ibid.
7. Ibid.
8. Ibid.

Chapter 21

HONEST MEN;
MEN OF PRINCIPLE

That evening, Roy and Eileen took the family to dinner at Wah-Q, a Chinese restaurant in the Twinbrook Shopping Center not far from their home. It was a special treat. With money so tight, the family almost never ate out. Little Sue, now eighteen months, wiggled her way through dinner. Bill was just thrilled to have escaped the boring courtroom. Linda chatted with her friend Mollie, who had joined them at the Supreme Court. Roy and Eileen, never demonstrative, pondered the case, what it meant, and whether it had been worth all the sacrifice.

The next morning, the vast majority of papers across the nation reported on only one story from the oral argument: Roy's case was moot. As the *Philadelphia Inquirer* noted, "come May 1" the "immediate object of Torcaso's suit before the court will cease to exist."[1] The *Baltimore Sun* reported the same. It noted that Roy "probably never will hold office even if the court rules in his favor."[2] Roy couldn't have read them, but similar stories cropped up across the United States.

Pfeffer, Sickles, and team toiled to get the mootness brief to the court by Friday. Their arguments were straightforward. Even if Roy couldn't hold his position, the question still needed answering. The oath requirement affected every public officer in the state. Maryland argued the opposite. Both sides filed their briefs on Friday, April 28, 1961. Roy's commission would expire three days later.

Nervous days passed. Roy's commission expired. Life remained the same. Roy found a job as an office manager of a plumbing and air conditioning firm in DC. The cool pleasantness of April yielded to DC's sweltering summer heat. Still no decision came. No one could predict how the divided justices would rule. The mootness question loomed. The justices had spewed out a series of hotly debated opinions that term, had issued seething dissents, and had argued openly with each other in public. All of it undermined the legitimacy of the court. Being able to avoid yet another close case might have been something all nine justices welcomed.

The court met every Monday to announce decisions. Roy waited for news. Pfeffer did the same in New York. Nothing came. The divide in the court was as evident as ever. It seemed every week they issued more five-four split decisions. Justice Frankfurter sat consistently on the side of the government's right to regulate. Justice Black rested reliably on the side of individual rights. Justice Potter Stewart remained the swing vote. No one could tell from oral argument how they would vote in Roy's case. Every week without a decision provided more evidence of intense infighting between the justices.

On the morning of Monday, June 19, everyone involved in the case would have woken with nerves in their gut. The Supreme Court would hold their last session of the 1961 term that day at noon. They had no choice. They had to issue a ruling on Roy's case.

Roy attended the session. He and Pfeffer sat together in the audience. Their stomachs churned. Roy had given up so much. Pfeffer, in many ways, had staked his professional reputation on the case. With so few other organizations willing to side with an atheist, he was alone, and it would be easy for others to leave him hanging if Roy lost.

The justices entered the grand chamber with all the pomp they had before. After they settled into their seats, some high, some low, they began issuing decisions. Their first was a five-four split that again resulted in a bitter and emotional dissent.[3] The justices most likely to vote for Roy were in the minority of that case. The next opinion cut the opposite way but was still five to four. So it went. In almost every case, a group of five men issued rulings that would affect the lives of every American for generations to come.

When they finally reached Roy's case, it was anybody's guess what direction they would go. There was no reason to think the divide wouldn't hold. It seemed to permeate everything. Then, from his lowered seat, his eyes barely visible to the packed courtroom, Justice Black eased toward his microphone.

Roy looked on in anticipation.

"Mr. Torcaso is right," Justice Black said in that gentle, elderly voice.[4]

The ruling was unanimous.

Roy would later describe that moment as one of the proudest of his life.[5] Never one to be demonstrative, it's unlikely he showed much reaction externally. Inside, he was beaming.

In his musical Alabaman accent, Justice Black read portions of the opinion, which he had written. Unlike so many of the other cases, there was no dissent.

Justice Black didn't even mention the mootness concerns. When the dust had settled and the justices had debated with one another in their conference room, it was apparent they felt the questions needed answering regardless of whether Roy could actually hold the position. After summarizing the Maryland constitutional provision, Justice Black wrote, "The power and authority of the State of Maryland thus is put on the side of one particular sort of believers—those who are willing to say they believe in 'the existence of God.'"[6] The Supreme Court justices identified something the lower court judges never perceived. Religious liberty is always threatened when the government places its mighty hand on the scale in favor of any group. That includes favoring one religion over another—the religious over the irreligious, the irreligious over the religious. To protect religious liberty, the government must remain neutral. It must not use its immense power to punish people for their beliefs, even when those beliefs run contrary to the vast majority of popular opinion.

"It is true," the justices continued, "that there is much historical precedent for such laws. Indeed, it was largely to escape religious test oaths and declarations that a great many of the early colonists left Europe and came here hoping to worship in their own way. It soon developed, however, that many of those who had fled to escape religious test oaths turned out to be perfectly willing, when they had the power to do so, to force dissenters from their faith to take test oaths in conformity with that faith."[7] Again the justices spied through the dark haze of history a common theme far too many others miss. When the law burdens one faith group—including atheists or agnostics—over another, it is only a matter of time before the unfavored group gains power. Once it does, it will use the law for its own ends. This results in factions vying for government power and turning it into a spear they can use to promote only their beliefs.

The opinion carried on: "This brought on a host of laws in the new Colonies imposing burdens and disabilities of various kinds upon varied beliefs depending largely upon what group happened to be politically strong enough to legislate in favor of its own beliefs. The effect of all this was the formal or practical 'establishment' of particular religious faiths in most of the Colonies, with consequent burdens imposed on the free exercise of the faiths of nonfavored believers."[8]

Roy should have basked in the opinion's language, in the vindication history provided him. Pfeffer likely breathed a sigh of relief. Justice Black noted that even in the colonies there were "wise and farseeing men . . . too many to mention . . . who spoke out against test oaths and all the philosophies of intolerance behind them."[9]

Pfeffer's faith in the Supremes had been justified, even as so many others had been afraid to stand with Roy.

In a direct shot at the Maryland Court of Appeals, Justice Black quoted from the Supreme Court's prior cases. "What was said in our prior cases we think controls our decision here."[10] The first statement was pithy—that the Free Exercise Clause "embraces two concepts,— freedom to believe and freedom to act."[11] The second quote was lengthy, but powerful:

> The "establishment of religion" clause of the First Amendment means at least this: Neither a state nor the Federal Government can set up a church. Neither can pass laws which aid one religion, aid all religions, or prefer one religion over another. Neither can force nor influence a person to go to or to remain away from church against his will or force him to profess a belief or disbelief in any religion. No person can be punished for entertaining or professing religious beliefs or disbeliefs, for church attendance or non-attendance. No tax in any amount, large or small, can be levied to support any religious activities or institutions, whatever they may be called, or whatever form they may adopt to teach or practice religion. Neither a state nor the Federal Government can, openly or secretly, participate in the affairs of any religious organizations or groups and *vice versa*. In the words of Jefferson, the clause against establishment of religion by law was intended to erect "a wall of separation between church and State."[12]

And finally, Justice Black quoted directly from his ideological rival, Justice Frankfurter, who had written in a different case, "We are all agreed that the First [Amendment has] a secular reach far more penetrating in the conduct of Government than merely to forbid an 'established church.' . . . We renew our conviction that we have staked the very existence of our country on the faith that complete separation between the state and religion is best for the state and best for religion."[13]

The Maryland Court of Appeals thought the Supreme Court had repudiated those statements. It was wrong, Justice Black wrote. "Nothing decided or written . . . lends support to the idea that the Court . . . intended to open up the way for government, state or federal, to restore the historically and constitutionally discredited policy of probing religious beliefs by test oaths or limiting public offices to persons who have, or perhaps more properly profess to have, a belief in some particular kind of religious concept."[14]

Pfeffer knew the significance of this. In later years, he would face attacks that he was somehow an enemy of religious people. Nothing could be further from the truth. The Supreme Court's statements and the principles it employed do not protect the irreligious over the religious. They don't undermine religion. They protect everyone. All people have some form of religious belief—that is to say, everyone has answers to the religious questions of "Why am I here?" "Where did I come from?" "Where will I go when I die?" among others. And government should not force answers to those questions upon anyone. The principles Justice Black embraced protect the Christian from the atheist as much as they protect the atheist from the Christian. When religious liberty is truly valued, government may not punish anyone for their beliefs, no matter who happens to control the reins of power in that particular moment. The principles the Supreme Court set forth don't ban religion from the public sphere or support the idea that religious people can't speak their mind in public. They stand only for the idea that government itself can't sway the debate.

In a footnote, Justice Black spoke of Oliver Ellsworth, a member of the Federal Constitutional Convention and later chief justice of the Supreme Court. In a 1787 letter, Ellsworth wrote, "In short, test-laws are utterly ineffectual: they are no security at all; because men of loose principles will . . . evade them. If they exclude any persons, it will be honest men, men of principle, who will rather suffer an injury, than act contrary to the dictates of their consciences."[15]

It's easy to imagine Roy reading that statement again and again. It described him. Contrary to all the accusations against him—being a communist, lacking moral accountability, being unfit—it deemed him an honest man, one of principle, willing to suffer rather than lie and claim he believed something he didn't. Even when the law tried to force him into having to choose between his beliefs and his career, he held firm.

"We repeat and again reaffirm," Justice Black wrote, "that neither a State nor the Federal Government can constitutionally force a person 'to profess a belief or disbelief in any religion.' Neither can constitutionally pass laws or impose requirements which aid all religions as against non-believers, and neither can aid those religions based on a belief in the existence of God as against those religions founded on different beliefs."[16] He noted that in the United States, religions that thrived but did not necessarily teach the existence of God included "Buddhism, Taoism, Ethical Culture, Secular Humanism and others."[17] And the opposite applied as well. Government couldn't favor nontheistic religions over others who did teach the existence of God. Everyone benefited.

Justice Black concluded, "The fact, however, that a person is not compelled to hold public office cannot possibly be an excuse for barring him from office by state-imposed criteria forbidden by the Constitution. . . . This Maryland religious test for public office unconstitutionally invades the appellant's freedom of belief and religion and therefore cannot be enforced against him. The judgment of the Court of Appeals of Maryland is accordingly reversed."[18]

The justices moved on to other split decisions. Roy and Pfeffer would have waited anxiously for their opportunity to leave the courthouse. When Roy finally did, amidst all the smiles and handshakes and feelings of vindication on the steps of the Supreme Court temple, the world was largely unchanged. Prejudices against him still lingered. Like weeds, attacks on his character sprung up almost immediately in various newspaper columns. To be an atheist still placed him lower than dirt in many people's estimations. But as he walked down those massive steps and took in the grandeur that is the United States Capitol, he should have known he could look his children in the eyes and tell them he had kept his integrity. He had won not just for himself but for anyone who valued liberty.

Notes

1. "Notary Public Job Denied Atheist," *Philadelphia Inquirer*, April 26, 1961, 2.
2. "Notary Job Doubted in Oath Case: Politics Probably Would Bar Torcaso, High Court Told," *Baltimore Sun*, April 25, 1961, 40.
3. "Drama Builds in High Court," *Christian Science Monitor*, June 20, 1961, 1.

4. Bill Torcaso and Linda Bernstein, in discussion with author, July 28, 2017.
5. Ibid.
6. *Torcaso v. Watkins*, 367 U.S. 488, 490 (1961).
7. Ibid.
8. Ibid.
9. Ibid.
10. Ibid., at 492.
11. Ibid. Note that the justices here quote from *Cantwell v. Connecticut*, 310 U.S. 296, 303–4 (1943).
12. Ibid., at 492–3; note that the justices here quote from *Everson v. Board of Education*, 330 U.S. 1, 15–16 (1947).
13. Ibid., at 493–94; note that justices here quote from *Illinois ex rel. McCollum v. Board of Education*, 333 U.S. 203 (1948).
14. Ibid., at 494 1961.
15. Ibid., at 494 n.9.
16. Ibid., at 495.
17. Ibid., at 495 n.11.
18. Ibid., at 495–96.

Chapter 22

PARTED LIPS

In the legal world, many scholars and lawyers often refer to Roy's case only for the principle that religious test oaths for public office are forbidden. It's true that his case had the immediate effect of invalidating similar provisions in Arkansas, Mississippi, North Carolina, Pennsylvania, South Carolina, Tennessee, and Texas. But in its historical context, it showed once again the importance of allowing people who believe differently from the majority the freedom to do so, without government interference.

Immediately after the decision was issued, newspapers across the country spilled columns of ink printing letters and sermons about the case. Many argued that the decision somehow undermined the United States' position as a nation with a religious history, that it attacked religion itself.[1] It did no such thing. If anything, the justices acknowledged the deeply diverse religious nature of the country's history and emphasized the importance of ensuring that government is not a weapon to be used to lift one form of belief over another. When religious freedom is truly valued, religions—including secular religions—must stand and fall on their own merits, without government hindering or helping them. They must attract converts by the power of their doctrines and the examples of their followers. New sheep will come to the fold through the spirit they feel when they enter a church house or attend a meeting of secular humanists. The government will give no advantage to any belief system. If people would be fishers of men, they must ensure their bait is enticing.

In that context, Roy's case highlighted the importance of the Establishment Clause—the source of the idea of separation of church and state. It is as crucial to religious freedom as protecting the free exercise of religion. That separation prevents any one set of believers from using government to burden those who believe differently. But it also prevents the government from corrupting religion.[2] It forces all people—believers and nonbelievers alike—to remember that they must be vibrant and enthusiastic in their way of life if they would have it flourish and attract others. By contrast, forcing people to attend church through government coercion does nothing but create a congregation of hypocrites. In countries where the government props up just one church, the result tends to be a watered-down faith that lacks any of the vitality we see in the United States. Many of the favored religion attend simply out of self-interest and to advance in government circles, others refuse to participate because they don't want to be coerced, and too many other religions suffer and wither.[3] Faith must be voluntary, or it has no power.

———

Roy and Eileen were married for sixty years, until her death in 2006. Roy bounced from one job to another. He took up various other causes. He continued to play chess. Linda, as a child watching so many lawyers traipse through her house, thought to herself, "I can do that." She did, graduating from one of the nation's most elite law schools and eventually becoming an administrative law judge.[4] Decades after the case, Bill would look back on his father's legacy with pride, even publishing some of his own thoughts on religious freedom in *The Boston Globe*. Pfeffer continued his crusade for religious freedom. By the time of his death, he had cemented his reputation as one of the most influential religious liberty lawyers in history.

As Roy progressed from middle age to his golden years, he

understood that his case had not been a victory for himself and like-minded people alone. It had been a victory for the liberty of all. Too often, people perceive "liberty" as something that should allow them to get what they want and everyone else to lose. They want liberty for themselves but not for anyone else. Those types of rules never work. A legal rule that benefits you when you're a majority can easily be turned against you when you become a minority. The law must be consistent in protecting everyone all the time. Today, the number of atheists, agnostics, and people unaffiliated with any formal religion is increasing dramatically. If religious freedom doesn't include them, it both disserves a large swath of the American public and potentially creates a situation where the official government religion could be atheism. Religious freedom recognizes that all religious beliefs should be protected and none should be made the official position of the state.

———

While Roy's case had been pending in the Supreme Court, the state senator from Montgomery County had recommended once again that Roy receive his notary's license. The governor had again approved. The county clerk held on to it until the Supreme Court ruled.

When the victory finally came down, Roy was ready to sign the oath supporting the Constitution and the laws of Maryland. Just more than two years from his original rejection, Roy again marched up the steps of the Montgomery County courthouse. The county clerk handed him the documents he would need to sign. Roy scanned them. They said nothing of his—or anyone else's—religious beliefs. The act was largely symbolic, of course. He no longer had a boss who wanted him to become a notary. He likely didn't even have much use for becoming one. That wasn't the point. He gladly etched his signature onto the page.

Shortly after, Roy's oldest daughter, Linda, decided she wanted to operate a ham radio. She had become fascinated with the technology and asked to practice with it. The rules at the time didn't allow just anyone to operate one. She needed to fill out an application for a license, and that application had to be notarized. On a hot, muggy day, wearing a white dress adorned with modest frills, she filled out the form. Reporters looked on.

One of Linda's enduring memories of her father was his stoic nature. He was never one to show his emotions. After completing the document, she slid it to him. Dressed in a baggy, light-colored suit and dark tie, Roy reached for the paper, his notary stamp ready. It would be his first official act. A man behind them clapped. A camera flashed. Roy's lips parted in a gentle smile.

Notes

1. "Atheist's Legal Victory Is Topic of Sermon," *Washington Post, Times Herald*, July 3, 1961, B1.

2. *See* Douglas Laycock, "Religious Liberty as Liberty," *Journal of Contemporary Legal Issues* 7, no. 2 (1996): 325.

3. See the following, for example: Andrew M. Greeley's discussion of surveys that show how participation in the established Church of England is significantly lower than participation in churches in the United States (*Religious Change in America* [Cambridge, MA: President and Fellows of Harvard College, 1989] 126–27); James Madison's argument in his 1785 "Memorial and Remonstrance" that the fruits of a legal establishment of Christianity are "pride and indolence in the Clergy; ignorance and servility in the laity, in both, superstition, bigotry and persecution," (in Edwin S. Gaustad and Mark A. Noll, eds., *A Document History of Religion in America to 1877*, 3d ed. [Grand Rapids, MI: Eerdmans, 2003], 235); R. Stephen Warner's exploration of the relationship between disestablishment and measures of religious vitality ("Work in Progress Toward a New Paradigm for the Sociological Study of Religion in the United States," *American Journal of Sociology* 98, no. 5 [March 1993]:1044, 1048–58).

4. Linda Bernstein, in discussion with author, July 28, 2017.

PART 3

A FORGOTTEN FAITH

The facts in cases involving the free exercise of religion all follow a remarkably similar pattern. They each involve a law or regulation that doesn't burden the religious practices of the people in power—otherwise the law wouldn't have passed in the first place. Instead, they each involve a religious dissenter who asks to be exempted from that law because of his or her religious beliefs. And they each involve the crucial question of whether the religious dissenter should receive an exemption to a law that applies to everyone else. This was the case for Anthony Kohlmann. It was what Roy Torcaso faced as well.

For decades, scholars have debated whether the Free Exercise Clause of the Constitution demands such religious exemptions. In popular media, a similar argument ensues every time a religious-freedom case makes headlines. No one argues that religious liberty should always trump every other concern. For instance, if a religious ritual requires sacrificing a human child, everyone agrees that the state's interest in protecting the child trumps the religious free-exercise rights of the person involved. The question is where the line should be drawn. Some argue religious freedom demands exemption unless the government has a compelling reason not to allow them. Others argue there should never be religious exemptions. Most take whatever position is convenient for them at the time and that agrees with their personal religious beliefs.

In many respects, the history of religious free exercise in the United States has been focused on how to address this particular question. There are, of course, numerous other issues related to religious freedom. Many involve the Establishment Clause and just how closely government and religion can influence one another. But for individuals trying to live by their beliefs, what matters to them is whether they can receive the religious exemptions they need to live their faith without facing retribution from the government.

By 1990, most scholars, judges, and lawyers thought the question had been settled. Then, an unknown Klamath Indian man rose up out of the mountains of Oregon, fought off government attempts to suppress his religious exercise, and demanded to be heard.

Chapter 23

SALVATION

On a cool morning in January 1957, more than two years before Roy refused to declare a belief he didn't hold, Al Smith had plummeted to rock bottom. He blinked awake to find himself in an alley in Sacramento, California.[1] His body ached. Bruises racked his muscles. If he'd had any money, it was gone now—wasted on booze. He reeked of alcohol and the filth of the street. Though thirty-seven years old, he might as well have been twice that age for all his body and mind had survived. His head pounded. His mouth felt as though he'd swallowed dirt.

He eventually forced his achy muscles to life, but moving through the dizziness and nausea was like trudging through tar. Life, it seemed, had beaten him. He had passed out between two cardboard boxes. There in the grime, struggling to stand, he might have still been physically alive, but for all intents and purposes, this world no longer held any meaning for him.

Anyone who had glimpsed pieces of Al's childhood or known what the government had done to his people wouldn't have been surprised. And anyone who spied him in that moment couldn't possibly have known that he would one day stand at the center of a sea change in religious liberty law.

Al was born on November 6, 1919, in Modoc Point, Oregon, in a small house along the Williamson River, which meanders through the foothills of the majestic Cascade Mountain Range. Towering, snow-capped peaks and soaring ponderosa pine ring the area. The pristine waters of Upper Klamath Lake, one of Oregon's largest natural bodies of fresh water, are just south of town. Today, when people skirt past it, they likely know nothing of the area's rich history. A two-lane byway carves through and disrupts the steady descent of the brush-covered mountain. Conifers dot the land. Below that, a single set of railway tracks hugs the lake's shoreline. The water looks like glass.

The culture and people that thrived on these lands, the lake, and its surroundings for thousands of years still abound, though many of their more ancient traditions have either faded or transformed. When Al struggled to his feet that morning in Sacramento, even he knew little of his own people. He really didn't even know who he was. By the time of his birth, the government had already spent decades trying to con-quer the world his grandparents and ancestors had known.

He was born a member of the Klamath tribe. For nearly ten thou-sand years, the Klamath had thrived in this region of mountains, lakes, marshes, rivers, and abundant wildlife.[2] At the time of Al's birth, the land, though still pristine and beautiful, was controlled by the United States government, which had been working for decades to impose a European lifestyle on the Klamath. Despite this, Al had enjoyed a largely Klamath early childhood. On that morning in Sacramento, as he struggled to his feet, he held just snippets of it, fleeting memories he tried to grasp the way someone strains to remember a fading dream: living with his mother and grandparents (he never knew his father), a small wooden house next to the Williamson River, fishing and canoeing with his grandmother,[3] a dog named Pal, gathering wocus seeds and letting them dry in the sun and using his slingshot to protect them from birds and squirrels.[4]

But even during those idyllic days, the flourishing lake of Klamath knowledge and tradition was at risk of drying up. He had sensed it as a child, even if he didn't understand it. The signs were there. His grandparents and mother would speak to each other in Klamath, but with him, they emphasized English, worried that Klamath would hold him back.[5] It's not surprising they felt that way. During their childhood years, at the schools the federal government had established on the reservation, Native American children were punished if they spoke in Klamath, with penalties that sound more like something out of a Japanese World War II prison camp. The white teachers would force older boys to slog around the schoolyard with a fence rail on their backs as punishment for speaking the language. Other times they would whip children with tree branches.[6] Whether Al's grandparents experienced any of these specific atrocities is unclear. But they certainly would have been aware of them.

And they experienced their own. When she was a young girl, Al's grandmother and the rest of the community had been forced by the government to watch while soldiers hanged Klamath and Modoc men who resisted the takeover. Etched in her memory through time and space were the images of women wailing while their husbands, sons, and brothers dangled from the hangman's noose.[7]

Al did not witness such violence, but he was subject to a number of government-imposed restrictions. He was not allowed to hunt. The ceremonies his ancestors had practiced for centuries were now forbidden to him.[8] Even the elders had stopped inviting young people like Al to participate in their ancient traditions and religious customs. Still, by the time Al was seven years old, he had enjoyed a stable life—a consistent home, the presence of loving adults, a strong cultural identity, a tie to his ancestral land, freedom, lessons in hard work, food, and a budding sense of who he was in the world.

That's when Al's arduous journey to the alley in Sacramento truly began.

———

Nearly fifty-five years before Al's birth, in December 1864, the federal government had forced the various tribes in the Klamath Lake region to sign a treaty that greatly reduced their lands and placed them directly under the supervision of a government agent. Part of the agent's duties, as recorded in federal statute, were "to promote the well-being of the Indians, advance them in civilization, and especially agriculture, and . . . secure their moral improvement and education."[9] It's hard to imagine a more patronizing view of an entire civilization. The man who helped design the treaty, J. W. Perit Huntington, wrote a letter to one of the first agents of the Klamath Agency:

> Your duty is to endeavor to make the Indian colony which is under your charge, strictly an *Indian* settlement, carefully guarding it against the contamination of white associations, and at the same time imparting to it so much of the intelligence, enterprise and stability of the Anglo Saxon Race as possible.[10]

The effects of those directions would change Al's life forever.

Government agents decided an education system would be the best way to engrain Anglo-Saxon cultural norms on Klamath children, so they established schools on the reservations. These schools, however, had only minuscule effect. As with any strong culture, the Klamath way of life could not be erased so easily. The agents needed something more drastic. In 1873, an agent to the Commissioner of Indian Affairs suggested the unthinkable: "Being fully convinced that a radical change in the Indian character can only be wrought in childhood and early youth, I would most respectfully urge the co-operation of the Government . . . of taking the children from their native haunts of degradation, and [then] clothing, feeding, and teaching them the habits and arts of civilization. Without a special appropriation for this object, little can be done to emancipate them from the thrall of ignorance and superstition which characterizes their fathers."[11]

The practice was adopted almost immediately.

And so, at seven-years-old, Al was torn from his family. He did not agree to it. Neither did his mother.[12] The agents at the Klamath Agency rounded up Al and a large number of other Klamath children and drove them to the relatively nearby town of Klamath Falls, where they forced them to attend Sacred Heart Academy, a Catholic boarding school. The erasure of everything Klamath in Al's life began.

The next twelve years represented the beginning of Al's unknowing descent toward the filthy alley in Sacramento. It was so gradual even he didn't realize it was happening. And how could he have? No seven-year-old boy could have the self-awareness to know where this forced cultural change would lead him. The protections of the Constitution's religion clauses had never been considered when it came to the Klamath or, in reality, nearly all other Native peoples. The late nineteenth and early twentieth centuries constituted a low period of religious freedom in the United States. The government engaged in wars with members of The Church of Jesus Christ of Latter-day Saints, atheists were pummeled in the streets, and Indians faced even worse atrocities. In violation of the Free Exercise Clause, the federal government and its agents did everything they could to wipe Klamath religion from the earth.[13] During the 1870s, they imprisoned Klamath shaman, the medicine men who played an important role in Klamath Society.[14] They prohibited religious ceremonies.[15] In 1897, shaman who practiced were sentenced to hard labor and prison.[16] At one point, an agent made clear that his goal was to "root[] out thier [sic] faith in thier [sic] own 'spiritual' medicine, and thus open[] the way for the white man's customs, laws, and religion."[17]

That led to decades of violations of the Establishment Clause. It wasn't enough for the government to wipe out whatever religion Al's ancestors had. They wanted to replace it.[18] Though it is clearly a violation of religious freedom for the government to force one religion on any group of people, no one seemed to think anything of doing just that to the Klamath. The government forced Christianity onto Al and his people. They built churches and ramrodded the Klamath into worship. They ripped Al from his family and locked him away in a Catholic school.

Many of the specifics of Al's early boyhood are lost, but always there was the freedom of the open land, the hills, the snow-capped mountains, the pristine lakes and rivers, his canoe gliding softly through the marshes, and the seemingly perfect-blue Oregon sky. In the prison that Catholic school became for Al, all of that vanished, replaced instead with walls, ceilings, locked doors, and strange women in odd clothes who would beat him with a switch if he didn't comply with their demands. They told him "how to dress, how to speak, and what to believe," one author described.[19] It's not surprising that Al raged against his new confines with the same intensity as a tornado trapped in a bottle. Having once known so much freedom, he couldn't stand being enclosed. He would not relinquish his childhood easily, especially because even then he sensed what was truly happening. Years later, he recalled, "They said they were reeducating me, but they were really breaking me from my native traditions. No one spoke the language or taught the Klamath culture. Instead, we were given Catholic religion every day."[20]

Not surprisingly, religion forced upon others through government coercion has little spiritual power to convert. Al's resistance started deviously. When the sisters asked him if he'd been baptized, he lied and said yes to avoid being forced into what he perceived as white religion.[21] But that wasn't enough. He longed for his family and his people. He started to sneak away, trying to get back to the river, the lake, and the soothing presence of his mother and grandmother. He never made it far. Sheriff's deputies often found him on the street, scuffling his way home, and they would lead him back to the school. He took comfort that at least he wasn't too far from his family.

That changed. Two years later, when he was nine, the government transferred him to a different boarding school more than two hundred miles to the north. This school was home to Native American and white students, and its goal remained wiping Klamath culture from the Natives' lives. Al continued to resist and struggled academically because of it. His mind never truly left the childhood it had known. The sisters could never keep him in hand. It reached the point that if they didn't watch him constantly, they knew where he would be: standing alone on a darkened highway, searching for a way back to his family and his way of life, which was slowly receding from his mind. The state police always brought him back.

By the time Al turned twelve, it was 1931, and faceless white adults again shipped him off, this time to a school in Beaverton, a suburb of Portland nearly three hundred miles from the Klamath lands. Al wouldn't have it. He convinced another student at the new Catholic boys' home to escape with him to Portland. They were only twelve, but they thought they might be able to survive in the larger city. Not surprisingly, they didn't last long. They made it as far as Portland Heights, about six miles away, where the police found them looking down on the city. The officers pushed the two boys into the patrol car, took them to the county jail, and fed them cookies and milk.

Then the priest came. When he had them back at the school, he locked them in a room, pulled out a leather strap, and beat them with it.

The other boy slunk back to his room, beaten and broken, refusing even to meet Al's eyes.[22]

Al only grew more determined. He marched back to the boys' dormitory. It was late in the night. He woke one of his Klamath friends, a boy named Skinny. "I'm going home," Al whispered. "Do you want to go with me?"[23]

Skinny blinked awake. Apparently he felt the same way Al did. They both gathered what they could and snuck out of the building.

For the previous five years, Al had learned that if he stayed on the highway, he would get caught. He and Skinny instead skulked across the road to the railroad tracks. Under cover of darkness, they followed the line to Oregon City. There, they waited for a freight train that would take them home. When it finally rolled through, he and Skinny hopped on.

They were headed back to their families.

For one hundred miles, they rode undetected, likely fantasizing about what life would be like once they were finally back in the one place they knew they belonged. When they reached Eugene, yard bulls found them and kicked them off.[24]

But Al was not one to give up. He and Skinny waited for another freight train. They repeated this again and again until, eventually, they made it home.

It didn't last. The mistaken governmental philosophy of the 1930s was that Native people needed to be lifted out of their state of living and taught a "better" way. When agents from the Bureau of Indian Affairs learned Al had returned, they came to his home. This time, Al and his mother convinced them to send him to a federal boarding school far away in Stewart, Nevada, where all of the students were Native Americans. The agents no doubt believed the distance would make it impossible for him to escape.

In some respects, they were right. The Stewart Indian School was far enough away that Al didn't try to escape again physically. This school was also a bit more tolerable for him than the Catholic boarding schools. The all-Native student body helped Al feel more at home, but its purpose was the same: assimilate Native American students into mainstream, white American culture. And most of the students were actually Paiutes from Nevada. They didn't think highly of the Klamath.[25]

The government's plan worked, but only in part. At Stewart, Al moved into the turbulent waters of adolescence. He tried to fit in. He played sports, even participating on the state championship basketball team. He experienced all the insecurities and questions everyone faces during that phase of life. But he had no family to guide him through it. The government had ensured that. The memories of his time with his grandparents had begun to fade. What little he knew of his native language and religion floated away like seeds in the wind. All that remained were fleeting, dreamlike memories. The government had indeed successfully stripped his culture from him. The little boy who had spent his free days "in the country looking for native plants with his family and picking huckleberries in the mountains near Crater lake"[26] was gone.

That didn't mean he had allowed the government's culture and religion to replace what he'd lost. Instead, there appears to have been a giant void—a great, expansive emptiness. That hole in his soul would define him for the next quarter of a century.

It is safe to say that up until his years at Stewart, Al had always been running *to* something. It was to the memory of "going up and down the river in the canoe. Being with my grandmother and my mom."[27] He had always wanted to return to those days. As the memories floated away, however, he no longer had that destination. Now he simply wanted to run *from* the desolation left in their wake. His singular focus was to flee that yawning hole.[28]

He had nowhere to turn. Everywhere he went, the menacing blackness was there, attached to him like a shadow. Escaping it began innocently enough. He would sneak drinks whenever he could. Beer, wine, whatever he could get his hands on. The sensation of the drinks "was as haunting, in a different way, as the memories of fishing the Williamson River."[29] Like most people, the alcohol didn't seem to hurt him much in his younger years. He did well enough in sports to be the captain of the football team and to get decent grades in math. But the drinking was always there.

It did start to have consequences. He got in fights. He stole wine from a farmer who neighbored the Stewart School, which got him expelled and sent back to a similar school in Oregon. There, he was always drinking. In his own words, he was a "live wire."[30] That school eventually expelled him as well. Around Christmas, while drunk, Al was stumbling around looking for the girls' dormitory when, through his stupor, he accidentally ended up in the faculty sleeping area, where he apparently woke one of the female English teachers.[31] There are few other details, but Al recalled later waking up with the police and the school superintendent looming over him. "They loaded me up with another kid, took us out of Salem, and told us that if we ever showed up at the school again we would be arrested."[32]

For the first time since he was seven years old, Al was free to return to his ancestral lands, to the childhood life he had sought for so many years. But it seemed to no longer hold any meaning for him. He stayed only for a few months before heading to Portland, where he ended up on skid row. He had become, essentially, a homeless alcoholic. He didn't know that and had actually never heard the term *alcoholic*, but his only goal was to panhandle to get enough money for booze and food. Life had devolved into nothing more than begging, street fighting, and escaping into the bliss that only alcohol seemed to provide.

When the Japanese thrust the United States into World War II, they seemingly provided Al a lifeline. He was drafted into the army. It might have been just what he needed to overcome the void in his spirit, but it was not to be. Again, alcohol seemed to be his only escape, and he didn't yet understand that while it may have provided him temporary relief, it was only making the emptiness that much larger every time its effects wore off.

Its impact in the real world was devastating. During basic training, he ended up in the stockade for drinking. He was later jailed for going AWOL. Eventually, after being stationed in Liverpool, England, he went AWOL so many times he received a five-year sentence in a prison in the southern part of the country. During that imprisonment, as German bombs quaked the earth around him, an army doctor diagnosed him as an alcoholic. It was the first time he had ever heard the word, but it led to his dishonorable discharge.

He didn't care. Just as the government had forced him from his home and then compelled him into the military, the army rammed him onto a ship back to the United States. Its destination was a federal penitentiary in Upstate New York. It was filled with prisoners. To Al, this was no different from what the government had been doing to him ever since he was seven years old. He went home from the war, he later said, "the same way I came over. I came over against my will, in a type of prison, and they shipped me back the same way."[33]

As difficult as the actual penitentiary was, it didn't hold a candle to the way Al felt spiritually. The darkness that had become his constant companion had finally overtaken him. He was surrounded by it. Escape was no longer a possibility. His only hope was to drink enough so that he didn't feel its presence any longer.

The day he was released from prison, he was called into a room. The guards handed him a black suit. They gave him a pair of brown army shoes, a tan shirt, and some cash.[34] He was back on the street. He immediately headed to Chicago and the women and liquor it promised. Just a few weeks later, he woke one morning in a strange, cheap hotel, hungover and shaking. The suit was stained. He had no money. He rifled through his pockets and found a train ticket back to Oregon, something he must have had the foresight to purchase before spending the last of his cash on booze. He stumbled through Chicago's streets to the train station and climbed on board. It was 1946. He was approximately twenty-seven years old.[35]

The next decade was crushing. If any memories from his childhood were still frolicking around in his identity, life obscured them in a fog of pain and alcohol while a gaping, insatiable darkness slowly replaced them. In 1950, in a hotel in Portland, Al's Mother slipped over a banister and crashed through a skylight.[36] The accident killed her. Al married but struggled to meet the demands of family life. He tried to work odd jobs, but the alcohol abuse found him too often back on the Portland streets, hustling. His health declined.

At one point, while working as an apple picker near Portland, he tried to make a wine run during a pounding storm.[37] He crashed his car. He and his friends salvaged whatever wine they could. They somehow made it back to the orchard, where they drank all night. When Al woke the next morning, coughs racked his body. He spit up blood. He managed to get on a bus back to Portland, where doctors discovered severe internal injuries and tuberculosis. He was on the verge of death.

The hospital transferred him to another facility that specialized in the disease. Internally, he was hemorrhaging. It was so bad the doctors couldn't operate. They gave him drugs to stop the bleeding. Eventually, they removed three ribs and sawed others in half so they could collapse his lung and then reform his entire rib cage.[38]

He healed physically. He even found some spiritual healing. During his recovery, he took art classes. His paintings seemed to invoke the muse of his long-lost childhood. One was of a Native man in full buckskin praying on a mountaintop, his hands in the air in the moonlight. It was done entirely in shades of blue.[39] He managed to stay sober for a couple of years, but the spiritual hits to his past continued to pummel him. The worst blow again came from the federal government. During Al's childhood, almost all members of the Klamath tribe had lived on historical tribal lands. By the 1950s, nearly half had moved away. They had migrated to other cities and states, largely at the hands of outsiders. Like Al, and many tribes during this era, the Klamath as a whole were losing their identity.[40] The Eisenhower Administration was terminating the federal government's relationship with tribes across the United States. For the Klamath, the loss intensified when, in 1954, the relationship between the federal government and the Klamath tribe officially came to an end. Through a statute known as the Klamath Termination Act, which many unwitting Klamath voted for, the tribe lost its land and its tribal sovereignty in exchange for a lump sum payment of $43,500 to each member.[41] The Klamath were now a people without a land and without any tribal center. Their traditional property belonged to the federal government. The migration intensified. It was nearly the final blow to Klamath cultural identity.

———

In 1957, after more run-ins with the law and brief periods of sobriety, Al once again found himself in a bar. This time in Sacramento.

There were some other Klamath there. He settled in with them. Through the din of cigarette smoke and revelry, time passed. The alcohol continued to flow. It washed over his brain like a soothing bath, but the comfort didn't last.

He ended up wandering the streets alone, in the dark. It was everywhere, surrounding him, squeezing him—the way some mythical creature might consume one if its victims.[42] He stumbled into an alley. There, on the ground, was a collection of cardboard boxes. Sleep beckoned. It was perhaps the only other way to escape the shadow. He eased to the ground and disappeared into its welcoming embrace.

In that alley in Sacramento, when Al finally rose to his feet the next morning, he felt the void again. If it were a mouth, it would have swallowed him whole. Panic struck him. He started to pat himself down and rummage through his pockets.[43] He needed coins. Or a bill. Something, anything, that would help him buy a drink. It was the only thing that would keep the gaping maw at bay. His search of himself became more and more frantic. Here, at the bottom, the darkness was as immense as it had ever been.

Then something occurred to him. Through the bruises and throbbing aches, he peered at a crucial realization: here he was, at just thirty-seven, knocking on death's door. And he wasn't ready. He stopped searching his pockets. If he was sick now, he told himself, he would only get sicker. If he didn't stop drinking then, he knew he never would.[44] The darkness that had been chasing him all those years had never yielded to alcohol. It had always returned, stronger than before. It was time to find another way. He stumbled from the alley and into the morning light.

––––––––

Almost everyone who tries to give up an addiction fails at least once. It's as if every past drink is a chain strapped to the addict's body. Even when you pull one off, the others are still there, dragging you down. The temptation is as ever present as the body's shadow. Al had been no different to this point.

He had heard of Alcoholics Anonymous, had even attended some of their meetings. On a cold day in January 1957, in a final effort to save himself, he eased through the doors of an AA meeting and took his seat in a room full of people. As part of its twelve-step program, AA required him to acknowledge that only a "higher power," something greater than himself, could help him recover. He had nothing to turn to. When he thought of God, he thought of angry nuns, boarding schools, prisons, being torn from his family, having his heritage stripped from him, and white religion being forced upon him.[45] He couldn't bring himself to embrace it. Indeed, thoughts of God mostly just led him back to the emptiness he had been trying to escape for nearly two decades.

It might have been enough to drive him away. Even here, in meetings supposed to help, the shadow found him with the undying persistence of a bounty hunter. It's easy to imagine Al pushing his hands against his knees, ready to rise, to give up. Perhaps even AA wasn't for him.

He was on the edge of a cliff. But then a distant memory reached through the darkness, like a beam of sunlight breaking through thick clouds. It touched him. He remembered his grandmother, when he was a child, before the government stole him away from her. It was a memory he had seemingly buried for years. Every evening, as he had settled into bed, she would wander through the tiny house along the Williamson River whispering something in Klamath, his forgotten language. It was a recitation, like a prayer, as comforting in its tradition as the sound of the river trickling over the rocks outside. He didn't understand the words or even if they constituted a prayer at all, but in that moment, in that AA meeting, as he looked upon the memory through three decades of pain and separation, he decided she must have been calling on some higher power for help. He determined that he would too. "That will be my God," he thought.[46] He didn't know what it was or who it was. But if his grandmother invoked its powers, he could follow her example. He could begin the journey to return to who he might have been had the government not torn him from his home all those years before. For the first time, he began to pray, to call on a source beyond himself for help.

It was January 15, 1957. For the first time, Al Smith reached for his Creator, a God he "didn't even understand."[47] It was the beginning of a lifelong spiritual journey. He asked the Creator for help. And for the rest of his life, for the next fifty-seven years, he never touched another drop of alcohol.

NOTES

1. There are conflicting writings regarding whether this happened in Sacramento or in San Francisco. The distinction is irrelevant for understanding Al Smith and his spiritual journey.
2. For a history of the Klamath people, see Theodore Stern, *The Klamath Tribe: A People and Their Reservation* (Seattle: University of Washington Press, 1966).
3. Carolyn N. Long, *Religious Freedom and Indian Rights: The Case of Oregon v. Smith* (Lawrence: University Press of Kansas, 2000), 23.
4. Jane Farrell (Al Smith's wife), in discussion with author, January 8, 2018.
5. Ibid.
6. Stern, *The Klamath Tribe*, 107.
7. Farrell, discussion with author.
8. Long, *Religious Freedom and Indian Rights*, 23.
9. Treaty between the United States of America and the Klamath, &c. Indians, October 14, 1864. 16 *Statutes at Large*, 708.
10. Letter of J. W. P. Huntington to Lindsay Applegate, November 18, 1867, Lindsay Applegate Papers, Special Collections & University Archives, University of Oregon Libraries, Eugene, Oregon.
11. *Annual Report of the Commissioner of Indian Affairs to the Secretary of the Interior for the Year 1873* (Washington: Government Printing Office), 324.
12. Long, *Religious Freedom and Indian Rights*, 24.
13. For an in-depth discussion of how the federal government treated Klamath religion, see Stern, *The Klamath Tribe*, 111–21, and the sources cited in those pages.
14. Stern, *The Klamath Tribe*, 110.
15. Ibid. at 113.
16. Ibid. at 114.
17. For an in-depth discussion of how the federal government treated Klamath religion, see J. Meacham to A.B. Meacham, Supt. (March 8, 1871), report for February.
18. Stern, *The Klamath Tribe*, 116.
19. Long, *Religious Freedom and Indian Rights*, 24.
20. Ibid.
21. Garrett Epps, *To an Unknown God: Religious Freedom at Trial* (New York: St. Martin's Press, 2001), 15.
22. Long, *Religious Freedom and Indian Rights*, 24.

23. Ibid., 25.
24. Epps, *To an Unknown God,* 15.
25. Ibid.
26. Long, *Religious Freedom and Indian Rights,* 23.
27. Ibid.
28. Farrell, discussion with author.
29. Epps, *To an Unknown God,* 16.
30. Long, *Religious Freedom and Indian Rights,* 26.
31. Ibid.
32. Ibid.
33. Ibid., 28.
34. Ibid.
35. Ibid.
36. Epps, *To an Unknown God,* 16.
37. Long, *Religious Freedom and Indian Rights,* 28.
38. Ibid.
39. Farrell, discussion with author.
40. Stern, *The Klamath Tribe,* 185.
41. Ibid., 252.
42. Farrell, discussion with author.
43. Long, *Religious Freedom and Indian Rights,* 30.
44. Ibid.
45. Epps, *To an Unknown God,* 18.
46. Ibid., 19.
47. Ibid.

Chapter 24

UNRELENTING ENEMIES

G iven his sad experiences, Al should have known the government wouldn't leave him alone forever. Yet, for a time, he felt
unfettered, able to follow his own spiritual path unmolested
by the state. He knew freedom. He used it to fill the hole in his life,
shovel by shovel. It wasn't easy. He had to learn to live all over again
without relying on alcohol, but he slowly succeeded.[1]

He found odd jobs. Now sober, he kept them long enough to advance. As the years progressed, he drew on his newfound strength to
help others. It started simply. While he was working in a furniture re-
finishing business in Los Angeles, his reputation grew in AA circles. He
spoke frequently on the AA circuit. Eventually, a group with federal
financing hired him to help people with addictions. Tired of speaking, Al accepted and returned to the Portland area. With a team of a
dozen recovering alcoholics, he scoured the Portland streets looking
for people wanting to escape the grip of addiction. They called themselves the Dirty Dozen.[2] They established shelters and reached out to
people of all races on skid row, offering food, housing, and a chance at
recovery. His work was successful enough that he landed a job with the
Bureau of Indian Affairs as part of its American Indian Commission on
Drug and Alcohol Abuse. This led to him traveling around the country,
assisting many tribes in establishing drug-and-alcohol-abuse treatment
programs. It also sparked a love of his Native American religion.

One week, on assignment in Wyoming, Al attended meetings that would alter his life forever. He couldn't have known it then, but his visit would also transform religious liberty law in the United States. It put him on a path to once again confront the government and its attempts to suppress his religious practices.

His boss had sent him to learn of various Native practices from a medicine man. At the time, it had become clear to professionals in the addiction-recovery field that many Native people were more likely to succeed if their spirituality found root in Native traditions. Al was tasked with better understanding those traditions.

In Wyoming, he participated in a sweat-lodge ceremony for the first time. He knew of the ceremonies, of course. They were even part of the Klamath tradition. But he had never taken part. Inside the lodge, as water hit heated stones and instantly burst into steam amidst intense prayer, something touched Al's spirit. He didn't understand the words or the deeper meanings of the prayers, but an immense feeling of gratitude washed over him. It was as if his spirit, or perhaps that little boy from so long ago, was reaching across time and space to thank him for what he was doing. Al learned from the medicine man most of the week, soaking in as much as possible.[3] In many respects, he had found a new spiritual awakening.

At the end of the meetings, Al climbed into his car and began the long drive back home, which was then in the Denver metro area. There was very little to see between Wyoming and Denver other than rolling brown prairies and farmers' fields. In the distance, the front range of the Rocky Mountains provided a stunning blue backdrop. Power lines paralleled the interstate. As Al sped along, he spied an eagle overlooking the road from a telephone pole. He eased to a stop to take in the scene. As it always does on that stretch of empty land, a breeze likely rustled the prairie grass and washed over Al. He stared at the eagle. It was almost like a spiritual visitor, there to tell him he was on the right path. To casual passersby, it would have been nothing more than a pretty bird perched on a pole. To Al, it was a vision, a confirmation: he was on the right path back to who he had always been. The high he experienced in that moment was as great as anything drugs or alcohol had ever given him. He plunged back into his work with renewed vitality.

As Al forged a new spiritual trail, elsewhere the country was roiling. The 1960s were a time of cultural upheaval on many levels, not the least of which was the use of psychedelic drugs. This led to the criminalization of a number of hallucinogens. In 1970, a federal law determined that certain drugs should be labeled as illegal "Schedule I" drugs because of their "high potential for abuse." This law included peyote on a long list with drugs such as heroin, cocaine, LSD, and marijuana. There was only one problem—peyote is nothing like those other substances.

It is a small, round cactus that looks almost like flattened balls of dough clumped together. Native to northern Mexico and parts of Texas, it hugs the ground of the Chihuahuan desert as inconspicuously as the dirt itself. The plant contains various alkaloids, and one is known as mescaline, a substance that can cause hallucinations and psychoactive effects that many describe as spiritual, leading to introspection and insights.

Research has shown that for thousands of years, certain Native groups have used peyote for prayer and in seeking spiritual enlightenment in tightly controlled religious ceremonies. Unlike other drugs, peyote is bitter and causes nausea, which means it has never been popular in recreational circles.[4] This makes it dramatically different from recreational drugs. Also unlike those drugs, modern research has confirmed that peyote is not addictive or habit forming, has no toxicity, and shows no harmful side effects.[5] For those who use it in religious ceremonies, small nickel-sized pieces of the cactus, or "buttons," are prepared through steaming or boiling until they are mushy enough to be eaten as the sacrament. Sometimes they are also dried, then ground and mixed with water to create an edible paste.

But from the time foreigners first spied Natives using it, they tried to suppress it. Beginning as early as 1886, federal agents forbade its use. By the time the 1960s rolled around, it was outlawed in almost all fifty states, although some were starting to grant exemptions for Native religious ceremonies. Federal laws listed it as an illegal substance; in practice, however, the regulations exempted religious use. The result was a hodgepodge of laws that made it illegal in those states where Native American groups didn't have enough clout to get a religious exemption and legal in places where they did. In short, there was absolutely no consistency in the law surrounding peyote.

Al, of course, knew none of this. At the time, peyote was as foreign to him as it was to most of white America. Yet his path would cross with it soon enough. If he was the moon, finally settling into a steady orbit around his world, the government's inconsistent regulation of peyote was a comet barreling from the outer reaches of the solar system. A collision was coming. The resulting explosion would change everything.

Al's time with the Bureau of Indian Affairs was coming to an end. He had continued to travel all over the country, both helping various tribes and learning more of Native traditions. But Klamath country now beckoned him—an almost imperceptible whisper calling him home. In the Denver area, he closed the door to his apartment for the last time and drove to a lot, where he traded in his little car for a pickup truck. He then began the trek west.[6]

After spending time near Klamath Falls and learning more Native traditions and how they could help people overcome addictions, Al landed a job at a treatment center near Corvallis known as Sweathouse Lodge. It served only Native clients. Al used Native American spirituality and other methods to help those who wanted it. He quickly gained a reputation for his no-nonsense approach to addiction recovery and his refusal to coddle new arrivals.[7]

One day, while Al was at work, a friend entered the office. His name was Herb Powliss. He was involved in something known as the Native American Church and was a key player in the American Indian Movement, a group formed to resist and protest government oppression of Native peoples.

Herb, a Paiute Indian, invited Al to attend one of the ceremonies of the Native American Church.

Al was curious. He wanted to learn more, but he expressed concerns. He knew peyote was part of the ceremony. Would just being around it risk a relapse? Would taking the peyote sacrament push him back into the darkness he had worked so hard to overcome?

"It's a sacred ceremony," Herb said.

Al had always been told peyote was a drug, like LSD.

"It's not dope," Herb said. "It's a sacred sacrament. Our ancestors were praying with that medicine."[8]

Al decided to consider it. The decision wasn't easy. On the one hand, the more he learned of Native spirituality, the more he kept the darkness at bay for himself and others. On the other hand, he held his sobriety sacred. He didn't want to take even a minor risk of losing it. The peyote ceremony could potentially invite that loss.

Al finally decided to attend. For a time, he merely watched the rituals without taking any of the sacrament. Finally, he decided it was time to partake.

When he reached the ceremony, he approached the roadman, who was Herb's son and who would lead the ceremony. "I'm a recovering alcoholic," Al said. "I don't want to be in relapse."

"You don't understand," the roadman said. "This is not a drug. This is a sacred medicine used for centuries by native people to come in communication with the Creator in their prayers. It's for healing; it's for doctoring; it's a sacred medicine."

Al felt an inexplicable wave of relief wash over him. He attended the ceremony. Through it all, in the back of his mind, the fear of where this decision might lead must have nagged at him. He had been sober for years at this point. Was it possible he could lose everything he had gained? Still, the lure of the potential spiritual benefits beckoned.

Inside a tepee, as the ceremony progressed, the roadman took the peyote buttons and passed them to everyone participating. Al opened his mouth and let the sacrament rest on his tongue. The taste was bitter.

He choked it down.

The group sang and prayed. Al didn't understand the songs. He didn't know the prayers. They were in a language foreign to him.

A wave of nausea passed over him. The experience was challenging. The queasiness grew worse, the night stretched on and on, and Al struggled to follow along. He eventually vomited. It was hardly a spiritual moment. But through the sickness and confusion, and the fatigue of the long ceremony, Al felt something familiar. It was not the return of the cravings for alcohol or the need for a high. This experience wasn't the trip that came from intoxication. That remained at bay. It was the same spiritual uplift he had felt that day on the highway, when he saw the eagle. It was the same gratitude. He felt again as though his spirit were thanking him, reaching through the eternities to express gratitude for Al acknowledging the ways of his ancestors. He felt that what he had done was right.

And he didn't relapse. Instead, he sensed that he had been led to a better place, where he could become a better man.[9] In the coming years, he never fully committed to the Native American Church as a member. Instead, it became a part of his broader efforts to connect with his ancestry and tradition and to heal the wounds that had crippled him for so long.

Even then, the government was coming. It was a distant threat at the time, so far away Al couldn't have possibly detected it, but it was coming.

———

The spring of 1982 yielded to summer. After years of experience and successful counseling of others, Al eyed a new position. He had enjoyed tremendous success at Sweathouse Lodge, where he had used Native spirituality and tradition, including peyotism, to help support scores of patients. He had eventually left, remarried, traveled with his wife, and welcomed a daughter into the world. With his new family obligations, he needed work. He interviewed at an agency called the Douglas County Council on Alcohol and Drug Abuse Prevention and Treatment, known by its acronym, ADAPT.

ADAPT was not Sweathouse Lodge. Its director, a thirty-two-year-old man named John Gardin, along with the rest of the organization, subscribed to the notion that absolutely any use of a mind-altering substance, including peyote, would risk sending the user into the uncontrollable spiral of relapse. They considered any use, for any reason, misuse. Although unwritten, their policy was to terminate anyone for misuse of such substances. When Gardin interviewed Al, the topic didn't come up. Gardin was impressed with Al's experience, his years of successful sobriety, his reputation in the field, and his ability to connect with ADAPT's Native American patients.

Al knew, deep down, that Gardin and the rest of the counselors at ADAPT would consider peyote a drug, but he agreed to work there anyway, suspecting that it likely wouldn't become an issue. While he found tremendous strength in Native traditions, he didn't need to use peyote to find his spiritual moorings. He was immediately well regarded. He offered insights that not only were helpful to clients but that also inspired his fellow employees. His perspective as a Klamath man and his comments stemming from his Native faith and spirituality were also unique and astute, offering a different perspective from what others brought to the table.

One counselor was especially drawn to Al. His name was Galen Black, and he was about to thrust Al into a fight the Klamath man never wanted. Black was a recovering alcoholic, white, just two years sober, but something about Native traditions intrigued him. Al didn't know him well. For one thing, they didn't work in the same area of

ADAPT, so they rarely crossed paths. For another, Black was significantly younger than Al, by almost thirty years.

But he had seen him around. One day, Black approached Al at ADAPT. Through giant eyeglasses and with a serious, eager expression, he asked Al about peyotism and whether he should try it, both as part of his own sobriety and as part of his helping others.

Al was honest. He encouraged Black to talk with people who had a more in-depth knowledge of peyotism. It wasn't a decision Al could make for him. Black would need to make a personal choice.

In the fall of 1983, he did, eventually choosing to participate in the ceremony and partake of peyote. He felt it was a spiritual awakening. Like Al, he didn't find himself stumbling into relapse; instead, he experienced a renewed transcendent strength. He didn't hesitate to tell people what he had done.

The fallout at ADAPT was immediate.

———

September 19, 1983, was a fair day in Roseburg, Oregon, with temperatures in the low sixties. At ADAPT, Director John Gardin was boiling. He called Al into his office. In his joyful moments, Gardin had a smile that would put people at ease. It was nowhere to be seen.

Al entered the office, unsure why he'd been summoned. He sat across from Gardin. The contrasts between the two men couldn't have been more glaring. Gardin was three decades younger, a white man with a master's degree in psychology on his way to a PhD. His hair was short and clean-cut—in many respects, he looked like the typical middle-class man who ran marathons to challenge himself since life hadn't done it enough on its own. He was the product one might expect of a culture not oppressed by powerful government agents. Al was in his early sixties. He looked like the quintessential Native American man, with dark skin and long black hair flowing over his shoulders. His education had grown from the school of hard knocks.

Gardin immediately confronted Al about using peyote, accusing him of taking it alongside Black. The younger man's tone was aggressive, his mannerisms tense.

Al tried to keep his composure. He explained that he hadn't attended the meeting. He would go if invited, but he hadn't been there. Despite the outward calm, a fire ignited inside him. Gardin may have been the director, but he was practically a child in Al's view. He stunk of the very culture that had stripped Al of everything he held dear in his youth. And he had no place accusing Al of anything.

You are not to use peyote at any time, Gardin told Al. It was forbidden by ADAPT's policy. Gardin's message was clear: if Al used peyote, he would be fired immediately. It was apparent that Galin Black was already charging forward to that result with the ferocity of a runaway train. In Gardin's view, he was merely trying to protect the integrity of ADAPT's treatment program.

Al heard only one message. It was that he couldn't go to church. He was shocked. This white man of the dominant society was telling Al he couldn't go to church. The same little boy who lied to nuns and hitchhiked on darkened highways to get home was still there, as fiery as ever. He wouldn't take this.

Gardin and Al would later remember what happened next somewhat differently. Gardin recalled that Al leaped to his feet and marched to the door in a fit of fury. Al remembered leaving, of course, but not in anger. He recalls his shock and amazement that his employer would try to control when and where he could go to church and how he could worship. Unwittingly, Gardin had tried to contain a tornado. But by 1983, after more than sixty years, Al was no longer in the business of being caged.

That night, Al and his wife, Jane, were at their home in Roseburg. A small green house with no yard and a gravel driveway, it wasn't much to look at, but it was theirs. They were happy. Furnishings were sparse, just whatever they could afford at local thrift shops.[10] Al would fix them up and stain them on the front porch. Their daughter, who wasn't yet two-years-old, could play with other neighborhood children.

Jane had decorated an old, doorless refrigerator box with crayons, and the kids would play in it for hours. As the autumn air cooled, Al and Jane faced a decision point.[11]

On the outside, the two of them were as contrasting as Al and Gardin. Jane was of French and Irish descent; Al, of course, was Klamath. Al was in his sixties. She was not yet thirty. But their connection was unmistakable. She was Pennsylvania born and bred and college-educated, but she seemed to have the restlessness of someone who had grown up surrounded by open land. She had trekked west after college, teaching in several inner cities, trying to satiate her wanderlust. When mutual friends first introduced her to Al, she didn't give it much thought. Then, roughly a year later, she attended a meeting with him on the Oregon Coast, where he spoke to an AA group. She heard his story about all he had overcome. It stirred something within her. They connected. They fell in love. It was inexplicable to outsiders, but like so many who become smitten, Jane and Al just let them look on in bewilderment. They didn't care. It worked for them.

By the time of that evening in September, they had known each other only four years and had been married even fewer. They faced an impossible choice. Al's paychecks were all that kept them in their home. They needed them not just for themselves but to provide for their daughter as well. If Al challenged Gardin and chose to follow his religious convictions, he would lose their sole source of income. If he bowed before Gardin's attempt to suppress him, he would abandon everything he had fought to restore. It would be, in many respects, the ultimate disloyalty, both to himself and to the heritage he was struggling to restore. The night waned on. The darkness deepened. Like Roy, Kohlmann, and countless others before them, Al and Jane stood before a fog, forced to decide whether they would leap into it.

NOTES

1. Garrett Epps, *To an Unknown God: Religious Freedom on Trial* (New York: St. Martin's Press, 2001), 18.
2. Jane Ferrell, in discussion with author, January 9, 2018.
3. Carolyn N. Long, *Religious Freedom and Indian Rights: The Case of Oregon v. Smith* (Lawrence: University Press of Kansas, 2000), 32; Epps, *To an Unknown God*, 46.
4. HR El-Seedi, PA De Smet, O Beck, G Possnert, and JG Bruhn, "Prehistoric Peyote Use: Alkaloid Analysis and Radiocarbon Dating of Archaeological Specimens of Lophophora from Texas," *Journal of Ethnopharmacology* 101, nos. 1–3 (October 2005): 238–42.
5. Thomas C. Maroukis, *The Peyote Road: Religious Freedom and the Native American Church* (Norman: University of Oklahoma Press, 2010), 111.
6. Epps, *To an Unknown God*, 49; Long, *Religious Freedom and Indian Rights*, 32.
7. Epps, *To an Unknown God*, 53.
8. Long, *Religious Freedom and Indian Rights*, 34.
9. Epps, *To an Unknown God*, 64–65.
10. Farrell, discussion with author.
11. Epps, *To an Unknown God*, 107.

Chapter 25

SCARE QUOTES
AND EAGLE FEATHERS

On October 3, 1983, Galin Black was fired. Gardin had demanded Black receive an evaluation from a counselor at the nearby Veterans Administration hospital to determine if he had relapsed. When the report returned, it didn't definitively reach that conclusion, but it did indicate he had demonstrated lack of judgment and that his thinking was skewed—the kind of thought processes that led to continued addictive behavior. Based on the report, Gardin gave Black several choices: he could seek treatment, resign, or face termination. Black threatened to sue, arguing the entire situation was nothing more than discrimination. Gardin fired him on the spot.

The report contained something else as well. A warning. Rumors of the events at ADAPT were swirling in the community. In his written assessment of Black, the counselor noted,

> I feel this is going to be a "political" issue in the local community and controversy may eventually be involved. There are those individuals who are going to support Mr. Black's decision to use peyote in the way he did and these include some recovering individuals. I have heard an argument about "freedom of religion."[1]

His use of scare quotes around the term *freedom of religion* is telling. It was then—and remains today—a common practice. Reporters, commentators, and even lay people use them whenever they don't value the religious beliefs of the people to whom they're referring. Extremists on both the right and the left tend to denigrate any religious beliefs with which they don't agree. The use of scare quotes is a clear indicator of that thought process. It's a subtle argument that the beliefs at issue aren't truly based in religion—or at least, in the writer's mind, a religion worth respecting.

It's also not surprising the counselor invoked them. Every religious tradition outside one's own sounds ridiculous and even potentially offensive. To devout believers in God who have experienced the presence of the divine in their lives, the notion that humans are nothing more than pointless organisms floating on a big blue marble that just accidently ended up in the perfect position in the cosmos to support them is just silly and almost comically depressing. But to atheists, to believe in an all-powerful God of the universe when humanity has, for most of its existence, clearly manufactured divine beings out of nothing is tantamount to sticking your head in the sand. Every religious belief—including atheism and agnosticism—sounds absurd when characterized to highlight its absurdity. Debates over religion often devolve into nothing more than sarcastically mischaracterizing others' religious beliefs to make them sound nonsensical. While that may be an accepted tactic between people of different beliefs trying to battle each other, when it comes to legal protections for religious liberty, it can have disastrous consequences. History has shown that few people have the self-confidence and ability to ensure the law respects the religious traditions of others, especially when those traditions conflict with something they value more.

Al was not dealing with those special few.

Black's termination raised the stakes. In the weeks and months that followed, it became clear that Black had no intention of going quietly into the night. Stories abounded that he was preparing some sort of legal action against ADAPT. He had already sought—and been denied—unemployment compensation from the state and was navigating Oregon's labyrinthine unemployment-compensation appeals process.

At ADAPT, Gardin was worried. His relationship with Al soured. In the office, they maneuvered around each other as if on eggshells. ADAPT also adopted a new policy to put into effect what Gardin had always believed was the rule but had never explicitly stated. It read,

> Use of an illegal drug or use of prescription drugs in a non-prescribed manner is grounds for immediate termination from employment.

This clearly targeted peyote. And, Al would later feel, it clearly targeted him. It was designed to box him in and set him up in case he ever decided to go to church.[2] Despite the positive effects peyotism had provided to Al and other Native Americans, it was still considered an illegal drug under state law. Al felt as if Gardin was setting him up for termination.

Outside the office, people in the Native community had their own concerns. If Black pursued his case on his own, it could be very damaging to Native American religion. Black was not, after all, a Native. In truth, he knew almost nothing about the Native American Church or peyotism. If he brought a lawsuit by himself, he would likely lose. Someone needed to join him, a true Native. Despite his concerns about providing for his family, Al felt the pressure mounting. The water around him was heating up, headed to a boil.

Jane advised him to follow his heart. She understood the gravity of his moral dilemma, and she would support whatever decision he made.

One morning at the beginning of March, while Black was still pursuing legal options, Al walked into the ADAPT offices. In the bank of interoffice mail slots, he found a wide manila envelope. Only his name was etched on the front. There were no other writings, not even a return address. Al looked at the envelope curiously. He finally opened it.

Inside, someone had inserted eagle feathers—a sacred symbol. There were twelve, each pristine; nothing else.

For Al, the eagle was sacred, a messenger between him and the Creator. Al had been invited to attend a peyotism ceremony that would be held at Coos Bay that coming weekend. He interpreted the feathers as not just an invitation, but a sign that he should attend. The decision he'd been agonizing over for months was now front and center. Al felt a new certainty that could come only from acting on faith and receiving spiritual approval. This was his faith. It had helped him stay sober. It had given him spiritual guidance toward a path of becoming a better man. It had given him a new lease on life and made him a better father and husband. The fear of losing his job still hovered like a menacing cloaked figure, but it was time to turn and face it.

He stepped into Gardin's office and told him he planned to go to the meeting.

Gardin, his face serious, didn't object to attendance, but he warned Al that if he ingested peyote, he would lose his job.

Al understood.

Gardin also tried to convince Al peyote was a harmful drug. It would put his sobriety at risk.

"I'll see you when I get back," Al said.

On Saturday, Al drove with Jane to the coastal mountain range east of Coos Bay. The weather was pleasant. A mild breeze blew from the north. He and Jane found themselves on a beautiful parcel of land surrounded by cedar, fir, and mountain meadows. Those who helped prepare for the ceremony had already gotten everything ready. A large tepee was set up in the center of a grassy field, firewood stacked beside it. Many people had come for this particular ceremony. They seemed to know the significance of what Al was doing.[3]

As the sun dipped below the skyline and twilight descended, Stanley Smart, the roadman who would lead the ceremony, guided all those who would participate in the ceremony along a clockwise path outside the tepee. He then ushered them in.

Al and Jane stepped inside. The entrance faced east. The ritual fire was already burning in the center of the space, the wood carefully formulated into an arrow pointing west. Smart had already prepared everything. A crescent-moon mound, symbolic of one's mortal life, had been meticulously formed near the fire. Beyond it, the drum, staff, gourd, sage, altar cloth, cedar bags, and peyote rested in their precise locations. Al and Jane took their seats in a circle along the outer edge of the tepee.

As leaps of faith go, Al hadn't completely reached the point of no return. He could still sit there all night but choose not to partake of the peyote.

The ceremony began. Smart, positioned opposite the entrance, led the group in prayers. He offered some initial instructions. Everyone prayed while holding tobacco wrapped in corn husks, watching as the smoke from the fire lifted their prayers to the Creator.

Eventually, the time came. Stanley Smart prepared the peyote buttons. Another man, known as the cedarman, sprinkled cedar on the fire in a symbolic form of purification.

Smart passed the peyote through the cedar smoke four times.

While he did so, helpers maneuvered among the participants, smudging each of them with burning sage and cedar as an act of symbolic cleansing.

Everyone knew what Al was there to do. He still had the option of saying no, of protecting the money and certainty of a steady job. But when Smart maneuvered around the circle, again moving clockwise, Al steeled himself. For six and a half decades, strangers, colonists, had been trying to tell him what religion he needed to follow. Al was no longer a seven-year-old boy. He would follow his own spiritual path.

When the moment came, with all eyes on him, he partook.

As night fully engulfed them, the temperature outside dropped. It was a damp cold. All around the area, the breeze turned into a strong wind, but the tepee was nicely tucked away from it. The roadman and the chief drummer would lead the group in songs and prayers. As the night progressed, the fireman would regularly tend to the ashes and coals forming in the fire. He would return again and again, adjusting the ashes and manipulating them into sacred symbols: an eagle, a water bird, a star, and eagle feathers.

Throughout the night, the group prayed. Some prayed for Al. Some likely prayed for those among them or their families who were sick or struggling. Al prayed for the resilience and courage he would need for what was coming. He prayed for others as well. Jane sat by his side. Their toddler slept peacefully behind them. There was no going back, and he had no intention of hiding from his choice.

Near the end of the ceremony, as morning approached, there was a sense that something would come from this, that it had set certain events in motion.

One thing was clear. When he emerged from the ceremony, Al and everyone around him knew he would lose his job.

The following Monday, Gardin summoned Al to his office.

Did you go to the meeting? Gardin asked.

"Yes," Al said.

Gardin asked if he took peyote.

"Well," Al said. "I took the sacred sacrament and prayed for you."

Do you want to resign? Gardin asked.

Smith said no. He hadn't done anything wrong by simply attending his church.

Gardin offered Al an opportunity to participate in an employee assistance program to help him with what Gardin deemed as substance abuse.

"I don't need rehabilitation for going to church," Al said.

Gardin didn't hesitate. "Have your desk cleaned out and let your clients know you'll be leaving at the end of the day."[4]

At nearly sixty-five, with a family to support, Al was out of a job.

Notes

1. Garrett Epps, *To an Unknown God: Religious Freedom on Trial* (New York: St. Martin's Press, 2001), 108.

2. Jane Farrell, in discussion with author, January 9, 2018.
3. For the details of Al's ceremony and ingestion of peyote, see Epps, *To an Unknown God,* 108.
4. The details of Al's conversation with Gardin and Al's firing can be found in Epps, *To an Unknown God,* 110; Long, 73; and interview with Jane Farrell.

Chapter 26

NEW ENEMIES

A l was largely willing to move on with his life. He had made his stand. He hadn't sacrificed his faith or principles for money. He would collect his unemployment benefits until he could find a new job, and he would always be able to look his children in the eyes knowing his integrity was intact. He marched to the county building. There, it took only a few minutes to fill out the form.

Eighteen days later, on March 22, 1984, Al received a letter. It was from the Employment Division, Department of Human Resources of Oregon. The letter indicated that ADAPT had opposed Al's request for benefits because Al had committed a "willful violation of the standards of behavior that an employer has the right to expect of an employee." It is not necessarily unusual for employers to oppose unemployment benefits for former employees, but it is also not always worth the fight. The only cost to an employer if a former employee receives benefits is a slight increase in their insurance premium, so many employers just decide it isn't worth investing the time to oppose. Not ADAPT. Under the Oregon statutes at the time, Al was entitled to receive unemployment benefits from the state unless he had "been discharged for misconduct connected with work,"[1] which was defined as an "act that amounts to a willful disregard of an employer's interest, or recurring negligence which demonstrates wrongful intent."[2] Given ADAPT's arguments, the Employment Division denied Al's request for benefits. He and Jane were left with nothing.[3]

This was a war cry. If ADAPT wanted to fight him, Al would fight. In his mind, he had done nothing but go to church. For that, he had lost his job. And now ADAPT had made the state his enemy as well. They were siding with his former employer, putting the state's official stamp of approval on what ADAPT had done. Al wouldn't stand for it. The only problem was that he had no idea where to start. All he knew was that months earlier, Galen Black had fought the same battle, had tried to navigate the same bureaucracy, and had lost miserably.

For Al, these days were demoralizing. His attempts to find a lawyer were as exhausting as swimming against the current of the Williamson River. He knew he needed one. He had absolutely no idea how to appeal the Employment Division's decision or even what his rights were. He felt like a child standing before an unchartered wilderness with no guide and no map. He sought help from the national Native American Rights Fund, but they wouldn't support him because, they said, they got involved only with tribes or cases of "national significance," a position that would later be so filled with irony it's almost laughable.[4] Traditional lawyers saw no money in it if they took it on contingency. Al couldn't pay anyone.

Eventually, he discovered Legal Aid Services of Oregon. At their office in Roseburg, he met a young attorney named David Morrison. Legal-aid attorneys offer free legal services to indigent clients, but they can take on only a fraction of the cases that present themselves. Morrison had entered law with the hope of creating social change. He wasn't seeking money, prestige, or power. He wanted to help people. And he did. He took on unethical landlords, used-car dealers, debt collectors, and more—all on behalf of people who had nowhere else to turn. By the time Al walked into his office, Morrison was coming into his own as an attorney, and he had developed a sense for which cases he should take: those where one side of the conflict was simply being unreasonable.[5] He also knew the facts of Smith's case. Indeed, after Galen Black had lost, Morrison had started helping him as well, so he was well versed in both ADAPT and the broader situation.

The difference was that, before seeking Morrison's help, Black had tried to navigate much of the process on his own and hadn't presented a fleshed-out religious-freedom argument in his appeal. He also wasn't nearly as well versed as Al in defending the Native American Church or peyotism. Al, Morrison thought, stood a much better chance of success.

Morrison likely explained the process to Al: once the Employment Division denied someone benefits, the next step was to appeal to an independent referee. After that, either the employee or the employer could appeal to the Employment Appeals Board. From there, if either side was unhappy and wanted to keep the fight going, they could appeal to the Oregon Court of Appeals. The first step for Al and Morrison was to build their case for the independent referee. They set to work.

———————

ADAPT was not going to back down. And it wasn't because of the money. The cost in lawyers and time alone would have outstripped the savings in unemployment insurance premiums. But for everyone involved, the case had become much more than a simple dispute over unemployment benefits. To Al, this was about outsiders once again trying to suppress Native American religion. To ADAPT, this was a simple case of employees ignoring an important policy and deliberately disregarding key principles of sobriety and addiction treatment, threatening the very principles on which the agency operated. Money was one thing; no one was willing to sacrifice principle.

For two and a half months, Morrison and Al prepared for battle. They amassed affidavits from experts in peyotism and from church leaders who could testify to Al's sincere involvement. Preeminent scholars signed affidavits on Al's behalf, testifying of the value peyotism had brought to countless recovering addicts. Al's own affidavit bore witness to his personal spiritual growth. Experts in the treatment of alcoholism provided lengthy statements that the use of peyote as part of the Native American Church didn't result in addiction; it actually achieved the opposite, and denying its use as part of religious ceremonies could even risk harming sobriety.

At the same time, Gardin and ADAPT were preparing their own case. Their arguments were straightforward. The center followed a strict abstinence philosophy, staff members had a duty to adhere to the center's teaching to be a role model to clients, and Al had violated that even after it was clearly communicated to him in writing. Indeed, Gardin would argue, he had explicitly warned Al that he would face termination if he ingested peyote. Al had no excuse. Under Oregon law, he had been properly discharged for misconduct.

The affidavits and policy positions were important, but it was the legal arguments that were potentially Al's most vital weapon. Morrison would have burrowed into them—and been pleased with what he found. In the cases, like Roy Torcaso's, from the early 1960s, one thing would have stood out to Morrison. Roy was not alone. Around the same time, the Supreme Court was finally lifting religious liberty to the pedestal the Founders had given it in the Constitution. The justices labeled it a preferred freedom, alongside racial equality and speech. In a series of decisions starting in 1963, the court established the legal principle that, under the Free Exercise Clause, if government burdened someone's exercise of religion, it needed to pass the most stringent of tests. That is to say, whenever government burdened someone's religious exercise, whether it intended to or not, it would need to prove two things: (1) that it had a compelling interest it was trying to meet, and (2) that it had chosen the least-intrusive means available for achieving it. If it could not pass that test, then the citizen whose religion was burdened would have to receive a religious exemption to the law or regulation.

This didn't mean religion would win every case. If someone's religious belief required them to sacrifice small children once a year, the government would have a compelling interest in stopping that, as long as it chose the least-intrusive method of meeting that interest—for example, government could probably stop child sacrifice by bombing the town where the religious group operated, but a simple arrest would do the trick. It couldn't use a hatchet when a scalpel would do. The test allowed government to perform its essential functions without allowing each religious person to simply become "a law unto himself."[6] Still, the "compelling interest test" meant those seeking religious exemptions to laws would likely receive them in most circumstances.

Al was bringing his case to the courts at the high-water point for religious liberty in the United States. Gone were the days of dragging citizens through the streets because of their religion. Many of the cases involving The Church of Jesus Christ of Latter-day Saints that had gutted religious freedom protections were almost certainly considered bad law. For more than two and a half decades, it had become the well-established law of the land that religious exercise deserved protection in all but the most compelling cases. And it had worked, providing exemptions where necessary but always allowing the government to prove why, in certain situations, religious freedom needed to yield to a greater concern, such as military requirements or the safe operation of prisons. It ensured government had little influence over religious practice, which was good for both government and religion. The powerful hand of the state couldn't be used to discourage certain religions, and religions saw no reason to try to unduly influence government.

The compelling interest test clearly gave Al an advantage. What would have excited Morrison even more was the fact that two of the cases establishing the compelling interest test involved people who had been denied unemployment benefits because they had been following their religious beliefs. The first involved a Seventh-Day Adventist whose employer had fired her because she couldn't work on a Saturday, her Sabbath. The state denied her unemployment benefits, arguing that she didn't have a good reason for not working on a weekend. The Supreme Court reversed. It held that the denial of unemployment benefits placed a burden on her religious exercise and that the state didn't have a compelling interest to justify it.[7] The second case ruled that a Jehovah's Witness was still entitled to unemployment benefits even though his religious beliefs prevented him from doing his job once his employer shifted all of its operations into making military weapons; he couldn't, according to his beliefs, help produce arms of war.[8]

Given the state of the law, Al had every reason to believe he would win.

———

On June 6, 1984, Al and Morrison arrived at the Employment Department on Pine Street in Roseburg. It was a triangular building with a glass entrance bookended on either side by stonework. An unusual chill lingered in the still air. The sky was clear.

A staffer ushered them to a closet-like, dusty room near the back of the building. Gardin showed up as well. Everyone was civil, but Morrison felt the tension heating the room like a boiler.

Eventually, an elderly lawyer named Robert Gruber entered. He was the special referee, a full-time officer with the state whose job was to hear appeals from the decisions of state agencies. He had a scholarly way of carrying himself and a pensive look that made people who met him feel as if he would give them a fair shake.[9]

The arguments went as expected, but emotions ran high. Gruber listened thoughtfully and asked questions when appropriate. The time came for the religious-freedom arguments. Morrison provided the legal background, but Al did much of the talking. In that tiny room, which felt more like a cupboard than a hearing space, he defended his religion, his beliefs, and how it had all helped him progress spiritually without him ever relapsing into drug or alcohol use. His Native religion had turned him from a man lying drunk in an alley to a responsible father and husband who was now helping others escape their own demons.

As he listened to Al talk, Morrison felt moved in a way he never had before. Fiscally, for both the state and ADAPT, there was little at stake. For Al, the case was the culmination of everything his people had been fighting since the first European colonizers stepped foot in Klamath territory more than a century before. Morrison knew he had taken the right case.[10] Whether Robert Gruber felt the same way remained to be seen.

Morrison was on edge. Although he felt confident about Al's case, he knew the referee or, later, the Employment Appeals Board, could still rule against them, just as it had ruled against Galen Black. He advised Al to talk with the federal Equal Employment Opportunity Commission (EEOC) to see if he had a valid religious-discrimination case against ADAPT. Al agreed to. In his mind, there was no question ADAPT had fired him for exercising his religion.

Later that month, he met with attorneys in the EEOC's Seattle office, where he explained his view of what had happened. Title VII of the Civil Rights Act of 1964 charged the EEOC with investigating complaints of discrimination in employment[11] and ensuring that employers comply with the law. Not surprisingly, it receives far more complaints than it can handle. With most, after a brief investigation, it declines to pursue any action itself but instead allows individual plaintiffs to sue on their own. In the most persuasive cases, however, the EEOC will agree to take them on and bring all of its resources to bear—a terrifying prospect for even the largest and most powerful corporations.

The EEOC's lawyers believed Al. After a thorough investigation, on July 18, 1984, they charged ADAPT with discrimination. They also issued a letter setting forth why they believed the agency had discriminated based on religion. The letter demanded that ADAPT and Al meet and try to reach a settlement through the EEOC's reconciliation process. The news would have been crushing to ADAPT. Reconciliation is the first formal step of an EEOC charge. The government uses it to force deep concessions from employers, such as admitting wrongdoing and giving backpay to people like Al. If the employers don't capitulate, what follows is nothing but expensive pain for the company in the form of litigating against a well-financed federal agency. At the time, the EEOC's pressure on ADAPT seemed like a tremendous victory for Al and for religious freedom. He would have been thrilled.

Only later would scholars look back and realize the EEOC's involvement may have been what ignited Al's obscure unemployment-benefits dispute into an explosion that would forever change religious liberty law in the United States.

At roughly the same time the EEOC issued its letter to ADAPT, the independent referee from the Employment Division issued his own missive.

Al won.

Robert Gruber determined that the unemployment statutes normally would disqualify Al from receiving benefits because he had clearly violated his employer's policies. But he also determined that the First Amendment's right to free exercise trumped the unemployment statutes. He applied the compelling interest test. The state's interest in those statutes for not paying individuals who had engaged in misconduct was to protect against "the undue depletion of the unemployment insurance fund."[12] That interest, Gruber determined, was not compelling enough to justify burdening someone's religious exercise. With that letter and the EEOC's enforcement efforts, Al was cruising to a total victory.

There was just one problem: the EEOC itself. Under normal circumstances, Gruber's decision would have been the end of the process. Employers almost never appeal past the referee stage. It just isn't worth the expense. It should have been a day of celebration for Al and an opportunity to move on with his life and provide for his family, but the party lasted only about twenty-four hours. ADAPT faced the concern that if they didn't appeal the referee's decision, it would look as if they were conceding wrongdoing and the EEOC would use that admission to bludgeon them. They felt they had no choice but to challenge Gruber's decision. The very next day, they filed an appeal with the Employment Appeals Board.

Al was dragged into yet another phase of his nightmare.

A month later, in August of 1984, a pall hung over the Smith home. The appeals board was taking its time. Morrison wasn't convinced the board would take the religious freedom arguments seriously. Al and Jane were barely able to make ends meet. They survived mostly on whatever substitute-teaching gigs Jane could get while Al tried to find other work.[13] The EEOC reconciliation process grinded on but was no closer to being resolved. Al needed to feed his toddler daughter. There had to have been moments where he wondered if standing for his religious convictions was worth it.

When the appeals board finally issued its decision, it made the cloud even darker. As it had with Galen Black, it ruled against Al. Two members of the three-officer panel concluded that Al's use of peyote was illegal. It didn't matter that he used it for religious purposes. Al's "ingestion of peyote was . . . contrary to the employer's legitimate interest and reasonable rules and disqualifies the claimant from benefits."[14] It disregarded the precedent from the Supreme Court regarding the compelling interest test. It dismissed any argument that peyote was not a recreational drug. It ignored the evidence that for Native American patients, peyotism actually helped with addiction recovery. In short, the panel dismissed everything Al stood for with the nonchalance of someone simply waving a hand.

As he had decades earlier, every time he stepped onto a new highway to find his way home, Al took the defeat as a challenge. He authorized Morrison to appeal the decision to the Oregon Court of Appeals.

This was a turning point in the case. His enemy was no longer just ADAPT. Once a party appeals an unemployment decision to the Oregon courts, the caption on the case changes. It ceased being merely *Smith v. ADAPT* and was officially transformed into *Smith v. Employment Division, Department of Human Resources, and ADAPT*. In other words, Al was now taking on the state. He was challenging not just ADAPT's take on the situation but the Employment Division's position as well.

When someone sues a state agency, the general practice is for the attorney general's office to get involved. They would represent the Employment Division. They would use their nearly unlimited resources to defend the appeals board's decision. Until that point, in the unemployment dispute, at least, Morrison and Al had been fighting against an opponent about as threatening as they were. The state had merely been the judge. But the Oregon attorney general's office entering the fray had the tide-turning effect of bringing a Gatling gun to a spear fight.

NOTES

1. Oregon Revised Statute 657.176.
2. Oregon Administrative Rule (OAR) 471-30-038(3) (1987).
3. Garrett Epps, *To an Unknown God: Religious Freedom on Trial* (New York: St. Martin's Press, 2001), 110–11.
4. Carolyn N. Long, *Religious Freedom and Indian Rights: The Case of Oregon v. Smith* (Lawrence: University Press of Kansas, 2000), 74.
5. Ibid., 74–75.
6. *Reynolds v. United States*, 98 U.S. 145, 167 (1878).
7. *Sherbert v. Verner*, 374 U.S. 398 (1963).
8. *Thomas v. Review Board*, 450 U.S. 707 (1981).
9. Epps, *To an Unknown God*, 134–35.
10. Long, *Religious Freedom and Indian Rights*, 80.
11. Title VII prohibits discrimination in employment on the basis of race, color, religion, sex, or national origin.
12. *See* Referee Decision, *In re Smith* (July 23, 1984) (No. 84-E-1181) (on file in the Supreme Court Library for the State of Oregon).
13. Jane Farrell, in discussion with author, January 9, 2018.
14. Garrett Epps, *Peyote vs. The State* (Norman, University of Oklahoma Press, 2009), 129.

Chapter 27

UNYIELDING FOES

D ave Frohnmayer was the kind of man whose warm smile, slightly tousled hair, and chubby cheeks masked his underlying intelligence and cunning. In his midforties, he was a politician of extraordinary skill who had risen quickly to the office of attorney general for the state of Oregon. Power players viewed him as the next governor. Some politicos saw even more potential. Perhaps his most remarkable gift was that his warmth wasn't forced. He genuinely cared for people. He seemed to have it all: a loving wife with three children and more coming, degrees from Harvard and Oxford followed by law school at Berkeley, an unlimited future, and a zeal for his work that was contagious.

Sitting in his offices in Salem, Frohnmayer observed from a distance as Al's case progressed through its various stages, including in the Oregon Court of Appeals. He personally touched it only enough to review and sign the briefs his team was filing. It was his belief system rather than his position that drove the case. His office had advised the Employment Appeals Board to rule against Al. His office, with all of its firepower, would challenge Al in the Oregon Court of Appeals. In Frohnmayer's view, the Free Exercise Clause didn't mandate that two men should receive benefits for doing something that was illegal to everyone else, even if they had a religious excuse. More important, he was convinced that nefarious actors were driving Al Smith and Galen Black. In his view, the case had nothing to do with religious freedom.

It had nothing to do with government oppressing Native religions. It was a drug case. And some drug reform group was cattle-prodding it forward as part of a plot to expand exceptions to all of Oregon's drug laws. Frohnmayer couldn't let that stand.

It appears he never took the time to explore the legitimacy or sincerity of Al's beliefs. Or if he did, he didn't care. This is common in religious freedom cases. The people in power pass laws or regulations that burden an obscure religious practice in a way they never anticipated. When the religious-freedom challenge inevitably comes, they don't understand it. Too often they assume it is simply a smokescreen to hide some other reprehensible purpose. Or they fear that allowing the one religious exemption will unleash a parade of horribles upon society. That fear and lack of understanding prevent any meaningful compromise.

For Al, it meant that he would, in time, become the boxer who, every time he knocked down his opponent, looked on in disappointed disbelief as his foe struggled up off the mat for one more beating. Every victory would carry with it the hollow feeling of knowing there were more blows coming. And the state's ability to climb up the ropes seemed endless. It occurred time and time again. When the court of appeals ruled for Al and Black on the religious-freedom argument, the victory was short-lived. Frohnmayer became personally engaged. He drove the case to the Oregon Supreme Court. When the EEOC forced ADAPT to settle with Al and pay him all of his back wages, it gave Al the money he and Jane needed to keep living, but it also removed any financial component from the case. It was now strictly about religious freedom versus state policy, so the state would keep fighting. When the Oregon Supreme Court ruled for Al, the attorney general refused to accept losing. The Oregon Supreme Court had conceded that the state's laws prohibited Al from receiving benefits, but it also determined that previous cases from the United States Supreme Court held that the Free Exercise Clause overruled state laws. Frohnmayer asked the Oregon high court for reconsideration. He would not let the case die.

Al was anxious. He was at home on September 3, 1986. The day had started off warm and only burned hotter from there. He and Jane had moved from Roseburg to a house near Eugene along the Willamette River. Rented from an old German couple,[1] it was a two-story home with a yard that was just a trail away from the water, where they enjoyed their own private beach. A huge cedar adorned the front yard.

The sun was baking everything that day.

Despite all the victories in the various battles, Al still hadn't won the war. Two and half years into his fight, he still hadn't received the declaration he wanted—that his faith deserved as much protection as anyone else's. It was that simple. He believed he was, in his own way, fighting for Klamath survival, taking on the government in a way his ancestors were never able.

While he and Jane and their daughter tinkered about the house, the phone rang. Al maneuvered to it with a spryness that belied his nearly sixty-seven years.[2]

Morrison was on the other line. He informed Al that the chief justice of the Oregon Supreme Court had denied the attorney general's request for reconsideration with a one-sentence order. The court understood Frohnmayer's arguments and rejected them.

Al felt the internal swelling that comes only from vindication. He took a deep breath, and one thought resonated in his mind: *Take that, Attorney General.*

Still, after all the temporary victories, somewhere deep in his subconscious, a question must have lingered with the annoyance of an itch he couldn't scratch. Was the attorney general truly beaten?

———

Frohnmayer hadn't reached his lofty position by curling into the fetal position every time the world dealt him a hearty blow. On the surface, it may have appeared as though he had never crossed a difficult river in his life. Certainly he had never experienced government agents dragging him from his mother, arresting him when he tried to return, and stripping his culture and religion from him. But reality is always more complicated than it appears to outsiders. In truth, Dave Frohnmayer had developed a fighter's spirit because life had demanded it.

Three years prior, he had returned home from work one evening to find that one of his young daughters had collapsed in the driveway. She had already been hauled to the hospital. What Frohnmayer and his wife discovered was that their seemingly perfect daughter suffered from a rare, genetic blood disease known as Fanconi anemia, where a patient's bone marrow stopped producing red and white blood cells and platelets. It almost always killed its victims.

A short time later, they learned that another of their daughters had the disease as well. Eventually, three of their five children would receive the diagnosis.

The doctors didn't equivocate: the Frohnmayers' daughters would not live into adulthood.

Frohnmayer put politics on hold. At the same time Al's case was meandering its way through the courts, the heavily favored politician opted not to run for governor. He stayed on as attorney general, but he launched all his efforts into saving the lives of his three daughters. He and his wife researched the disease, organized fundraisers, and traveled the country trying to form coalitions that could result in a cure. At every turn, when physicians and researchers told them their plight was impossible, they pushed forward, scrapping and searching for a miracle.

By the time the Oregon Supreme Court ruled against him, Frohnmayer had known defeat. He'd become bedfellows with the crushing emotions that assailed someone every time hope got battered from their lungs. And he understood how to mush forward into a strong onslaught.

Despite the challenges he faced at home, he couldn't tolerate the Oregon Supreme Court's ruling. A religious exemption to the normal rules regarding drug laws would, in Frohnmayer's view, unleash chaos upon Oregon's drug-enforcement efforts. After he read the one-sentence rejection from the chief justice, he quickly dismissed his disappointment and huddled in his offices in Salem with his team. It was a powerhouse group. It included a senior assistant attorney general, the deputy attorney general, the solicitor general for the state of Oregon, and the assistant solicitor general. Supporting them was a team of lower level attorneys and staff. How this lone, poor Klamath man with just one legal-aid lawyer had defeated them time and again was mind-boggling.

Frohnmayer likely listened to his team debate their options. The situation was stark. They could just give up, or they could try to convince the United States Supreme Court to take the case, always a dim prospect. If they let the Oregon Supreme Court's decision stand, Al and Black would receive their unemployment benefits. It wasn't the end of the world. It would have been the easy path, at least in the short term. Frohnmayer knew that was true, but he couldn't escape the haunting notion tickling his gut that it would be far more painful for the state in the long run. Someone with improper motives had to be driving this, they believed, and if the decision became the law of the land, their next move would be to push for exemptions to all sorts of illegal substances. Not just in Oregon but everywhere. One important aspect of the Oregon Supreme Court's ruling was that the justices didn't reach their conclusion under state law; rather, they had ruled that the federal Free Exercise Clause supported Al. Other states might piggyback off that ruling. In Frohnmayer's view, this meant the US Supreme Court might be interested in the case.

Whatever else was said in that meeting, Frohnmayer's opinion won the day. Unbeknownst to Al, the top attorneys for the state of Oregon marched out of that office with instructions to prepare a petition for writ of certiorari to the highest court in the land.

Notes

1. Jane Farrell, in discussion with author, January 8, 2018 and subsequent follow-up communications.
2. Ibid.

Chapter 28

OUTGUNNED

A l's defiant smile toward the attorney general didn't last long. His phone rang with two morsels of bad news. The first was that the attorney general had appealed to the Supreme Court. In the marathonic universe of civil litigation, lawyers understand something that drives their lay clients to fits of fury: litigation takes forever. That is especially true in cases where neither side is willing to yield. In December of 1986, when Al received notice that Frohnmayer was petitioning the Supreme Court, his response was exhaustion. The state just wouldn't go away.

The second piece of bad news was that Al's longtime legal-aid attorney, David Morrison, had no choice but to hand the case off to someone else. The man who had successfully navigated the case twice through the Oregon State Supreme Court would no longer be at the helm. He had decided to leave legal aid to launch his own private practice. He simply couldn't take the pro bono case with him and meet the demands of trying to build a business. It fell instead to a baby lawyer just three years removed from law school. Her name was Suanne Lovendahl. She had never practiced in the federal appellate courts, much less the United States Supreme Court. She stood alone between Al and Frohnmayer's army of attorneys.

In a cramped office in Roseburg, in a building that looked as if it had been designed more for a laundromat than a law firm, the thirty-seven-year-old Lovendahl pored over the state's cert petition. She had life experience, but her legal career was just beginning. As part of the legal-aid team, she had assisted Morrison in the Oregon Supreme Court. She had also handled numerous unemployment cases and other minor disputes. But now she stood alone.

In her office, she scanned the state's arguments, looking for ways to oppose them. She needed to convince the Supreme Court to reject the case. Frohnmayer had focused on the illegality of peyote under Oregon law, trying to make the court think the case was about someone trying to get around criminal statutes. He had even suggested it was time for the court to consider overturning the compelling interest test for religious-freedom cases. He acknowledged that Al was seeking only unemployment benefits, but he hit hard the notion that allowing someone to receive those benefits when they had violated the law would undermine Oregon's drug-regulation efforts.

Lovendahl still should have been confident. There was a reason Al and Black had won at nearly every stage of the case. The law protecting religious free exercise stood as a well-assembled wall that the Supreme Court had been fortifying for decades, decision by decision. In its request to get the justices to take the case, the state wanted to take a sledge to that barrier. Lovendahl knew she needed to emphasize that this was nothing more than an unemployment-benefits case. It had nothing to do with criminal law. In fact, the Oregon Supreme Court hadn't ruled on the illegality of peyote. It had simply determined that the state's only interest was in preserving the integrity of the unemployment-benefits fund, and that interest was not compelling enough to trample on Al's religious freedom.

She set to work.

The special-interest groups who had refused to help Al in the early stages of his case because it wasn't "national" enough now materialized like ants drawn to sugar. The matter had climbed to the national stage. Newspapers had taken notice. The ACLU, the Native American Church, even the American Jewish Congress—all came to see Al's plight as a chance to make a splash on a bigger stage. Oddly, Lovendahl would have none of it. It's hard to know her motivations.[1] Most likely she worried about losing control of the case; it often happens that when well-heeled special-interest groups begin exerting their influence over litigation, they push for their own arguments, often at the expense of the original parties. Later events suggest she may have just been insecure about allowing others to review her work. Either way, Lovendahl resisted any outside help.

Day after day, alone, she prepared her response brief. She consulted with Morrison, one of the few people she knew she could trust.

Al lingered largely in the dark. He took whatever jobs he could find to provide for the family, and he and Jane enjoyed a supportive community life. Still, the case was like an albatross dangling from his neck. He simply couldn't be rid of it. His position was clear. He didn't believe the state should treat him differently simply for following his religious convictions. How Lovendahl presented that argument to the Supreme Court was out of his hands. He trusted her to do it well.

In early January 1987, Lovendahl prepared forty orange booklets. Each one contained her brief in opposition. She mailed them to the court. She and Al could do nothing but wait.

As soon as Lovendahl's brief was filed, Frohnmayer and his team of attorneys and staff would have set into tearing it apart. While she sat alone in her offices in Roseburg helping other poor people who couldn't afford attorneys, they compiled arguments against her. They didn't know if the Supreme Court would take the case, but if it did, they would be ready.

Meanwhile, in Washington, DC, after all the briefs had reached the Supreme Court, the only thing that followed was excruciating silence. On February 25, 1987, four weeks before Jane and Al's second child was born, the justices broke that silence, but not with anything that related to Al's case. They ruled in a different matter. But the facts were remarkably similar. The state of Florida had determined that a woman couldn't receive unemployment benefits because her boss had fired her for refusing to work Friday evening and Saturday shifts, which occurred during her Sabbath. The Florida courts had upheld the denial of benefits. In an 8–1 ruling, the US Supreme Court reversed the decision. It reaffirmed that the compelling interest test governed these types of cases. And it concluded that Florida had not met that test. Under the Free Exercise Clause, a state couldn't deny someone unemployment benefits if they had lost their job for exercising their religion.

Al and Lovendahl would have been thrilled. Frohnmayer and his team would have felt foolish. In their petition, they had suggested the court abandon the compelling interest test. The court instead affirmed that all of its prior cases building up the compelling interest test were solid, good law. In many respects, it would have made no sense for the court to grant the state's cert petition in Al's case. All Al needed to do at that point was wait for the denial and finally move on with his life. He and Jane could lie down at night, their four-year-old daughter sleeping peacefully nearby, knowing it would all be over soon.

NOTE

1. Lovendahl passed away in 1991, when she was in her early forties, so much of her thought process and work product passed with her.

Chapter 29

COUNTERREVOLUTION

I n the quiet halls of the Supreme Court, where so few Americans ever get to set foot, something was happening, and Al couldn't have known about it. At the time, even the most careful observers only barely perceived it. In the fall of 1986, as Al's case was still churning in the Oregon Supreme Court, a short, fifty-year-old Italian-American jurist and scholar stepped into his offices at the United State Supreme Court for the very first time. Even then, his cheeks were pudgy, and his thinning, jet-black hair was slicked straight back. Ronald Reagan had nominated him, the United States Senate had confirmed him 98–0, and he had served as a law professor at the University of Chicago, one of the nation's elite law schools, but it still must have been a surreal feeling for him to step into an office in those vaunted chambers and know they would be his until death clawed them from him or he decided to relinquish them of his own volition. His name was Antonin Scalia.

He was, perhaps, the final chess piece moved into position to alter the direction of the court. It was a move the political right had been anticipating and planning for decades. At long last, the court was theirs.

It wasn't by accident. It was a direct reaction to a key strategy from the political left. Beginning in the 1950s, just before Roy Torcaso's case, many on the political left realized they could never achieve their goals through normal political channels. There was simply too much resistance in the legislatures across the land to get what they wanted implemented. Instead, they took to litigation, hoping judges would use the Constitution to do what politicians would not. They were not disappointed. Under the direction of Chief Justice Earl Warren, the Supreme Court took upon itself the role of expanding individual constitutional liberties. When politicians in the South enacted laws to keep black citizens oppressed, the justices helped stop them. When schools refused to integrate, the justices forced them. When free speech faced grave threats, the justices protected it. In the name of individual liberties, the Supreme Court and lower court judges expanded the power of criminal defendants, women, minorities, and suppressed voters. It also swelled its own power, as well as that of the federal government.

On the surface, this sounds like something most fair-minded Americans could support. It was a bloodless revolution. It seemingly meant more freedoms for all. Indeed, the increased protections for religious liberty and religious speech that formed at the same time were not accidental. Roy Torcaso, the compelling interest test, protections for minority religions, religious parents' rights to determine the education of their children—all formed like protostars in the ever-expanding universe of constitutional rights. The revolution resulted in the most robust protections for religious freedom in any country in the history of humanity.

But few expected the revolution to swell as far as it did. Those on the left continued to push for more and more constitutional rights. Unable to find any direct support in the text of the Constitution and believing they could never get a constitutional amendment passed, they asked the Supremes to expand the meaning of already existing terms. In other words, they sought rights that the Constitution never specifically mentioned. The justices obliged. The court found a right to privacy implied in the Constitution, although the word *privacy* itself appears nowhere in the text. From that they found a right to birth control. They granted criminal defendants rights that many felt crippled law enforcement and made America's streets unsafe. They upheld state programs that gave preferences to racial minorities. The courts created so many new rights that many Americans began to feel as if there were no rights at all. After all, if every human desire rises to the level of being a constitutional right, then nothing does—they all cancel each other out.

When the revolution first began, resistance was limited to small pockets of people who were opposed to a particular right and whom many didn't take seriously: racists in the South or backwards legislators in a particular state. By 1973, however, when the Supreme Court declared a constitutional right to abortions, the opposition matured from easily dismissed fledgling clusters of disconnected resistance to a fully organized counterrevolution that included many well-respected, mainstream people from the political right.

Roe v. Wade stunned many of them. The left's strategy of seeking judicial rulings to achieve their political aims had worked to remarkable success. The only way to combat it, many on the right reasoned, was to change the judges themselves. Politicians began scouring for justices who would stop expanding federal power *and* stop creating constitutional rights. They sought judges who would place police above criminals, who viewed the role of the judiciary as being limited to interpreting existing laws, not creating new ones—a task, they believed, the Constitution left only to legislatures.

Throughout the 1970s, while Al was finding his Native American roots, pushing for Native human rights, and building his reputation in the world of Alcoholics Anonymous, President Richard Nixon began slowly stacking the court with judges who would push back on the rights revolution. That paused for a time during the Ford and Carter years, but Reagan followed suit. It took more than a decade to place them in the majority. Antonin Scalia was the final piece that would tip the court's balance. It was now poised to unravel the tapestry of constitutional rights the court had spent the previous four decades weaving together.

When Justice Scalia walked into his chambers for the first time and eased into his leather-backed chair, a new reality was born. He was charismatic, intelligent, fun-loving, and skilled at drawing people into his camp. Whether anyone recognized it or not, Al Smith's fate now rested in this new justice's tiny hands.[1]

NOTE

1. Personal meeting with Justice Antonin Scalia.

Chapter 30

OUT OF CONTROL

In early March 1987, in her tiny office in Roseburg, Lovendahl would have received a single paper. It was the order from the Supreme Court. It was brief, just one sentence. She likely scanned it quickly. Here is what it said:

> Petition for writ of certiorari to the Supreme Court of Oregon granted. The cases are consolidated and a total of one hour is allotted for oral argument.

The joy she had felt when the Oregon Supreme Court had slammed the door in Frohnmayer's face dissipated as quickly as it had come.

She spoke with Al. Lovendahl had a serious voice, raspy and middle-toned. It conveyed gravity. Her talk with Al likely underscored it.

He was already painfully aware of the roller coaster of emotions litigation could cause. So one more instance of the legal system tossing him about like a rag doll wouldn't have surprised him. What did bother him was the justices' decision to consolidate his and Black's cases. In his mind, alarm bells began to ring. It probably made perfect sense to legal professionals to consolidate the cases so that there weren't two sets of briefs and arguments for what seemed like identical facts and legal questions. To Al, that was the problem. The justices and their clerks, hiding away in their cloistered marble tower three thousand miles away, most of them coming from lives of privilege, clearly didn't understand what this case meant to him, to his people. They were treating it as if it were nothing more than a boring piece of fiction about people who didn't really exist. And if that was their view, what chance did he have to win?

In Al's mind, these were not identical cases. As sincere as Galen Black may have been, he was not Native. He had only a passing involvement with the Native American Church. He had never experienced the struggle of government stripping his culture from him. For Al Smith, *his* case was about more than unemployment benefits. In truth, it had almost nothing to do with that. It was about whether the Constitution would now protect the people it had failed to shield in his youth—him, his grandparents, his mother, his ancestors, his *entire* tribe, every Native person who shared the devastating effects of American colonialism. Would it finally defend Native people's rights to practice their religion without being punished? For Al, the stakes couldn't have been higher.

As he spoke with Lovendahl and pondered these questions, a darkening realization settled over him as steadily as the descending night: Attorney General Frohnmayer would never, ever give up. He would push until Al broke.[1]

―――――――

As the seasons changed, Al watched in wonder as the case spiraled out of control. The briefing in the Supreme Court wrapped up. Lovendahl traveled to DC for oral arguments. One way or another, the case should have been near its end.

Four months later, the justices refused to rule. Instead, they remanded the case back to the Supreme Court of Oregon so it could decide if the use of peyote was illegal under state law. The Supremes felt that the legality of peyote use in Oregon was unclear. More consequential, however, was their opinion that the three unemployment-benefits cases that had become precedents in Al's case were different from his in that the religious employees had engaged in *lawful* conduct. If Al's behavior was *illegal* under state laws, the justices said, and those laws were valid under the Constitution, then denying Al benefits was perfectly acceptable under the Free Exercise Clause.[2] Of course, they provided no guidance as to whether the laws were in fact valid under the Constitution.

The Oregon justices would need to decide the same case for the third time.

It seemed as if Al's long nightmare had no discernable end. While he awaited anew the process in the Oregon Supreme Court, Lovendahl inserted another wrinkle into his case. It's unlikely Al knew of her reclusiveness, her refusal to work with other lawyers, but it was costing him.

For nearly a year, she had kept Al's case close to her chest. After the US Supreme Court issued its opinion, higher ups at the statewide offices for Oregon Legal Services took notice. They recognized that the case had moved beyond being just an unemployment benefits case. When the Supreme Court asked Oregon to determine if the use of peyote was legal under state law, the case was converted to a criminal matter. The key question now wasn't whether these two men should receive unemployment benefits. It was whether a state government could criminalize religious worship under the Constitution.

Lovendahl's superior, a man named Bernie Thurber, picked up the phone to let her know he wanted to help her craft a legal strategy that would address this shift. He had found an Indian law expert named Craig Dorsay, who could also serve as a tremendous resource.[3]

Huddled in her office, Lovendahl mostly refused to speak to either Thurber or Dorsay, just as she had refused assistance from the ACLU, the American Jewish Congress, and the Native American Church. Instead, she slaved away on her brief to the Oregon Supreme Court in blissful solitude.

They called her repeatedly, begging to discuss strategy. In the days prior to email and shared network drives, it was nearly impossible for the two men to glimpse her work, short of driving all the way to

Roseburg, bursting into her office, and demanding she hand over the physical copy.

She either refused or sometimes simply failed to respond. Her phone rang, but she didn't answer. When they could reach her, she kept everything close to the vest. She wouldn't discuss the specifics of her strategy.

But the case was too important for them not to keep pushing to influence the legal strategy before any brief was filed. They offered suggestions, not knowing if she was using them.

For some reason known only to her, she couldn't stand anyone reviewing her work product.

Thurber became aggressive. The stakes were just too high. Finally, as the deadline for filing drew near, he convinced her to hand over a copy of her draft brief.

With it in hand, Thurber and Dorsay immediately set to work. For the next few days, they revised, inserting key facts and legal concepts unique to Indian law, and, most important, trying to posture the case in a way that would ensure it ended forever. Ruling the religious use of peyote legal would do just that. But in her draft, Lovendahl had asked the Oregon Supreme Court *not* to rule on the legality of peyote under state law because no criminal case was before them.[4] In essence, she advised the state court to ignore completely the US Supreme Court's question. Instead, she requested them to hold that even if religious peyote use were illegal under state law, it still had to be allowed under the US Constitution's Free Exercise Clause.

Thurber and Dorsay panicked. That argument, if the Oregon Supreme Court adopted it, was essentially a slap in the US Supreme Court's face and would almost certainly trigger yet another round of review there. If the Oregon Supreme Court simply ruled that state statutes or the state constitution allowed religious use of peyote, the US Supreme Court would have no reason to get involved. It generally doesn't care if states choose not to regulate something. But if the state court invokes the federal Constitution, which governs all fifty states, then the Supreme Court would want to take a closer look.

Thurber and Dorsay finished their changes as quickly as they could. Prior to the filing deadline, they scrambled to their fax machine, inserted the revised draft, and sent it to Lovendahl in Roseburg. They waited as the beep and grind processed page after page.

It was too late. Over the phone just a few minutes later, she informed them in her gravelly voice that she had already filed her brief, without even looking at a single one of their changes.

Less than two weeks later, on September 8, 1988, Dorsay was listening to his radio. The broadcaster announced that Lovendahl and the attorney general's office had argued the case before the Oregon Supreme Court. The justices had scheduled oral argument early, and Lovendahl hadn't told a soul. Once again, she had refused to seek strategic advice from anyone.

The news stunned Dorsay. Any chance of persuading the Oregon justices to end the case under state law had just vanished.

———

Al languished waiting for the Oregon Supreme Court's decision. In the years since ADAPT had terminated him for practicing his religion, his little daughter had grown from an infant to a toddler to a young girl. Jane had given birth to another child, a boy. Al had found some work in the addiction-recovery field, but mostly the case was too toxic and people were afraid to hire him. He and Jane had converted the house next to the Willamette River into a lovely home. In the living room, they had made a makeshift desk from filing cabinets and a maple board. Old, worn Persian rugs overlapped one another to hide stained rental carpet. Political posters hung on the wall, and Pendleton blankets covered the furniture. In the backyard, during the warm months, their daughter built forts, splashed in the river, and cuddled next to a makeshift outdoor fire pit, where friends gathered to drum and sing and enjoy the evening air. Time marched on. Still, Al received absolutely no certainty in his case.[5]

Finally, the Oregon Supreme Court issued an order. It ruled that peyote was in fact illegal under state statutes but that it didn't matter because the federal Free Exercise Clause trumped the state criminal code. In other words, the state criminal ban on peyote eaten for religious purposes was unconstitutional under the federal Constitution because there was no true compelling interest in stopping the religious use of peyote.[6] Following Lovendahl's brief, it refused to rule whether Oregon's state constitution trumped the criminal laws because that would be an advisory opinion on a hypothetical case.[7]

Al had won. Again.

Frohnmayer wouldn't stand for it. Again. He immediately ordered his team to begin preparing a second appeal to the United States Supreme Court.

With the victory, Lovendahl no doubt felt justified in how she had approached the case, but when Frohnmayer filed his second petition for review in the United States Supreme Court, Dorsay's and Thurber's worst fears were coming true. Frohnmayer emphasized that the Oregon court had based its ruling on the federal Constitution, that its reasoning was wrong, and that the Supreme Court needed to reverse it.

Oregon Legal Services called Lovendahl and informed her that, going forward, Dorsay would need to approve all briefs she filed in Al's case.

Lovendahl was not happy. She protested.

Her superiors would not change their minds. Her insistence on shutting people out was threatening not just Al but religious liberty for Native Americans across the entire country.

Rather than agree to work with someone else, Lovendahl withdrew from the case. It may be that she also realized she was simply outgunned—the attorney general's office just had too many resources.

Going forward, Dorsay would handle everything. The only question was whether he was getting involved too late to stave off disaster.

Frustrated and worried, he did everything he could to stop the justices from taking the case. Al was no longer alone—the major newspapers in Oregon began to lambast Frohnmayer for keeping the case alive, suggesting his motives were born of nothing but hostility, or indifference, to Native American religions. Law professors from the University of Oregon urged the attorney general to back down. But on March 20, 1989, the justices agreed once again to decide *Employment Division v. Smith*.

There would be no remand this time. The case had run its course. It should have ended years earlier. From its humble beginnings over unemployment benefits, Al's dispute had morphed into a Frankensteinian monster that would determine whether the United States Constitution forbade states from criminalizing religious worship. The answer would affect every person in the country.

NOTES

1. Garrett Epps, *To an Unknown God: Religious Freedom on Trial* (New York: St. Martin's Press, 2001), 183.
2. *Employment Division, Department of Human Resources v. Smith*, 485 U.S. 660 (April 1988). A summary of the court's decision said this: "The Free Exercise Clause did not prohibit legislative control over religious activities that posed some substantial threat to public safety, peace, or order. The prohibition on the possession of peyote was a valid legislative proscription and was not unconstitutional under the Free Exercise Clause. If the use of peyote were illegal under state law, then its use constituted willful [*sic*] misconduct. Because it was unclear whether its use was illegal, the action was remanded."
3. Carolyn N. Long, *Religious Freedom and Indian Rights: The Case of Oregon v. Smith* (Lawrence: University Press of Kansas, 2000), 150.
4. Courts are generally wary of making what are called "advisory" opinions, which are opinions on hypothetical cases, instead of ones that are actually in front of them. Lovendahl essentially argued that the US Supreme Court was asking the Oregon court to issue an advisory opinion.
5. Jane Farrell, in discussion with author, January 9, 2018.
6. *Smith v. Employment Division*, 307 Or. 68 (October 1988).
7. Ibid., at 73 n.3, reports: "Because no criminal case is before us, we do not give an advisory opinion on the circumstances under which prosecuting members of the Native American Church under ORS 475.992(4)(a) for sacramental use of peyote would violate the Oregon Constitution."

Chapter 31

PRESSURE

With the arguments in the Supreme Court just weeks away, the pressure, Al discovered, was beginning to come from more than just the attorney general's office. A peculiar anxiety had begun to seize all of the special interest groups watching the case. The ACLU, the Native American Church, the American Jewish Congress, the Native American Rights Fund (a public-interest law firm known in the legal world as NARF), and the Council on Religious Freedom—each saw in the changed case a gun pointed at religious peyote and religious freedom more broadly. As the case barreled toward the Supreme Court, they eagerly worked with Dorsay to draft amicus briefs on Al's behalf, but some of them were looking for a way to get the conflict dropped altogether. NARF, in particular, wanted the case to go away.

Miles away, in Eugene, Al was just trying to survive. At nearly seventy years old, and with a family to feed, he had landed a job at Goodwill collecting donations outside a large semitrailer in a mostly unused parking lot. He was highly regarded for his long-held sobriety and commitment to Native recovery and program development, yet the publicity of the case and the general public's skepticism toward peyote meant he couldn't get a job in his field. He had been reduced to collecting used, throwaway clothes and loading them onto a truck.[1]

Still, he and Jane were excited. Though they had little money, Craig

Dorsay had somehow obtained tickets for them to fly to Washington, DC, to hear oral arguments. It was now just a couple of weeks away. Their trips were planned. Dorsay had practiced several mock arguments. The briefs were submitted. The long journey through nearly every aspect of America's legal system was approaching its end. Al had fought the good fight, and Jane had supported him every step of the way. He had won at every turn. They clung to that knowledge and hung on.

In mid-October, they received an invitation from a local attorney named Roy Haber, a well-known civil-rights lawyer originally from New York. He and Al knew each other a bit and were friendly. He invited Al and Jane to come to his home, where a number of attorneys from NARF and several other community leaders wanted to meet Al. The couple accepted.[2]

On a crisp fall evening, they arrived at the party. At the front door, Haber greeted them warmly. He shook Al's and Jane's hands and welcomed them to his home. His smile was as wide as they come, and his black hair was fluffy and curly. What stuck with Al was just how friendly Haber was being. The two knew each other, but they were only acquaintances—not best friends.[3]

Al and Jane immediately felt something was amiss. The house itself was far nicer than anything they were used to, but that wasn't what felt askew. It was something else. The attire, the furnishings, the drinks, the spread, the forced friendliness—to Al and Jane, it all seemed contrived.[4]

Haber guided them to a dinner table and introduced Al to a number of key religious leaders from around the country. Two of the men present were Steven Moore and John Echohawk, preeminent lawyers with NARF out of Boulder, Colorado. They had dedicated their careers to Native American rights. Moore had joined NARF several years earlier and was the lead attorney representing the interests of the Native American Church as they related to Al's case. Echohawk was a Pawnee man, one of the founders of NARF, and its executive director. He carried himself with an intense quietness that could both intimidate and placate anyone talking with him. It made him a powerful advocate and a persuasive negotiator.[5]

Other people Al and Jane had to navigate were ministers, pastors, and religious leaders from around the Northwest. It was not their normal crowd.

Al was mostly in a state of confusion. He thanked profusely each person who greeted him, but he had no idea why they were being so friendly. For the first time, he realized the level of national interest in the case. All night long, strangers clasped his hand, patted him on the back, and smiled at him. He didn't understand why, but he was thankful for what he perceived as true support for his cause.

He felt as out of place as a white man attending his first sweat. The night droned on. Before, during, and after dinner, guests at the party talked with Al about the case, its importance, and the impact it could have on all Native peoples. Moore and Echohawk both spoke at length with Al. They informed him that they were putting pressure on Frohnmayer to back down. They simply didn't understand—and they informed Frohnmayer of this—why he was so doggedly pursuing the case.[6] Haber continued to schmooze Al, smiling and checking on his comfort.

At one point during the dinner, Echohawk and Moore pulled Al aside. They expressed the concerns of the church, that if the case went badly, it would be devastating for the peyote religion for decades to come. They were affable and friendly.

Al nodded. He understood. He said he wanted what was best for the church. He also expressed his feelings that he wished the case had never come to him. He wished it had fallen on someone else's shoulders. But he was willing to do what was necessary to see it through and protect Native people's interests.[7]

When the evening ended, Al and Jane climbed into their van to head home. What had the whole night been about? Neither had any idea.

Al would learn soon enough. Just two weeks before the oral argument, while he and Jane and their kids were hanging around the house, the cordless phone above their makeshift desk rang. Al sauntered to it and pressed the button.

"Hello?"

It was Craig Dorsay. He informed Al that, apparently, Moore and Echohawk were not in town as mere supporters. They were there for their own purposes. The Native American Church had hired NARF to protect it, and they had asked Roy Haber to represent them locally. From the church's perspective, the case was nothing but trouble. In NARF's and the church's view, given the makeup of the Supreme Court and the counterrevolution happening among the justices, Al's case was a threat to the church. If it went the wrong way, the entire church would lose its right to legally practice its most central ceremonies. They needed to end the dispute before that happened. Under the Supreme Court's rules, if the parties agreed to settle a case before it was decided, the court would automatically dismiss it. NARF saw this as the best path for protecting the broader church. They wanted Al to settle.

Listening to Dorsay through the phone, Al bristled. When his case had first begun five years earlier, he had gone to NARF for help. They had rejected him, saying his matter wasn't high profile enough.[8] Now he felt like they were asking him to sell out for them.

Suddenly the purpose of the fancy dinner came into focus for Al. He and Jane were not used to political machinations. They hadn't perceived the ulterior motives behind the food and special treatment and extra-charming smiles. Now it all made sense. They had been trying to loosen him up.

Dorsay wasn't finished. Al was not the only one NARF had been wining and dining. At a meeting shortly after the dinner to schmooze Al, Echohawk and Moore had met at the Hilton in Eugene with Frohnmayer and his staff. They had demanded that Frohnmayer drop the case, and they had been aggressive in letting Frohnmayer know why he was wrong. Since then, behind the scenes, Moore and Echohawk had been working with the attorney general's office on some sort of settlement.

What would a settlement look like? Al wanted to know.

Dorsay didn't have any details. They were still hashing things out. But Frohnmayer seemed willing to consider it.

"Why are they doing it without me?" Al asked. "This is my case. It makes me very uncomfortable."

Dorsay understood and promised to check back in as soon as he knew more. He too felt as if they were being left out of the loop. And he wasn't happy. Still, he explained, the reality was that Moore and Echohawk were required to represent the best interests of their client, just as Dorsay was obligated to represent Al. And in the church's view, its central ceremony was now on trial and no member of the church was actually involved in the case.

But Dorsay reassured Al that at the end of the day, NARF and the Native American Church were not parties in the case. If they were going to settle, Al would have to agree to it.

Al again let Dorsay know how uncomfortable all of this made him. He ended the call and eased the phone back into its cradle.

One evening, that same week, long after the sun had set and the little ones were already fading into their dreams, Al and Jane sat in their living room. It was late. Al was tired and ready for bed himself.

The silence was interrupted by the beeping ring of the cordless phone.[9]

Al grunted, got off the couch, and walked over to it. "Hello?" he said.

On the other end, a faint, almost imperceptible voice seemed to be speaking from across a vast distance. "Why are you hurting our church?" the elderly voice said. The words came in broken English with a thick, obviously Native American accent. The faintness came not from a bad connection but from humble timidity and age. It was a Native elder from Minnesota.

Al explained in a friendly tone that he didn't want to hurt the church. He was trying to help it.

"Don't take our medicine away," the elder said. He asked Al to drop the case, to settle, so that the Supreme Court wouldn't hurt the church.

Al listened. He didn't get angry. He was mostly surprised at where this was coming from.

It was the first of many calls. Every night, late, the phone would ring, sometimes more than once, and distant followers of the Peyote Road would plead with Al to let the case go. They begged him not to harm their way of life, as if he, not Frohnmayer, were the one pushing the case forward.

As Al listened to the plaintive cries for him to throw in the towel, he felt a knot forming in his stomach. Self-doubt crept into his thoughts like a thief in the night. Even though he felt someone was putting these poor people up to this, even though he knew they really didn't understand the case, he wondered if perhaps he should just give in. Perhaps he should simply take whatever settlement NARF negotiated without him and walk away.

———

Oral arguments drew near, thirteen days out. In Salem, Moore and Echohawk poured everything they had into reaching a deal with the attorney general and his staff. For three days, they stayed at a hotel near the Oregon Department of Justice, sleeping little and waking each morning for a new round of negotiations. Like them, Frohnmayer believed the new makeup of the Supreme Court cut in his favor. He saw no reason to back down. And he clearly didn't value peyotism as a valid religion.[10] Every time the two NARF attorneys thought they were making progress, Frohnmayer would return to the same point: if the state allowed peyote for religious use, what would it have to do when the "Church of Marijuana" came out of the woodwork and asked for an exemption to the drug laws? Or the "Church of Heroin"? Moore and Echohawk were aghast. Peyote had no history of recreational use like those other drugs. There was absolutely no evidence of abuse or harm from peyote. Frohnmayer's dogged insistence to lump it in with other, more harmful substances showed his complete lack of respect and understanding of the Native religion. They pushed and pushed.

Tensions ran high. Frohnmayer found Echohawk particularly persuasive. Eventually, the attorney general expressed a willingness to find some common ground, but there had to be conditions. As the group negotiated, they finally invited Dorsay to the meeting to see if he could sign off for Al.

After the third day, ten days before oral arguments, at three o'clock in the morning, NARF and the state struck a deal.

There was only one problem. None of them represented Al Smith. Soft spoken, even gentle, Dorsay was not one to get angry, but his temper had been rising as steadily as water in a heated pot. He emphasized again and again that Al had to agree to any terms. And he wasn't sure he would. The settlement ensured the case would never go to the Supreme Court and therefore protected the Native American Church, but it gutted all of Al's wins in Oregon.

In the attorney general's office, Moore, Echohawk, and Frohnmayer asked Dorsay to sign the settlement on Al's behalf. Dorsay agreed to add his signature with the understanding that it was not binding until Al agreed to the terms. "This is something I have to run by Al," he said.

Moore and Echohawk took heart. They didn't know of Al's misgivings. From their conversations with him at the dinner party, they believed his goal was aligned with theirs to protect the church and the practice of the peyote ceremony at all costs. Confident Al would take the deal, they drove from the attorney general's office to the airport and boarded a red-eye back to Colorado.

All eyes turned to Al. A sleep-deprived Dorsay sat down with him and explained the settlement. He couldn't in good conscience tell Al that it was a fair deal for him. The church was asking him to fall on his sword for a greater good. Dorsay also couldn't tell Al to take or reject the deal. The choice was entirely his. Stated simply, the settlement would vacate Al's victory in the Oregon Supreme Court, require Al to pay back the unemployment benefits he had received, result in the Oregon Supreme Court reversing the Oregon Court of Appeals' judgment in Al's favor, and conclude with the Employment Division denying Al benefits. Al and Galen Black would also have to pay for some of the state's costs. NARF would cover these expenses.

Dorsay handed Al a copy of the settlement document.

Al needed to think. He had told Echohawk and Moore that he wanted to protect the Native American Church, but it had never occurred to him he would have to completely surrender. The attorney general was offering him nothing.

He took the papers home and handed them to Jane. With her by his side, he phoned Stanley Smart, the roadman who had presided over the peyote meeting that led to Al's being fired from ADAPT. Smart advised Al to stay the course. He had won. He shouldn't just throw out the ruling from the Oregon Supreme Court. More important, in Stanley's view, it was time to stop hiding. The day had come to see if the First Amendment would finally protect Native Americans.[11]

Al must have swallowed hard. He had received all the advice he was going to get. The decision now rested solely with him. Jane told him she would support him no matter what. The night waned, and he and Jane eventually went to bed.[12] The two lay side by side discussing all the pros and cons until Jane drifted off, leaving Al alone with his thoughts.

He eased off the mattress. There, in the dark, he paced the room. The wood floors creaked beneath his feet. The voices of elders from across the country cried to him. *Don't take our medicine away.* He worried about them. With their nearly silent, timid voices pleading for him to drop the case, he imagined their devastation of no longer being able to take the sacrament central to their religion. It pained him, but an anger toward the pressure to cave burned inside him as well.

Earlier that day, Jane had scribbled her thoughts onto the back of the settlement documents. They captured perfectly how she and Al were feeling and, perhaps, how the members of the church were feeling about him:

> Craig [Dorsay] says to be on g[u]ard for possible character bashing. Steve Moore has already commented to Craig—Al was just a flake, not a *real* member, just hangs out w/ white women, *not* traditional. This hits below the belt—all trust is gone. How can Al take advice from these men who have shown themselves this way[?] . . . Al's case was negotiated away to nothing. NARF's stand was a heavy pressure on Al to give up whatever he had to "save the church"—threatened him with full responsibility of "killing the church because he was too pigheaded to back out."
> . . . They are willing to sign away everything that was gained here in Oregon. . . . Is not the same persecution NARF has pleaded to end? Is this moral support for Smith? How can one deny an individual his freedoms and justice in order to save those freedoms for this larger community?[13]

Jane's words reverberated in Al's mind. He had journeyed so far down the Red Road, clawing and scraping his way to take back what the government had stolen from him and his ancestors so many epochs before. Could he abandon it now? Or, in clinging to the case, would he end up destroying the very path he wanted to follow? All he wanted was to do what was right. If he signed, he felt he would be admitting he had done something wrong simply by going to church.

As he paced in the dark, a faint memory, tinged with regret, slipped peacefully into his thoughts. Decades earlier, after the federal government had officially "terminated" any recognition of the Klamath tribe, it had also sought to swallow all of the Klamath ancestral lands into the national forest. It would have been the final step in literally wiping an entire culture off the face of the map. The government had offered to pay each remaining Klamath tribe member a vast sum for his or her portion of the land. Like almost all of them, Al had taken the money. He had blown it on "fast cars and suits and foreign-made shoes."[14]

One man, Edison Chiloquin, had refused the money. He was the only one. He had stood alone in the forests of Klamath country and demanded that the government give him his portion of the land so that the Klamath way of life wouldn't fade forever. The government had sent him a check. It had pressured him to cash it. He had refused. Instead, he had called on Native supporters who helped him form a camp, erect tepees, and maintain a sacred fire. He declared the fire would not go out until the land was his, to be used to build a traditional Klamath village, where young people could learn of their ancestors' way of life. He eventually won.

In the quiet of his house, his children's rhythmic breathing the only sound present, Al pondered Edison Chiloquin. He lamented that, back then, he hadn't had the courage and conviction to turn down the money and stand shoulder to shoulder with that man. In the years since, other tribes had called the Klamath "sell outs." Thinking of Chiloquin, Al couldn't bear the accusation of selling out again.

The night had grown long. It was already early morning. Al pivoted from the window and looked down on his sleeping children. His daughter was now seven years old. She filled her days with building forts in the backyard by the river and playing kitchen in the cubby at the top of the stairs, but it wouldn't be too long before she turned into a teenager.[15] The realities of just how cruel and unrelenting the world could be would soon rest on her little shoulders. Al's son would follow. Al could see other people surrounding his grown children. "*Smith?*" they would say when they learned his children's name. "*Farrell-Smith?* Is your dad *that* Al Smith? The one who sold out?" And he saw it then, the image that would steel his resolve and set his path: his children hanging their heads, ashamed of who their father was.

He couldn't do that to them.

The next morning at NARF headquarters in Boulder, Echohawk wouldn't have been more flabbergasted if a bomb had exploded in his office. He had just received a call from Dorsay, who had told him that

Al felt the settlement agreement should be torn up. Like it or not, they were all headed to Washington.[16]

Echohawk let out a long, slow sigh. His first reaction was shock. They had wasted all that time. He and Moore had already told their client, the Native American Church, that they had succeeded up in Oregon. The more he thought about the situation, the more his shock turned to anger. Al Smith was putting a church he didn't even belong to on trial. In his view, Al was simply changing his mind. Out of what? Pride? How could he do this?

Through his fatigue and frustration, Echohawk picked up the phone, hoping to get Roy Haber on the line quickly.

———————

Outside the Goodwill donation truck in the parking lot of a local grocer, Al was sorting clothes and other donations. He glanced up to see Roy Haber, his fluffy hair bobbing frantically, rushing toward him.

Haber pulled Al aside from the Goodwill donations, begging to know what Al didn't like about the deal.

Al told him: he was being asked to admit that he'd done something wrong. It was as if going to church were criminal.

Haber pleaded with Al to reconsider and somehow convinced him to call Echohawk and Moore, just talk to them about everything one more time.

Al said he was willing to listen to anyone.

In a matter of minutes, he was on the phone, listening as Echohawk and Moore launched into their last efforts to close the deal.[17]

After Echohawk finished talking, Al said he understood their point of view. "But," he said, "I have to see how this is going to turn out."[18]

"I'll tell you how it's going to turn out," Echohawk said, his tone rising. "We're going to lose our constitutional rights!" Echohawk's fears were not misguided. In the 1970s, Native Americans had enjoyed a string of victories in the Supreme Court; but as the counterrevolution had taken hold, the justices had begun turning on them. By the time of Al's case, Native American leaders had become convinced that the justices on the court, including Scalia, would show very little respect to their religion.

Al ended the call. If there was one consistent aspect of his personality, it was that he wouldn't tolerate being told what to do, especially by people who seemed to care only about their own interests. He had constitutional rights to go to church as well. And he had won them in the Oregon Supreme Court. Why should he be forced to give them up now?

He stormed back to tell Haber to take a leap, but he might as well have been marching right into the faces of the Supreme Court justices.

NOTES

1. Jane Farrell, in discussion with author, January 8–9, 2018.
2. Ibid.
3. Ibid.
4. Ibid.
5. Steven Moore and John Echohawk, in discussion with author, January 10, 2018.
6. Carolyn N. Long, *Religious Freedom and Indian Rights: The Case of Oregon v. Smith* (Lawrence: University Press of Kansas, 2000), 168–69.
7. Moore and Echohawk, discussion with author.
8. This is not unusual. Public-interest law firms often can't take cases that are too narrow in scope. With very limited resources, it is common for them to focus what money and time they do have on cases that will influence the broadest number of people.
9. Farrell, discussion with author.
10. Moore and Echohawk, discussion with author.
11. Garrett Epps, *To an Unknown God: Religious Freedom on Trial* (New York, St. Martin's Press, 2001), 202; Farrell, discussion with author.
12. Farrell, discussion with author.
13. Epps, *To an Unknown God,* 203–4.
14. Al Smith, speech given in Berkeley, California, 1990.
15. Farrell, discussion with author.
16. Moore and Echohawk, discussion with author.
17. Details of the parking lot exchange as remembered and retold by Jane Farrell are from discussion with author.
18. Ibid.

Chapter 32

SHOWDOWN

It was November 6, 1989, and to signify his seventieth birthday, Al Smith walked through metal detectors at the United States Supreme Court. He wasn't alone. Piled in the bins on either side of him were mounds and mounds of Native American jewelry. Indians from all across the United States, from multiple tribes, had come to support him, many wearing their finest turquoise and silver. To get through security, they took it from off their wrists, necks, boots, and belts. It was a scene unlike any the court had ever seen.

Reporters massed inside and out. They shoved microphones in Al's face, trying to get him to comment on the story. He felt the quiet strength that comes from numbers. A week earlier, once he had made his decision final, a single thought had taken hold in the minds of those who cared about Native American rights: Al Smith needed to win. Echohawk and Moore offered full support to Dorsay. They helped him engage in more than six mock arguments in one week. The Native American Church sent legions of its members to the steps of the court. As many as could get in filled the benches of the august courtroom.

And then there was Al. He stood out as much for his skin color as he did his clothes. His black hair, alive with flashes of gray, draped around and hugged his shoulders. He wore a brown wool suit jacket and gigantic bolo tie, an eagle symbol etched into the silver, which popped off his maroon shirt. To top it off, a massive cowboy hat, the color of desert sands at sunset, left his face in shadow. Stanley Smart and Jane were with him.

They entered and took their seats on the front row, in chairs specially reserved for the parties.

The room looked as intimidating and royal as it had for decades. The formal proceedings began as they always did. When the justices entered from behind the curtain, Al felt only resentment. Where did they get off lording over everyone? he wondered, and he was certain none of them would have tolerated putting their own religion on trial.[1]

When it was time for oral argument, Dorsay took his seat at the counsel table. He was young, with a crisp black beard, pale skin, and hair that was already thinning. As a show of solidarity, Echohawk and Moore took the seats next to him, even though they would have no role in the argument.[2]

Frohnmayer rose to the podium.

A long hush ensued, and all eyes turned to the attorney general. The silence lingered for an uncomfortably long time as Frohnmayer organized himself. Al watched him, struggling to understand why this man couldn't simply leave him be. Why did these people, from the days of Al's youth and all the way to that moment, feel they had a right to control Al's people, to change their religion? He just couldn't comprehend it.

Finally, in his deep bass, Chief Justice Rehnquist leaned into the microphone and said, "General Frohnmayer, you may proceed."

The pressure that had been gathering in the room vented itself through a barrage of questions from the justices. For Frohnmayer's time, the arguments went as expected. The justices delved into the state's interest in regulating peyote. Did the state truly have a compelling interest in stopping Native American Church use of peyote? Wouldn't it destroy the church if Oregon were allowed to criminalize peyote use in church ceremonies? Couldn't the Oregon Supreme Court have resolved all of this by simply ruling that peyote was allowed by the state constitution? If the federal government thought it should exempt religious use of peyote from enforcement of federal laws, how compelling could the state's interest really be here in criminalizing it? Was there really any evidence of people using peyote outside of church services?

Frohnmayer strained to bat the questions away. He was a master at downplaying the answers that hurt him. He emphasized the hallucinogenic nature of peyote, he tried to distinguish it from wine in a Catholic mass, and he failed to provide any real evidence that peyote was harmful to the practitioners of the peyote religion. Once he had finished using his time, it was unclear where the justices stood.

As soon as Craig Dorsay took to the podium, Justice Scalia pounced. Dorsay, in a higher-pitched, somewhat nasally voice, tried to argue that alcohol was far more destructive to Native Americans than peyote ever could be. His point was that from a white man's perspective, peyote seemed dangerous. To a Native man, however, alcohol had devastated so many lives that it, not peyote, should be the regulated drug. That, in a nutshell, was the problem with this case. What compelling interest could the state possibly have in regulating the religious use of a drug that was actually helping Native American people?

But Scalia mangled the argument. He misconstrued it entirely, thinking Dorsay was arguing that peyote was the same thing as wine at a Catholic mass. It was, of course, in many respects. A devout Catholic, Scalia refused to accept that. "I don't see a correlation between the wine and the peyote," he said flatly.[3]

And it became clear that no matter what arguments Dorsay volleyed, Scalia wasn't interested in accepting them. In his view, peyote was dangerous. Wine was not.

Dorsay pressed. "There is . . . no evidence that peyote, as used by the Native American Church, has been misused in the sense that is has been misused in society . . . [W]e have a long history with this church of hundreds of years, and there has been no documented evidence."

In fact, as Dorsay reminded the court, the evidence demonstrated the opposite: while alcohol had devastated many Native communities and tribes, the use of peyote in traditional religious ceremonies showed the ability to help people overcome those addictions.[4]

Scalia seemed skeptical.

Still, even those arguments focused merely on the technicalities of whether the state truly had a compelling interest. That had been the test for nearly three decades in determining whether government could burden someone's religion. Did the state have a compelling interest, and had it taken the narrowest path for achieving that interest?

Then something changed. The moment came and went like a flash of lightning. To a casual observer, it might have gone unnoticed. Justice Scalia seemed to change the conversation, if only for a moment. Dorsay was emphasizing for the third time, that it wasn't enough for the state to have a general fear of a drug. It needed to show that the drug caused some sort of harm, or resulted in some sort of abuse, or could be used recreationally. "It is my position," he said, "that [the state] ha[s] to justify that position by showing some actual harm. Otherwise, there would really be no free exercise right, because the state could outlaw any kind of conduct and say—"

"So long as it does it generally, I think . . . why isn't that right?" Scalia interrupted.

Dorsay paused. He wasn't quite sure of Scalia's point. He started to rephrase his statement, but Scalia cut him off a second time.

"So long as it does it generally and doesn't pick on a particular religion. It has a generally applicable law for good and sufficient reasons."

"Well the problem," Dorsay responded, "is this law and the 'neutral' . . . prescription *does* affect a particular religion only."

"Well," Scalia said, "I suppose you could say a law against human sacrifice would, you know, would affect only the Aztecs. But I don't know that you have to make . . . exceptions."[5]

Not surprisingly, the notion of sacrificing humans spurred Dorsay back into a discussion of what constituted an interest so compelling the state should be able to crush a religion to stop it. The arguments, like the briefs, continued to focus on that singular concept.

What faded into the collective forgetfulness was Scalia's comment that it would be okay under the Constitution for a state to burden a religion as long as the law didn't pick on a particular faith and was applied generally. Aside from Dorsay's pointing out that such a rule would obliterate any constitutional protection for the free exercise of religion, no one even responded to it.

The idea was almost like a scene from a B-horror movie, where a writhing, fanged monster slips into our world from another dimension, vanishes before anyone even recognizes what it is, and then is forgotten as it lurks about the land, waiting to unleash itself.

As soon as arguments ended, news reporters overran everything. Frohnmayer basked in the attention. On the steps of the Supreme Court, a gray, overcast sky behind him, he continued to peddle his argument. Surrounded by microphones, he addressed questions from reporters.

"Will you identify for us first what the . . . compelling state interest is in this matter?" a reporter asked. Others shoved microphones into Frohnmayer's face.

Calm and cool, no doubt aware that he still had a bright political future, Frohnmayer fielded the question as if reading from an outline. "Well, it's threefold. One is that there is a general concern about the use of any hallucinogenic drug. . . . The second is a compelling interest of the state in neutrality among religions."[6]

Reporters interrupted him again and again. He never made his third point in that moment. But one thing was clear: the compelling interest test was the lens through which everyone viewed the case.

Across the street, Al's supporters gathered for their own press conference. Steve Moore stood to the microphones. People of many Native American traditions surrounded him. They prayed. They performed several ceremonies to support their way of life. Craig Dorsay offered some comments. Leaders of the Native American Church spoke and prayed. Still lingering in the air was the resentment many in the church held toward Al for bringing the case. He could feel it. Yet they still invited him to the microphones. In contrast to Frohnmayer, Al wasn't seeking the strange celebrity necessary for politics. He was as uncomfortable standing in front of the microphones as Frohnmayer would have been sitting in a tepee. He explained briefly what the use of peyote had done for him.

He finished simply: "Let our people be."[7]

Inside the Supreme Court, the justices were churning. As Al left the grounds to go celebrate his birthday with his family, all he could do was wonder about how the court would rule.

Both sides felt confident. Frohnmayer rested assured that there was likely no more compelling interest for a state government than to ensure its drug laws were enforced consistently. Dorsay believed that if the court truly looked at the record, it would find no evidence of peyote being harmful to anyone. It just wasn't like other drugs. Even if the state had a compelling interest in battling harmful drugs, crushing the Native American Church was not the narrowest way to achieve that interest.

Both Dorsay and Frohnmayer returned to Oregon confident they had done all they could do. The justices would either find a compelling interest or they would not.

Winter gave way to spring. The absence of news about one of the biggest cases in their lives likely drove everyone to watch their televisions, papers, and fax machines with added vigilance. Finally, one morning in mid-April 1990, Craig Dorsay was in the midst of trying to survive a bout with a Stairmaster at the gym next to his office. Other exercisers toiled away around him. Weights clanged in the distance. The televisions anchored high on the walls blared out the day's news.

Al's case showed up on the screens. Dorsay sprung off the machine and stared at the television. The report was as sparse as one might expect from media personalities who knew nothing about the substance of what they were covering, so it didn't tell Dorsay much.

All he knew was that Al had lost.

Heartbroken, he cleaned himself up and rushed to his office, hoping a fax with the opinion would be waiting for him. Lingering in his thoughts was poor Al, whom he knew would be vilified for whatever the Supreme Court had done. When he finally got to his office and was able to get his hands on the actual opinion, his heart sank.

It wasn't unusual for David Frohnmayer to receive phone calls before sunrise. When his phone rang on the morning of April 17, 1990, he answered it with relative nonchalance. The person on the other end was Linda Greenhouse, the Supreme Court reporter for *The New York Times*.

Greenhouse informed Frohnmayer that Oregon had won in Al's case. She wanted a few quotes from him.

He obliged.

As the call progressed, however, she asked one question that troubled him. Wasn't he worried that the Supreme Court had "taken away" religious freedom?[8]

After he hung up, the gravity of that question pulled his mind into its orbit. He kept swirling around it, wondering what she'd meant. He needed to get his hands on the opinion.

Virtually no one could believe what the Supreme Court had done, Dorsay most of all. Justice Scalia had written the opinion. Justices Rehnquist, Stevens, Kennedy, and White had joined him. It started off innocuously enough. He recounted the history of the case, misstating a few facts as he went. After explaining the case's many twists and turns through the court system, he wrote, "Now that the Oregon Supreme Court has confirmed that Oregon does prohibit the religious use of peyote, we proceed to consider whether that prohibition is permissible under the Free Exercise Clause."[9]

Nothing about his analysis to that point suggested anything was out of the ordinary. In fact, any reader of the case would have expected, at that point, for Scalia to launch into the compelling interest test discussion.

He didn't.

Reminiscent of the cases dealing with The Church of Jesus Christ of Latter-day Saints and polygamy, the court invoked the distinction between belief and action. Justice Scalia affirmed that government may not constitutionally regulate someone's beliefs. "But the 'exercise of religion,'" he wrote, "often involves not only belief and profession but the performance of (or abstention from) physical acts."[10]

He then reached a conclusion that shocked Dorsay to the core. "There being no contention that Oregon's drug law represents an attempt to regulate religious beliefs, the communication of religious beliefs, or the raising of one's children in those beliefs, the rule to which we have adhered ever since [the cases involving the Church of Jesus Christ] plainly controls," Scalia wrote.[11] The only problem was that Scalia completely ignored the rule that had been the governing law over religious free-exercise cases and instead manufactured a new one from whole cloth. Dorsay couldn't believe it. No party had argued for the test Scalia was creating. Neither party had discussed it in the briefs. No one had even been able to explore its pros and cons.

And the rule itself essentially obliterated any constitutional protection for religious freedom in the United States. It held that if a law was neutral and generally applicable, it didn't matter if it happened to burden someone's religious exercise.

As Dorsay pondered the opinion, the examples likely exploded in his mind. If a state decided to prohibit alcohol across the board, it could prevent Catholics from celebrating Mass. It wouldn't matter that Mass was central to Catholic worship. Under Scalia's rule, the state would be acting constitutionally as long as it didn't target Catholics.

It could do the same to the Jewish Seder. Under this test, Anthony Kohlmann would have lost. Essentially, any religious group whom the majority didn't consider when passing statutes could be annihilated.

Even as Scalia claimed his test had actually been the law for decades, it was clear he was talking out of both sides of his mouth. He spent the remainder of the opinion discussing all the times the court had invoked the compelling interest test and why it didn't really apply in this situation and why it shouldn't apply in religious-freedom cases more generally.

The only bone he threw religious freedom was a meatless and unhelpful one. Near the end of his discourse, he explained that state legislatures and the federal government were certainly entitled under the Constitution to provide religious-freedom protections. They simply weren't obligated to do so. In other words, if the state of Oregon wanted to protect Al Smith and the Native American Church, it could. But if a religious sect wasn't influential enough to convince politicians to protect it, so be it.

The scope of the opinion was breathtaking.

Al Smith had lost.

The Native American Church had lost.

Religious freedom had lost. The only thing protecting it now were the whims of whichever majority happened to have control of government.

The counterrevolution on the Supreme Court charged ahead in full, unashamed earnest. The bloc the political right had been forming through multiple presidencies finally had control, and they were determined to return power to the states. If there were casualties of things they held dear along the way, they either didn't mind or, more likely, didn't notice.

Notes

1. Garrett Epps, *To an Unknown God: Religious Freedom on Trial* (New York: St. Martin's Press, 2001), 5.

2. Steven Moore and John Echohawk, in discussion with author, January 10, 2018.

3. Transcript of Oral Argument, *Employment Division v. Smith*, 494 U.S. 872 (1990) (No. 88-1213), 1989 U.S. Trans. LEXIS 94, at *27.

4. Ibid., at *28–29.

5. Ibid., at *43–44.

6. *Employment Division v. Smith*, https://www.c-span.org/video/?c4584870/employment-division-smith.

7. Ibid.

8. Epps, *To an Unknown God*, 215; Carolyn N. Long, *Religious Freedom and Indian Rights: The Case of Oregon v. Smith* (Lawrence: University Press of Kansas, 2000), 196–87.

9. *Employment Division v. Smith*, 494 U.S. 872, 876 (1990).

10. Ibid., at 877.

11. Ibid., at 882.

Chapter 33

"YOU'RE NEXT"

The news stunned nearly everyone. On the phone with Dorsay, Al and Jane tried to comprehend what Scalia had done. Dorsay explained the contours of the decision.

"Maybe a battle's lost," Al said to Dorsay, "but the war's not over. I've lost battles before." As his life had proven time and time again, Al Smith was not one to give up easily. Yet deep inside, he was heartbroken. His mind wandered to all of those members of the Native American Church and other Natives who no longer had a right to practice their religion. And he felt sorry. Had he done this to them?

Dorsay further explained the sweeping nature of the ruling.

Al ended the call with a question. "If the First Amendment doesn't protect me, how the hell's it going to protect you?"[1]

Frohnmayer was equally in shock. As he pondered the new standard Scalia had created, he struggled to wrap his mind around it. They hadn't briefed it, they hadn't argued it, not one justice had questioned him about it, and he had never even suggested it. The court had just reaffirmed the compelling interest test a few months earlier. All Frohnmayer had expected from the case was a ruling that the state had a compelling interest to uniformly enforce its drug laws; nothing more.[2] But a dark realization may have crept into the recesses of his mind. For all his accomplishments, he would be remembered as the man who destroyed religious freedom in the United States.[3]

The reaction on the court was swift. The justices who dissented from Scalia's opinion blasted it as "distorted"[4] and "a wholesale overturning of settled law concerning the Religion Clauses of our Constitution." At the end of the dissent, drafted by Justice Harry A. Blackmun, the justice concluded only, "I dissent." In earlier drafts, Blackmun had closed in the customary way, writing, "I respectfully dissent." Before the opinion was published, however, he deleted the word *respectfully*.[5]

Even Justice Sandra Day O'Connor was livid about the ruling. She agreed with the result the court reached because she believed the state *did* have a compelling interest to regulate peyote, but she did not agree with Scalia's opinion. She tore into it with ferocity. "To reach this sweeping result," she wrote, "the Court must not only give a strained reading of the First Amendment but must also disregard our consistent application of free-exercise doctrine to cases involving generally applicable regulations that burden religious conduct."[6] She called out the ruling for what it was: "The Court today . . . interprets the [Free Exercise] Clause to permit the government to prohibit, without justification, conduct mandated by an individual's religious beliefs, so long as that prohibition is generally applicable."[7] She pointed out how inconsistent Scalia's reading of prior cases was, how he largely just ignored everything the court had been doing for nearly five decades. She continued, "A State that makes criminal an individual's religiously motivated conduct burdens that individual's free exercise of religion in the severest manner possible, for it 'results in the choice to the individual of either abandoning his religious principle or facing criminal prosecution.'[8]"

She wasn't finished. "The Court today gives no convincing reason to depart from settled First Amendment jurisprudence. There is nothing talismanic about neutral laws of general applicability . . . for laws neutral toward religion can coerce a person to violate his religious conscience or intrude upon his religious duties just as effectively as laws aimed at religion."[9]

In her conclusion, she pointed out the absurdity of Scalia's reasoning. "Finally," she wrote, "the Court today suggests that the disfavoring of minority religions is an 'unavoidable consequence' under our system of government and that accommodation of such religions must be left to the political process. In my view, however, the First Amendment was enacted precisely to protect the rights of those whose religious practices are not shared by the majority and may be viewed with hostility. The history of our free exercise doctrine amply demonstrates the harsh impact majoritarian rule has had on unpopular or emerging religious groups."[10]

The picture Justice O'Connor painted was chilling. Under Scalia's rule, any religious group whose beliefs or practices were unpopular with the majority was now under threat.

The dissenting justices were just the beginning. The popular press, legal scholars, liberals, conservatives, academic journals—all of them almost uniformly condemned the decision.

But it was set in stone. Without argument or fanfare, without input from anyone other than his clerks and fellow justices, Scalia had decided to singlehandedly rewrite the law of religious freedom in the United States. The only question was how long it would take for majority rule, unchecked by the Constitution, to start crushing the religious exercise of anyone who dared challenge society's norms.

———

As a quiet panic settled over the legal landscape, Al Smith received an invitation to speak at the University of California—Berkeley School of Law, Dave Frohnmayer's alma mater.

He stepped to the podium, his familiar long hair, now more gray than black, draped over a denim jacket. A blue curtain hung behind him. He peered across the crowd through large glasses. With his age, his cheek bones were more pronounced than before. He spoke calmly.

"I'm really surprised and pleased to be here," he began. But then he looked over the audience and paused. In a stilted cadence, he said, "I want to speak to my brothers and my sisters that are in this audience. . . . I want to apologize to you, my brothers and my sisters who are Natives of this land." As he spoke the words, he shook his head and smirked in disbelief. "If in any way this case has harmed you, if in any way it has made the practice of going to church in any respects bad or harmful, I apologize for that. I think in the long run . . . we'll be stronger for it. This has been going on for a long time. This treatment."

He then pivoted. He turned to his own story, all he had overcome, what the government had taken from him and his people, how that had ravaged his life, and how he wished the case had never come to him. "I wish it had been somebody else," he said. "Why me?"

It broke his heart to know that some of his own people looked at him and wondered what he had done.

As he continued, it was hard not to see in this one man the gut-wrenching experience of an entire people. But then he rammed home a poignant point: "It no longer just affects Al Smith and Native Americans. It affects you. You Americans. You two-leggeds . . . It affects *all of us*. . . . We need to look at each other as neighbors and relatives. We need to stand together. We need to care about each other. We need to treat each other as family. We need to pray together, raise our children together."

He talked of his kids, of the power struggle the government had created in his case. Knowing he was talking to a group of young law students, he said, "I encourage you to do what you know is right. Follow the dictates of your heart. . . . I don't know if this can be changed or not."[11]

In the years that would follow, Al would slide out of the national spotlight the same way he had stepped into it: with Jane by his side and his kids on his arms, his spirit always ready for another sweat lodge. His message that day at Berkeley resonated not just with law students, but with Natives across the country, spanning multiple generations.

They heard it from an Elder, and it inspired them to keep up Al's fight. It would take time, but because of Scalia's opinion, in the years that followed, the leaders of America's major religions slowly came to fear a stripping of their religious freedom the same way Native American people had for centuries.

Al would not be a part of that battle. Dementia eventually slowed him. And on November 19, 2014, five days after his ninety-fifth birthday, his spirit crossed over and began his journey back to his Creator. What did remain, chilling and lingering in the minds of anyone who had heard Al speak that day at Berkeley, was his single, two-word phrase: "You're next."

NOTES

1. Carolyn N. Long, *Religious Freedom and Indian Rights: The Case of Oregon v. Smith* (Lawrence: University Press of Kansas, 2000), 196.
2. Garrett Epps, *To an Unknown God: Religious Freedom on Trial* (New York: St. Martin's Press, 2001), 215–16.
3. Long, *Religious Freedom and Indian Rights*, 196–97.
4. *Employment Division v. Smith*, 494 U.S. 872, 908 (1990).
5. Ibid., at 921.
6. Ibid., at 892.
7. Ibid., at 893.
8. Ibid., at 898; note that Justice O'Connor is quoting from *Braunfeld v. Brown* (366 U.S. 599, 605) in the latter half of this remark.
9. Ibid., at 901.
10. Ibid., at 902.
11. https://www.youtube.com/watch?v=v8gL5P9-rkI.

PART 4

IT'S JUST CAKE

People's views of religious freedom tend to change with how much power they have. When a particular group controls the levers of government, they give little thought to religious liberty. And why would they? No group is going to pass a law or regulation that burdens their own religious exercise. Almost always, when religious freedom faces a threat, it is because the dominant group fails to recognize the concerns of a religious minority. Or, occasionally, they target people with whom they disagree religiously. For Protestants, requiring all people to testify in court likely didn't pose a problem, because in their religious tradition, it doesn't. For a mostly Christian state to require a belief in God for a government position was largely unremarkable, until a man of conviction who didn't share that belief needed employment. Outlawing the use of peyote in religious ceremonies didn't raise flags for the vast majority of citizens in Oregon because none of them used it in their religious traditions.

But power is fickle, societies change, mores evolve, and those in control shift. When the powerful become the powerless, they tend to value religious freedom greatly. When the powerless then gain control, they often become the oppressors who no longer cherish the religious freedoms of those opposed to them.

These shifting views on the value of religious freedom posed a constant problem in Europe before the founding of America and continue to threaten the United States and other countries today. They lead to battles over control of government. Insecurity and uncertainty reign. The rule regarding religious freedom should be a constant fixture in our constitutional stars. Instead, it is as unpredictable as the next election. And those who cherish religious liberty only when they need it may well find it isn't there when that time comes.

Chapter 34

TWENTY SECONDS IN JULY

Working in the back of his shop, he couldn't see the customers walking across the roasting parking lot—two men and a woman.

It was July 19, 2012. Denver was boiling. The high would reach one hundred degrees that day, just one notch below the record. If there was a cloud in the sky, the sun quickly fried it. In the Denver suburb of Lakewood, Colorado, born-again Christian and baker Jack Phillips was running his bakery, putting the finishing touches on a few cupcakes. In the front, his daughter chatted with some customers about various items they might need. In the corner of the store sat a small table where Jack often consulted with clients about custom cakes. His tousled hair and goatee, perhaps showing his fifty-plus years on earth, had finally started to thin. Wisps of gray were mixed in with his natural sandy color.

Outside, the customers had closed the gap between their car and the storefront.

Jack had operated his business for close to twenty years. Driven by a lifelong talent and love for painting and drawing, he had wanted to run his store in a way that would allow him to be an instrument in God's hand. Naturally shy, with an unobtrusive, even hesitant voice, Jack never sought attention. Located in an unremarkable part of the Denver area, his shop matched the vibe of the neighborhood around it and the personality of its owner. The only thing that drew attention to it was Jack's skill as an artist, which had earned him recognition as one of the best wedding cake designers in all of Denver.

———————

David Mullins and Charlie Craig sought Jack out precisely for that reputation.

They had called ahead and made an appointment. As they passed through the parking lot, they felt a flurry of excitement. Their first date had been on December 5, 2010.[1] After two years, they were in the final stages of planning their wedding. Charlie's mom, Deborah, walked beside her son. She had made a special trip from Wyoming. This would be the only day she could participate in the planning.

In the tradition of so many who had gone before them, Charlie and David wanted to dedicate their lives to one another. They were prepared to commit to complete fidelity to each other and no one else. To dance together. To buoy each other up in times of trouble. To commit their whole hearts to the cause of being together for the remainder of their lives. They would make that commitment in Massachusetts, one of the few places where same-sex marriage received government recognition at the time. They would wed there, on the opposite side of the country, then have a larger reception in Colorado.

Like any couple planning a wedding party, they had a million details to finalize. Getting the cake was on that list. The host for their reception had recommended Jack's shop. She had used it before. And after looking at the website, Charlie and David felt it would be a good fit.[2]

Above them, in a half-circle, black-and-white sign was the word "Masterpiece," a phone number underneath. Next to it hung the word "CAKESHOP," in red, all-caps block letters, the kind common to a store in a strip mall.

Excitement bubbling inside, they reached the door, grabbed the handle, and pulled it open.

———————

With a firm belief that God could use him if he engaged in his profession while also living the precepts of his faith, Jack had named his shop Masterpiece. In Jack's view, the name held dual meanings. It referred to the notion that each of his custom creations was a work of art.³ But it also referred to the Sermon on the Mount, in which Christ exhorts his followers, "No man can serve two masters: for either he will hate the one, and love the other; or else he will hold to the one, and despise the other. Ye cannot serve God and mammon."⁴ The name was a reminder to Jack that his master was not money. And he wasn't opening the shop for money; he was doing it to try to help others. Just like the brushes and tools he used to craft his cakes, he wanted to be a paintbrush his Lord could use to create a brilliant piece of art on this earth. Jack's belief was that if he operated his shop the way God asked him to, and lived his faith to the best of his ability, God would use him and his store for good.

Over the years, he had done exactly that. As with anyone, how he defined "living his faith" was intensely personal. There were things he believed God wanted him to do, such as caring for the poor or promoting good causes. At one point, Jack discovered a young couple living in a car in the parking lot outside his shop, the teenage girl pregnant, her boyfriend unsure what to do. Jack helped them, arranging for them to go to a pregnancy center that could put them on the right track. A few doors down sat an Alcoholics Anonymous center. Jack would always open his door to those who went there for help. They would step in and talk with him, and he would listen, and they would feel his friendship on their path to recovery. With each person he helped, he sincerely believed he was simply acting as an instrument for his God.⁵

There were also things Jack believed God forbade him from doing. Those primarily involved participation in any activities that were in opposition to God's will. Jack believed that using his artistic talents to facilitate those activities would be akin to dishonoring the very God who had blessed him with those talents in the first place. He never turned away people, but he did turn away events. In Jack's belief system, the modern celebration of Halloween, with its focus on the occult, witchcraft, and satanic imagery, was one such activity. So when customers asked him to create cakes celebrating Halloween, he politely declined, inviting them to go to a different baker. They did. When someone entered his shop and asked him to bake a cake celebrating their divorce, he had to say no, believing that God would not want him participating in rejoicing over the ending of a marriage. They found a different shop. Other times, people came to his store asking him to bake cakes that would celebrate bachelor or bachelorette parties. Believing that what often occurred at those parties contradicted God's will, Jack again asked his customers to go to a different baker; he simply couldn't be a part of it and still obey his Lord. They did. There were even instances of people coming to his shop and asking him to bake custom cakes containing derogatory messages, including negative messages about LGBT individuals, racist slurs, and anti-American sentiments. He declined them all.[6]

There were times when Jack turned down more cakes in a day than he accepted. It was not a financially savvy way to run a business, but he knew whom he obeyed. It was the only way Jack felt he could operate his shop and follow his religion. Of course, in the world of religious freedom, the concept of "sin" or "God's will" is an interesting one. What one person views as sinful, someone else sees as a lovely, redeeming, sometimes even God-commanded activity. Still, Jack believed he could follow his beliefs without punishment even if others didn't understand them. For nearly twenty years, he had done just that.

———

When Charlie, David, and Deborah stepped inside the shop, the smell of baked goods and sugary frosting filled the air. In his hand, Charlie clung to a binder filled with ideas for the cake. Cupcakes, cookies, brownies, birthday cakes, and pastries filled the glass counters and added to the ambience. On the wall, a newspaper story from 1993, when the shop had opened, discussed how it had been Jack's dream to open the store and how he had saved for more than ten years before finally realizing it. "Walking into the store," the story read, "is akin to walking into an art gallery of cakes."[7]

In the far corner of the store sat Jack's consulting table, surrounded by roughly a dozen Styrofoam wedding cakes decorated to highlight all the possibilities of Jack's artistry. He had painted each of them with his own special icing concoction. Some were adorned with pine trees and forests, others with hand-painted designs or icing flowers, still more with golden ribbons of icing Jack had painstakingly brushed on.

David, Charlie, and Deborah made their way through the shop and eased into the black chairs in front of the table. As they waited for someone to come, they perused Jack's book of photos and design ideas.

Jack's daughter was busy working at the store's counter, and another employee was occupied elsewhere, so Jack, being the only one free at the time, walked around the counter, a notepad in hand, and greeted them. His smile was affable, his voice tender, as always.

David, Charlie, and Deborah all introduced themselves.

Then David said, "We're here to look at wedding cakes."

Jack had his pen and notepad in hand, ready to take notes. He asked whose wedding it would be.

"It's for our wedding," said Charlie.

Jack leaned back. His mind raced a little as he looked for a polite way to tell them he couldn't do a same-sex wedding. "I'm sorry, guys," he finally stammered. "I can't do cakes for same-sex weddings."[8]

Charlie and David broke into wide-eyed surprise. "Really?" Charlie said.[9]

A hush filled the space between everyone at the table.

To relieve the pressure, Jack continued, "I'll make your birthday cakes, shower cakes, sell you cookies and brownies. I just don't make cakes for same-sex weddings."[10] In Jack's view, God had commanded that marriage and sexual relations should be solely between a married man and woman. Just as with other events, Jack couldn't use his artistic talents to endorse a wedding he believed was contrary to God's will. He was happy to sell the couple anything else in the store. He had, in fact, served without prejudice plenty of LGBT customers over the years. He had even employed a gay man in his shop. But he couldn't create a custom cake for an event he believed went contrary to God's commands.

David and Charlie burst from their chairs. They marched from the shop. On the way out, David spun and swore at Jack, causing others in the store to turn their heads. He flashed a well-worn obscene gesture and bounded into the parking lot.[11]

The entire exchange lasted only twenty seconds.

Their reaction broke Jack's heart. With a sigh, he returned to work. He wasn't happy with how the meeting had turned out, but he figured the incident had passed and he would eventually be able to set it behind him and continue with his work. He took some comfort in knowing that there were plenty of other bakeries that could serve them. He also knew he had no choice. He had to stay true to who he was, to what his faith required of him.

In the parking lot, near their car, Mullins was fuming. He snapped a photo of the shop. The Colorado native had never in his life experienced something like this.

Charlie burst into tears. For him, old wounds had been torn open again. He had grown up in small-town Wyoming, where people throughout his teenage years had taunted and bullied him for being gay. Like many in the LGBT community, he hadn't chosen his orientation, but he had suffered for it. Although he had survived the bullying of his youth, it had left him wary.[12] Later, he attended the University of Wyoming, where, years before, a twenty-one-year-old gay student named Matthew Shepard had been brutally robbed, beaten, tortured, and left to die while tied to a barbwire fence in a field just outside Laramie. All signs pointed to the crime being motivated by anti-LGBT animus. Living so close to where that heinous crime had happened left Charlie cautious. And given his own experiences, he had learned to keep his guard up.[13] One of his reasons for moving to Denver was the hope that he could live in a place where he wouldn't face any of that again.

Still, on most days, Charlie maintained a wall of emotional protection, unsure of what the world might throw at him. But on that afternoon, he let down his guard. It was supposed to be a day to celebrate, to let go of the demons of his past and enjoy an afternoon with his mom and fiancé. As he had walked into a bakery moments before, he hadn't thought anything could go wrong.

Jack's inability to serve them unearthed all of Charlie's past tenderness. His mom hugged him. He wept in her arms. She told him she loved him and that they would get through this.[14]

David embraced Charlie as well. Feeling his fiancé sob on his shoulder, David decided one thing. He wasn't letting this go.

David had never been turned away for anything based on his sexual orientation. He had long known there were people out there who condemned his lifestyle, but he had tolerated it with delicate restraint. This time he turned to Facebook. In a post he wrote immediately after being turned away, he typed out a message to his friends and followers. It began: "So, I'm about as pissed as I've been in a long time." He explained how Jack had refused to bake a cake for a gay wedding.

"I AM FURIOUS!" he wrote.

He attached a photo of Jack's storefront. Below that, he included Masterpiece's contact information. Finally, he wrote, "If any of my friends out there is interested in making a statement in support of us and the right of gays to marry, I would most appreciate it if you might drop them a line or an e-mail." David didn't expect much from the message. He had hoped his family would see it, perhaps some of his friends.[15]

Instead, news of the incident spread like a virus.

Inside the shop, the phone rang.

Jack answered. "Masterpiece Cakeshop," he said.

"So are you the baker who just turned away the gay couple?" someone on the line said.

"No," Jack said. He explained that he turned away the opportunity to bake a cake for a same-sex wedding but that he would never turn away a gay couple.[16] He would always and gladly serve anyone who came into his shop, but he simply couldn't participate in certain events.

That wasn't enough. The caller swore at him and abruptly ended the call.

Jack was shocked. He would have liked to explain his dilemma more, to have people understand why he couldn't do this. To people from a variety of religious backgrounds (including many people who have no traditional religion), the concept is not difficult to understand: participating in something that you believe to be a sin actually facilitates the sin and is, therefore, a sin itself. It doesn't matter that other people outside one's faith don't see the behavior as sinful—that doesn't change anything from the standpoint of the believer. Just as Jack couldn't participate in a same-sex wedding, many LGBT cakeshop owners couldn't participate in events denouncing same-sex marriage. In their view, that event would be promoting the sin of intolerance. But Jack didn't get to explain that.

Wondering about the magnitude of the maelstrom he may have walked into, Jack hung up the phone.

He turned to the two women who worked for him. "I think I'll answer the phone for the rest of the day."

Moments later, it rang again. He picked up and received the same treatment as before—swearing and a quick hang up. No willingness to discuss the issue, to understand anything about him.

For the next hour, the pattern repeated itself. More and more calls poured in, all filled with swearing, false accusations, and a complete unwillingness to talk. In one hour, until closing, he received six of those calls.

———

Charlie and David were exploring options. Still stinging from being turned away, they took comfort in the warm flow of support they felt from friends and family. Online, David's Facebook post had grabbed the attention of hundreds of supporters. The same people who had called Jack and sworn at him were posting positive messages to David and Charlie on Facebook and other venues. Several made it clear they had every intention of trying to shut down Jack's store. They shared the story with their friends, who forwarded it to their own networks. A groundswell was forming. More and more people from all over the world began discussing ways to ruin Jack's business.[17]

The next day, Charlie's mom, Deborah, called the cakeshop. Charlie was the oldest of her three boys and, like any mother, she wanted to protect him.[18] When she had Jack on the phone, she didn't follow the pattern of so many of the other callers. She sincerely wanted to know why Jack had turned them away, perhaps so she could try to convince him to rethink his position.

Jack explained as best he could about why it violated his Christian beliefs.

Munn pushed back. She was a Christian as well, she explained. "I serve a loving God whose son taught us to love and not judge others," she said.[19] But the conversation quickly followed a fruitless path common to almost all religious-freedom cases. Often, when someone takes a stand for their religious convictions, opponents don't challenge them on purely legal grounds; instead, they debate them on *theological* grounds. That is to say, they try to explain why the religious party's beliefs are wrong. In Munn's view, the Bible didn't prohibit someone from participating in an event like this. In Jack's view, it did. That difference in belief was a chasm too far to cross. And the call ended with nothing being resolved.

But it did raise a specter of what was to come.

It is one thing for private citizens to proselytize and persuade one another to change their religious beliefs. It was appropriate for Munn to do precisely that as she explained her beliefs to Jack. What violates religious freedom, however, is when a judge or government is permitted to do this. The reasoning is simple: it allows the government to take sides by labeling the beliefs of one religion correct and another false. In such a scenario, the party who wins in religious-freedom cases would do so not by successfully arguing a legal standard, such as the compelling interest test, but by successfully finding a judge who agrees doctrinally. True religious freedom forbids that method. Because of that, most judges and government actors understand that commenting on the validity of someone's religious beliefs is to venture into forbidden territory. Most, but not all.

That same day, Charlie and David believed they had exhausted their options. Aside from trying to start a boycott or pushing their contacts to call Jack, they really didn't know what else they could do. Neither had been heavily involved in LGBT rights issues.[20] Neither was a lawyer.

At some point, a relative of Charlie's reached out to them, telling them that Colorado had laws prohibiting exactly what had happened to them. They should look into it.

They did. Of course, they could have let the matter drop. They were not in a situation like what African Americans had faced under Jim Crow laws prior to the civil rights movement of the 1960s, where it was impossible to receive a number of services, goods, or accommodations. This was different. In fact, rather than facing a world where services could be denied them by nearly every store they entered, Charlie and David may have stumbled into one of the only bakers in the entire Denver metro area who *wouldn't* participate in their wedding. The very next day, at least two other bakeries caught wind of their story and offered to bake their wedding cake for free.[21] Even over Charlie's and David's protests, these bakers wouldn't accept any money.[22] So to some outsiders, it seemed like it should have been easy for them to forget about Jack's refusal and move on with their lives. The sting would have lingered, of course, but it would have eventually faded.

Still, for David and Charlie, this wasn't just about the magnitude of the burden they faced. And it wasn't about cake. It was, in their view, about equal treatment. It was about knowing that they and other LGBT citizens could walk into any store, just like everyone else, without having to worry about being turned away. There is a dignitary harm a person experiences when a storeowner refuses to serve them. In David's and Charlie's view, no other LGBT citizen should have to go through what they experienced.

They started exploring legal options. And they continued to fan the flame of support that had ignited on the internet. For the next several days, they pondered their next move.

A few days later, Jack was on edge. He was working in the shop with his daughter. Things were quiet. The phone rang. At this point, every time it did, Jack grew tense. He didn't know what to expect.

The situation had gotten out of control. By 2012, all of the social and technological trends of the internet age were in full force. The modern era of viral internet posts had not only dawned but was by then a pulsating, unhinged force. Biased people from every walk of life, both the right and the left, could now exist in their own, personally crafted echo chambers. They could hear only one side of any argument and consider themselves informed. And they could attack people they didn't even know just by stroking a few keys. All they needed was a target.

They had found it in Jack.

For Jack, the phone calls had climbed into the dozens, all laced with profanity and vitriol. He had tried to change the shop's number, but Charlie's and David's supporters online quickly figured that out and posted his new digits to their followers. The calls continued to pour in.

On the crowd-sourced reviews site Yelp, prior to the incident, Jack had enjoyed a high rating and had received consistent praise as one of the best custom cake shops in the Denver area. Within days, his rating had fallen to below one star, all based on false and made-up reviews from people all over the world who believed they were supporting Charlie and David. Yelp quickly discovered the bad reviews were not from actual customers of the shop. It deleted them. The posters picked up on this and devised a strategy to get around it. Instead of complaining about Jack's policies, they manufactured false reviews about the quality of his cakes. Yelp sifted many of those out, but some still lingered. His ratings remained well below what they had been prior to the incident.[23]

On social media sites designed to help Charlie and David, some supporters posted that they would drive Jack out of business. Others encouraged the couple to call local reporters. Still others indicated that Jack and his views were not welcome in society. All of it was happening at a blistering speed.

By the time the phone rang this time, Jack was hesitant. He reached for it and picked it up, almost afraid to answer.

A man was on the other end. "I'm coming and I'm going to shoot you in the head," he said. Jack froze. His face flushed. Before he could hang up, the caller told him what street he was on and where he was turning. He was close.

Jack caught his breath.

The caller hissed that he also knew Jack's daughter was at the store.

Jack ended the call. He turned and surveyed the shop. His daughter was working near the counter, her four-year-old daughter—his granddaughter—playing idly next to her. Suddenly, the tiny store with its sugary smell, which had always been a sanctuary of sorts for many years, felt like a death trap.

He drew close to his daughter, out of earshot from his granddaughter. "You need to get in the back. Someone's threatened to come and kill me." When Jack tells the story now, his voice cracks, and tears fill his eyes. "So go to the back," he continued to his daughter. "Don't come out until I tell you."[24]

His daughter whirled to her own child and led her into the back kitchen.

Jack snatched up the phone and called 911. He explained what had happened, and the dispatcher immediately sent units to the shop.

In silence, Jack watched the windows. Tense moments passed. His own breath sounded like waves crashing in his ears. On the streets outside, every car that passed dragged the possibility of death along with it. Whether Jack knew it or not, this wasn't unusual in these cases. In New Mexico, a young wedding photographer had refused to photograph a same-sex marriage. She was a mother with young children. As soon as her case received publicity, people started calling her home. Hidden behind a veil of anonymity, they threatened to burn her house to the ground, with her, her husband, and children inside. In Washington, a florist who declined to make arrangements for a same-sex wedding received so many death threats she had to reroute her way to work and install security systems to stay safe.[25]

But in that moment, knowing he wasn't alone wouldn't have helped Jack. All he cared about was making sure his sweet daughter and granddaughter weren't killed for their religion. He couldn't change the will of God, even though that would've been the far easier path. All he could do was pray. And watch. And wait.[26]

Online, supporters of Charlie and David formed a website to boycott Masterpiece Cakeshop. David shared it with his friends to encourage them to sign up. They flocked to it in droves, all the while rejoicing that Jack would be out of business soon.

At the shop, Jack stared into the vast expanse of the parking lot beyond his windows. Cars could come from a multitude of directions. His shop was in a corner space, so two of the walls were all glass, easy to shoot through. Beyond the parking lot sat so many of the stores that made up the shopping center: a hobby shop, a sandwich place, some restaurants, a massage parlor, and many others. The sun reflected off the windshields of the cars baking on the asphalt.

As Jack took it all in, a steady calm stayed with him. He worried about his sweet granddaughter and her mom. As for himself, he took comfort in knowing that if God wanted him to remain on this earth, He would protect him. If it was time for him to leave this life, then it would be God's will.[27]

Eventually, the vehicles that turned into the parking lot were police cars. Watching them roll up to the building, Jack released a slow sigh. The officers entered and secured the building. After talking with Jack, his daughter, and granddaughter, they tried to trace the call to see who had placed the death threat. It didn't work.

Once they left, Jack stood alone, wondering what else could happen.

Within the next few weeks, everything exploded. Jack's choice to live by his faith ensured he would not drift back into a life of anonymity anytime soon. David and Charlie organized protests. They rallied in front of the shop with rainbow flags and signs that read, "Let them eat cake." Jack could only look through his windows in frustration. He had no problem with selling them cake; it was his forced participation in the event he simply couldn't do. The profanity-laden phone calls continued, as did death threats, which were now coupled with calls from supporters. It was a deluge of attention.

Soon, reporters invaded everything. They called the shop in waves, some hostile, others supportive, a few just seeking quotes. They interviewed David and Charlie. They took positions on what Jack should or should not believe. A local Denver news website mockingly ran stories of other people whom Jack had turned away for things like celebrating Halloween or tarot cards. It clearly showed a lack of understanding of Jack's religious motivations. National LGBT rights websites and magazines picked up the story. Online, more and more people began to take entrenched positions on either side of the fight. Jack's supporters flowed into his shop just as those in David and Charlie's camp took their business elsewhere.

Part of it was the unyielding nature of both sides in what appeared to be a minor dispute. No matter their position, advocates reduced their arguments to the same thing:

"It's just a cake, so bake it," or

"It's just a cake, so get one from someone else."

But clearly, for everyone involved, the fight was about far more than cake.

For LGBT citizens, there is a real and serious dignitary harm to being turned away from a business. It can't be ignored. It shouldn't be dismissed. It is not fictitious—there is something inherently troubling about the law allowing people to be treated differently by places of public accommodation. And there is a dark shroud that hangs over the history of the United States, where minorities and others have been denied access to basic goods and services simply because they were not part of the majority. African Americans, ethnic minorities, religious minorities, women—all faced discrimination in places of business throughout the country's history. Charlie and David simply felt they could not let it stand.

At the same time, asking someone like Jack to abandon his faith commitments or give up his occupation—as Charlie and David's supporters were doing—invokes an equally ugly stain on human history. The burden that grows from having to make such a choice cannot be ignored or flippantly disregarded as nothing more than the cost of doing business. As one scholar explained, excluding people from certain occupations because they are "unwilling to violate their faith commitments . . . [has] an odious history. The English Test Acts and penal laws long excluded Catholics from a range of occupations, including positions of responsibility in the civil and military service, solicitors, barristers, notaries, school teachers, and most business with more than two apprentices."[28] Throughout human history, one of the central methods for oppressing dissenting religious views has been to exclude certain believers from various occupations. Believers in God have done it to atheists. Atheists have done it to theists. Protestants did it to Catholics. Catholics did it to Protestants. Muslims have done it to Christians, and Christians have done it to Muslims.

The reality was that neither Charlie nor David could change their sexual orientation. It was a core part of their identity. And they had legitimate reasons for why it shouldn't affect how they were treated in public. At the same time, Jack could not change his religious beliefs. They were also a core part of his identity. Changing them was not like putting on a new shirt. And he too had legitimate reasons for feeling he shouldn't have to choose between his beliefs and his job.

But what should lawmakers and courts do when faced with such compelling interests on both sides? How should they resolve the dispute when the people involved couldn't seem to find a compromise on their own?

Jack, Charlie, and David were about to find out.

Notes

1. "Meet the Gay Couple at the Center of the Masterpiece Cakeshop Case," *Washington Blade* (website), accessed October 12, 2018, http://www.washingtonblade.com /2017/11/21/meet-the-gay-couple-at-the-center-of-the-masterpiece-cakeshop -case/.

2. Ibid.

3. Jack Phillips, interview by Ryan T. Anderson, "Justice for Jack: Free Speech and Religious Liberty at the Supreme Court," *Heritage Foundation*, September 6, 2017, https://www.heritage.org/religious-liberty/event/justice-jack-free-speech -and-religious-liberty-the-supreme-court.

4. Matthew 6:24 (King James Version).

5. Personal Interview with Jack Phillips, February 23, 2018.

6. Phillips, interview by Ryan T. Anderson.

7. "Couple Launches Dream with Cakeshop." *Looking at Lakewood* 9, no. 6 (November 1993).

8. Phillips, interview by Ryan T. Anderson.

9. Deborah Munn, "It Was Never about the Cake," *Huffington Post*, December 9, 2013, https://www.huffingtonpost.com/deborah-munn/it-was-never-about-the -ca_b_4414472.html.

10. Joint Appendix at 168, *Masterpiece Cakeshop, Ltd. v. Colorado Civil Rights Commission*, 138 S. Ct. 1719 (2018).

11. Michael Roberts, "Gay Couple Discriminated against by Shop That Refused to

Bake Their Wedding Cake, Judge Rules," *Westword*, December 6, 2013, https://www.westword.com/news/gay-couple-discriminated-against-by-shop-that-refused-to-bake-their-wedding-cake-judge-rules-5858535.

12. https://www.nbcnews.com/feature/nbc-out/meet-couple-behind-masterpiece-cakeshop-supreme-court-case-n826976.
13. Munn, "It Was Never about the Cake." See also https://www.nbcnews.com/feature/nbc-out/meet-couple-behind-masterpiece-cakeshop-supreme-court-case-n826976.
14. Munn, "How It Feels When Someone Refuses to Make Your Son a Wedding Cake," *Time,* October 27, 2017, http://time.com/4991839/masterpiece-cakeshop-supreme-court-gay-discrimination/.
15. https://www.westword.com/restaurants/masterpiece-cakeshop-yelp-removes-negative-comments-while-supporters-create-facebook-group-5746438.
16. Phillips, interview by Ryan T. Anderson.
17. David Mullins, Facebook post, July 19, 2012.
18. Munn, "It Was Never about the Cake."
19. Munn, "Is It Legal to Discriminate against My Gay Son?" *Newsweek,* July 5, 2017, http://www.newsweek.com/it-legal-discriminate-against-my-gay-son-632012.
20. "Meet the Gay Couple at the Center of the Masterpiece Cakeshop Case," *Washington Blade.*
21. https://www.westword.com/restaurants/masterpiece-cakeshop-yelp-removes-negative-comments-while-supporters-create-facebook-group-5746438.
22. Ibid.
23. Kelsey Whipple, "Masterpiece Cakeshop Refuses to Bake a Wedding Cake for Gay Couple," *Westword*, July 12, 2012, https://www.westword.com/restaurants/masterpiece-cakeshop-refuses-to-bake-a-wedding-cake-for-gay-couple-5727921.
24. Phillips, interview by Ryan T. Anderson.
25. Warren Richey, "For Those on Front Lines of Religious Liberty Battle, a Very Human Cost," *Christian Science Monitor*, July 16, 2016, https://www.csmonitor.com/USA/Justice/2016/0716/For-those-on-front-lines-of-religious-liberty-battle-a-very-human-cost.
26. Personal Interview with Jack Phillips, February 23, 2018.
27. Phillips, interview by Ryan T. Anderson.
28. Douglas Laycock, *Same-Sex Marriage and Religious Liberty: Emerging Conflicts*, edited by Douglas Laycock, Anthony R. Picarello, Jr., and Robin Fretwell Wilson (Lanham, MD: Rowman and Littlefield, 2008), 201.

Chapter 35

WINNER TAKE ALL

The burning summer heat faded. In early September, 2012, Charlie and David were in the final stages of planning for their wedding, which was just a few weeks away. Before jetting off to Massachusetts, however, with the help of the ACLU, they each filled out initial information on a one-page form. At the top, in large, bold letters, it read, "CHARGE OF DISCRIMINATION." They submitted it to the Colorado Civil Rights Commission. After talking with several LGBT rights organizations, the couple had learned that Colorado law forbade businesses like Jack's from refusing services to anyone based on "disability, race, creed, color, sex, sexual orientation, marital status, national origin, or ancestry."[1] There were no exemptions for people who had a sincere religious reason for not wanting to comply. All Charlie and David had to do was file a charge to enforce the law's protections.

Both Charlie's and David's forms provided identical information. And that information was accurate . . . with the exception of one key difference. After explaining how they got in the store, both David and Charlie wrote, "The Owner replied that his policy is to deny service to individuals of our sexual orientation based on his religious beliefs."[2] That was not Jack's position, nor was it what he had said. The parties would later agree on that point. But for the time being, the allegation lingered unchallenged. At the bottom of the forms, David and Charlie scrawled their signatures.

That sparked an investigation.

For the next six months, the Civil Rights Commission dug into the allegations. They asked for a response from Jack. They reviewed news reports. They considered affidavits filed by other LGBT couples for whom Jack would also not make wedding cakes.

During the same time, Charlie and David got married. They celebrated their marriage in Colorado with a rainbow-layered wedding cake provided for free. They continued to participate in news articles and advocacy. People from all over the globe, from every continent, offered them support.

Jack carried on with business as usual. The protests and the attempted boycotts had little effect on his bottom line, which actually increased as supporters from around the city stopped in to offer their backing.[3] Lawyers affiliated with the Alliance Defending Freedom, a Christian-based religious liberty law firm, helped him respond to the investigation. In his stronger moments, none of the attention or the legal proceedings fazed Jack. He couldn't change the will of God any more than an atheist could choose to believe in God just to save his job. If staying true to his faith meant he lost his shop, so be it.

On March 5, 2013, the investigator for the Colorado Civil Rights Commission made his determination. It was only the first step in the process. If he decided there was probable cause for Charlie and David's case to move forward, then it would finally have legs, and Jack would need to defend himself before various officers of the commission. If the investigator decided the claim lacked support, then it would stop dead in its tracks.

The investigator found there was probable cause to believe Jack had violated the statute. He, Charlie, and David were ordered "to attempt amicable resolution of these charges by compulsory mediation."[4]

The statute governing discrimination claims provides that once the director of the Civil Rights Commission is "satisfied that further efforts to settle the matter by conference, conciliation, and persuasion will be futile, he shall so report to the commission," which can then order the case to proceed.[5] That is exactly what happened with Jack, David, and Charlie.

Mediation didn't work. And how could it? This wasn't a case about money, where the parties could have met in the middle and gone their separate ways. One side or the other would have to yield a deeply held belief. Both sides believed the other was engaged in an egregious wrong. Both sides believed history favored them. Both felt mistreated, mischaracterized, and misunderstood. And both were confident they were fighting for a greater good beyond themselves.

As soon as mediation failed, the commission sent to Jack and his attorneys a written complaint, requiring him to respond to the charges at a formal hearing before an administrative law judge. The stage was set. One party was going to win, and one was going to lose. There would be no compromise.

Up to this point, Charlie and David could have walked away, as other couples had done before them. Despite the dignitary harm they suffered, it was a fleeting moment. They had received a cake within two days, they had gotten married, and they were moving on with their lives. They could have embraced the long-honored American tradition of live and let live.

But that philosophy has never characterized the debate between those on the religious right and those on the LGBT left.* Instead, each side has always sought only its own interests without compromise.[6] And both sides are guilty.

There is no question that this story began back when the religious right had all the power in the United States and saw no need for compromise. The laws during the early years of the country and into the

---

* In this section, I refer to the "LGBT left" and to the "religious right." To be clear, the LGBT left does not represent the entire LGBT community, and the religious right does not represent the entire religious community. They represent two specific groups with particular views about the law, which I explain in this section.

twentieth century punished those engaging in same-gender sexual activity with heavy fines, prison, and even corporal punishment. That is to say nothing of the abuse and bullying LGBT individuals faced just in the ordinary course of their lives, often without any protection or even sympathy from those on the religious right. This isn't astonishing. History teaches that it is rare for those in power—from either the right or the left—to protect those with whom they disagree. Few people in the world have ever shown such foresight or compassion. And even those who do often fail to do it consistently.

During the initial period of the United States, the pendulum of power fully and decidedly rested on the religious right's side. This meant that LGBT citizens had to live in secret, all the while scraping and clawing for every bit of legal protection and recognition they would ever receive. As they did, the pendulum began to break through rust and dust and swing in their direction.

But it was slow in coming. During the same rights revolution that expanded religious freedom protections prior to Al Smith's case, the Supreme Court similarly expanded constitutional protections for Americans' sexual activity. As each decade passed, the Supreme Court ruled more and more that the Constitution prevented government from intruding into people's bedrooms. At first, those protections extended only to married heterosexual couples, when the justices ruled that government couldn't ban the use of birth control.[7] It then later expanded that ruling to unmarried individuals.[8] As late as 1960, same-gender sexual activity was criminalized in all fifty states. In the decades since, many of those laws were repealed, but others remained on the books. In 1996, the justices determined that states could not adopt state constitutional amendments that prevented sexual orientation from being a protected class under discrimination laws.[9] Finally, in 2003, a majority of the justices ruled that the Constitution forbade states from criminalizing same-gender sexual activity.[10]

On the legal side, the pendulum was swinging to the center. But the legal shift was not alone. During this same period, public attitudes toward the LGBT community transformed. It was driven largely by big media, especially in entertainment. By the 1990s, news stories, sitcoms, talk shows, movies, novels, theater, and magazines began changing their portrayal of LGBT people; perhaps not exclusively, but enough to begin changing public perception.[11] It was sometimes subtle messaging. But for the first time in the entertainment the public consumed, LGBT citizens were being seen as normal people—humanized and complex.

Where the LGBT rights movement saw a continued progression and expansion of the very liberties that had made America a light to the world, folks on the religious right began to see a decline in the values that they believed had made the United States the most powerful country on earth. Not surprisingly, they fought it. They pushed for laws to incriminate intimacy between people of the same gender. They fought against treating sexual orientation as a protected status under the nation's anti-discrimination laws. They looked to ban LGBT citizens from serving in the military. In their own media, they railed against what they believed to be the slanted views of the more traditional outlets, which they saw as undervaluing and undermining the very family structure they felt was the backbone of the most successful society in history.

Then they perceived in the distance a far greater threat. As the pendulum of power swung toward the center and they lost battle after battle, the religious right saw that it would not stop there. Its momentum would eventually swing the balance of influence away from them. In time, they feared, the LGBT left wouldn't settle for equal treatment under the law; it would attempt instead to force itself upon dissenting people of faith. This wasn't an irrational fear. History has shown time and again that victims have no qualms with being oppressors once they control the levers of power.

The two places that worried the religious right the most were same-sex marriage and anti-discrimination laws. As to marriage, the religious right believed that if it were ever considered a constitutional right to have government recognize same-sex marriage, the next move from the LGBT left would be to force religious people to participate in and acknowledge those marriages or face stiff government penalties. Courts, for example, could force churches to perform same-sex marriages or face penalties[12] Religious institutions that refused or didn't acknowledge those marriages could lose their tax exemptions for doing so.[13] At one point, Donald B. Verrilli, Jr., solicitor general of the United States, admitted in open court before the justices that these would be issues the LGBT left would pursue in the future.[14] As to anti-discrimination laws, the religious right believed that if LGBT status ever rose into the lofty heights of other protected categories (such as race, religion, ethnicity, or gender), then the LGBT left could punish people who disagreed with it based on their religious teachings.

In the religious right's view, they needed to stop the pendulum before it was too late. They decided to force the issue. Beginning in the latter half of the 1990s, in states across the country, they rallied voters to place state constitutional bans on government recognition of same-sex marriage.[15] They also fought any state anti-discrimination laws that would include sexual orientation as a protected category. In their view, the strategy would rally voters and finally block any threat from the LGBT left.

It backfired. The religious right underestimated the power of media on behalf of LGBT equality. Although various ballot measures did pass in a number of states, every vote gave the movement for marriage equality far more attention than it was achieving on its own. It became the *cause célèbre* of the new century. Soon, in television, music, movies, online, and even in the news, many who opposed same-sex marriage were labeled bigots and hypocrites. Where many in the media had finally begun portraying LGBT citizens as the well-rounded, multi-dimensional, and sympathetic people they are, a similar number of outlets began portraying those from the religious right as flat caricatures: ignorant, hateful, judgmental, and closed-minded.[16]

By 2010, in many parts of the country, the LGBT left had gained the upper hand in both political power and media clout. The power pendulum hadn't even paused in the middle. It had swung firmly into their camp. The only question was what they would do with that power now that they had it. Of course, this wasn't universal. In traditionally red states, the religious right still had enough influence to protect their interests and to refuse to protect LGBT citizens. But in blue or purple states, many majorities favored placing LGBT interests over any contrary religious beliefs, even if that meant going beyond legal equality and forcing religious objectors to support events or practices with which they vehemently disagreed. In that respect, the earlier fears of the religious right were justified. In every state where the political and media power had swung into the LGBT-left camp, they mirrored the behavior of their counterparts on the religious right and refused to protect their interests.

Just as when Protestants split away from the Catholic Church in the 1500s to create a new, separate, and equally powerful religious group, so the LGBT rights movement had created a similar divide in the United States by early 2010. The country was equally divided. The Pew Research Forum showed that by that time, the nation was split down the middle on whether same-sex marriage should be recognized.[17] And it was a religious divide not between two traditional "religions," as we normally think of the term, but between two groups that had staked tents on either side of what was essentially a religious question: what types of sexual relationships are moral? One side followed the longtime religious tradition of sexual purity. The other followed a newer religious tradition of belief in sexual freedom. And just as with Protestants and Catholics during the European religious wars prior to the founding of the country, both sides were willing to use the power of government to protect themselves and no one else. The fight was no longer about mere equality. Neither the LGBT left nor the religious right wanted equality for the other, and that was evident by the differing laws passed in the various states—they reflected the interests of who had control, not of equality for all.

They faced off. Neither was willing to compromise. In red states, the religious right refused to pass any laws that would protect LGBT citizens from discrimination in areas like employment, housing, or hospital visitation rights. In blue states, the LGBT left refused to grant any religious exemptions to laws that protected their own interests. Both sides feared that if they gave even a little, they would risk losing everything. To be clear, there were plenty of religious and LGBT people willing to seek compromise, to embrace the time-honored American values of "justice and liberty for all" and "live and let live," but the fringes controlled the debate and the money and the policy positions. And they would not yield.

Five hundred years after the Protestant Reformation launched Europe into a series of bloody wars, humans were making the Protestant-Catholic mistake all over again. Whoever could gain control of the government had but one dogged focus: ensure the law protected only their views.

In that singular moment in history, with that winner-take-all refusal to compromise ruling the landscape, Charlie and David walked into Jack's shop. And in Colorado, the power of government was on their side. They could have chosen not to wield that power and thus destroy Jack's business. There were plenty of other bakeries. They had unfailing support. Like Joseph of old, they could have shown mercy to those over whom they now had power.

It's not surprising they didn't. Across the nation, the far right refused to acknowledge same-sex marriages or unions in any shape or form or to protect LGBT citizens. In that milieu, it would have been shocking if Charlie and David had shown the strength to back down. It's hard to yield a weapon when your perceived enemy is pointing one back at you.

NOTES

1. Colorado Rev. Stat. § 24-34-601.
2. Charges of Discrimination, on file with author.
3. Interview with Jack Phillips, February 23, 2018.
4. Joint appendix at 95, *Masterpiece Cakeshop, Ltd. v. Colorado Civil Rights Commission*, 138 S. Ct. 1719 (2018).

5. C.R.S. § 24-34-306(4).

6. Douglas Laycock, "Religious Liberty and the Culture Wars," *University of Illinois Law Review* 2014, no. 3 (2014): 839–80.

7. *Griswold v. Connecticut*, 381 U.S. 479 (1965).

8. *Eisenstadt v. Baird*, 405 U.S. 438 (1972).

9. *Romer v. Evans*, 517 U.S. 620 (1996).

10. *Lawrence v. Texas*, 539 U.S. 558 (2003).

11. See Tina Fetner, *How the Religious Right Shaped Lesbian and Gay Activism* (Minneapolis: University of Minnesota Press, 2008), 127.

12. Supreme Court Justice Antonin Scalia asked during *Obergefell v. Hodges,* "once [same-sex marriage is] . . . made a matter of constitutional law, . . . is it conceivable that a minister who is authorized by the State to conduct marriage can decline to marry two men if indeed this Court holds that they have a constitutional right to marry? Is it conceivable that that would be allowed?" See Transcript of Oral Arguments, *Obergefell v. Hodges*, 135 S. Ct. 2584 (2015) (No. 14-556) (No. 14-562) (No. 14-571) (No. 14-574), 2015 U.S. Trans. LEXIS 40, at *20.

13. Supreme Court Justice Samuel Alito, in reference to a case focused on a religious university, asked in *Obergefell:* "The Court held that a college was not entitled to tax-exempt status if it opposed interracial marriage or interracial dating. So would the same apply to a university or a college if it opposed same-sex marriage?" See ibid., at *34.

14. In response to Justice Alito's question referenced in note 14 above, General Verrilli responded, "It's certainly going to be an issue. . . . I don't deny that. . . . It's going to be an issue."

15. It is important to note that the debate over whether same-sex marriage should be "legal" is somewhat mislabeled. After 2003, the question wasn't whether same-sex marriage was legal or illegal. It was clearly allowed under the law. The question was whether government would recognize such marriages the same way it recognized heterosexual marriages. It was a question of equal treatment, not criminality.

16. Fetner, 127; for many examples of this and an in-depth study of it, see also John W. Cones, *Patters of Bias in Hollywood Movies* (New York: Algora Publishing 2012), 49–65. For just two examples, note the character of Angela Martin from the television series *The Office* on NBC or Jonathan Franzen's treatment of Christian characters in his critically acclaimed novel *Freedom: A Novel* (New York: Farrar, Straus and Giroux, 2010).

17. "Changing Attitudes on Gay Marriage: Public Opinion on Same-Sex Marriage," Pew Research Center, http://www.pewforum.org/fact-sheet/changing-attitudes-on-gay-marriage/.

Chapter 36

AN UNCLEAR PATH

Jack huddled with his lawyers. On May 31, 2013, a notice had arrived. The Colorado Civil Rights Commission had ordered that he appear before an administrative law judge on September 23, 2013, to determine whether he had violated Colorado's law. If he had, if his attorneys couldn't find a way to protect him, the commission held the power to hound him, fine him, even close his business.

He had just four months to build his case.

The good news for Jack was that by the time the hearing date arrived, the parties didn't really dispute the facts. They largely agreed on what had happened that day more than a year before. Jack didn't hide from his decision. He had declined to bake the cake because he believed his religion required it of him. It was that simple. And everyone agreed he wouldn't hesitate to serve Charlie and David any other product in nearly any other setting.

When the date of the hearing arrived, the judge decided to change things up. The parties concurred. Instead of holding a full-blown trial to resolve disputed accusations, the judge would simply rule based on how the law should apply to the agreed-upon facts. He would give the parties a bit more time, until December 4, 2013, to craft their arguments and submit them in written form. The real issue was whether the Constitution or other laws gave Jack a defense against Colorado's Anti-Discrimination law.

Jack's lawyers set to work.

Charlie and David's did as well.

From the beginning, though, Jack's team faced a major, glaring obstacle. It was something Charlie and David could use as a powerful
weapon: Justice Scalia's opinion in Al Smith's case. In many respects, it
would drive everything that was about to happen. Somewhere from the
annals of time, Al's voice, saying "You're next," echoed with resounding
vibrancy.

After Justice Scalia shocked the nation with his opinion in *Smith*,
people all over the country panicked. No matter what Scalia had been
thinking in his chambers when he wrote it, the conclusion from everyone else was clear: the Constitution no longer protected the free exercise of religion, or at least it did in only the most superficial way.[1]
That begged the question: What should be done next? If the First
Amendment didn't protect religious freedom, that meant protection
would come only from legislatures and Congress. If they were gracious
enough to protect someone's religious practice when passing a law that
was neutral and generally applicable, wonderful. But if they weren't,
the burdened religious group had almost no recourse.

In a remarkable display of unanimity, groups who are often opposed to each other on nearly every issue joined together. Scalia
had, in essence, attacked not just the Native American Church or
Al Smith; he had threatened every religious group in the country.
Conservative Christian groups such as the Christian Legal Society
and Pat Robertson's American Center for Law and Justice joined
with the ACLU and Americans United for Separation of Church and
State; Republicans held hands with Democrats; the American Jewish
Congress stood alongside the National Association of Evangelicals. If
everyday people had woken up to find cats and dogs living together,
they wouldn't have been more surprised. It was a mix of some of the
strangest bedfellows anyone had ever seen and one of the broadest,
most unified coalitions to ever work together. For a peculiar, surreal

moment in time, Scalia had united the nation in a way he would never do again. He gave everyone a common enemy.

Together, with the help of some of the nation's leading religious-freedom scholars, the coalition drafted a statute known as the Religious Freedom Restoration Act. It would quickly become known by its acronym RFRA (pronounced RiffRah). As its name suggests, it was meant to restore the religious freedom the Supreme Court had stripped away. Everyone agreed on that point. It would be a superstatute, one that trumped all other statutes, laws, or regulations, whether they were passed by the federal government, a state, or even a city. Essentially, it would order judges to apply the compelling interest test any time government placed a substantial burden on anyone's "exercise of religion even if the burden results from a rule of general applicability."[2]

In its opening lines, RFRA lambasted the Supreme Court. It began, "The Congress finds that—

(1) the framers of the Constitution, recognizing free exercise of religion as an unalienable right, secured its protection in the First Amendment to the Constitution;

(2) laws "neutral" toward religion may burden religious exercise as surely as laws intended to interfere with religious exercise;

(3) governments should not substantially burden religious exercise without compelling justification;

(4) in *Employment Division v. Smith*, 494 U.S. 872 (1990) the Supreme Court virtually eliminated the requirement that the government justify burdens on religious exercise imposed by laws neutral toward religion; and

(5) the compelling interest test as set forth in prior Federal court rulings is a workable test for striking sensible balances between religious liberty and competing prior governmental interests.[3]

And the statute applied to everything, including any laws or regulations passed before RFRA. It was sweeping. It was monumental. It ensured government couldn't overstep its bounds and burden people's religious exercise without a compelling justification and, even then, it had to use the narrowest means available.

After some wrangling over abortion rights, RFRA passed the House of Representatives on May 11, 1993, with a unanimous vote. The Senate approved it 97–3. President Bill Clinton happily signed it into law in November that same year. In the ceremony, with Vice President Al Gore smiling behind him, President Clinton said, "The power to reverse legislation by legislation, [as well as] a decision of the United States Supreme Court, is a power that is rightly hesitantly and infrequently exercised by the United States Congress. But this is an issue in which that extraordinary measure was clearly called for."[4]

If everything had stopped there, the law for cases like this would have been easy to understand. Colorado would have tried to enforce its anti-discrimination statute, Jack would have held up RFRA as a shield, and courts would have applied the statute's compelling interest test. That wasn't a guarantee that Jack would have won the case, but at least the test would have been straightforward.

Life is never that simple.

When Jack and his lawyers evaluated their options for defending the charge of discrimination, they didn't find a well-marked and obvious path across the legal landscape. They faced a bog.

From the beginning, there was one obvious problem with RFRA. It was a statute, not a constitutional provision. If enough people changed their minds about religious freedom, Congress could always repeal it. And unlike a constitutional provision, which (at least in theory) remains as a fixed check on government power (subject only to decisions of the Supreme Court), a statute still left religious freedom to the whims of majority rule. There was also the possibility of the Supreme Court striking RFRA down if it believed the law surpassed Congress's authority. At the time of RFRA's passing, with nearly unanimous support from everyone in the country, it was hard to believe either outcome was possible.

It turns out they both were.

First, just four years after Clinton signed the bill in his grandiose press conference on the White House lawn, the Supreme Court struck down RFRA as it applied to any state or lower level laws. In a case titled *City of Boerne v. Flores*,[5] the court ruled that the federal Congress didn't have the authority to pass such a statute against the states using the rationale it did. It could only pass it against the federal government. No one who drafted RFRA saw this coming. Congress had passed all sorts of laws just like RFRA, but this particular statute clearly took a jab at the Supreme Court, which was still in the beginning stages of the counterrevolution that would pull back on federal rights and give more power back to the states to regulate as they saw fit. The same mentality that led to the *Smith* decision pushed this result as well.

Second, when the original drafters of RFRA tried to pass a bill that would get around the *City of Boerne* decision, they found that members of the coalition that had passed RFRA were now at complete odds with one another. From 1993 to 1998, something had changed. In just five years, support for religious freedom had devolved from unanimous to fractured. All of the groups on the left had abandoned the statute. Without their support, the new bill floundered and died in committee hearings.

What happened was simple. During the 1990s, as the LGBT left gained momentum, it dawned on its leaders that people from certain religious groups who believed same-sex intimacy was sinful could potentially use RFRA as a legal protection for decisions to deny services, housing, or other benefits to same-sex couples. They wanted any new religious freedom statute to say explicitly that it wouldn't apply if LGBT rights were involved. The religious right couldn't agree to that. The coalition collapsed.

Going forward, RFRA would apply only to federal law.

Because the Colorado Anti-Discrimination Act was a state statute, Jack could not invoke RFRA as a defense against it. He and his team needed to look for other options.

Other laws to protect religious freedom did pass Congress, but they applied only in very limited circumstances. To solve the very specific result in *Smith*, Congress passed a law that ensured peyote could be used by Native American tribes for religious purposes.[6] It applied to federal and state law. So despite the ruling in Al's case, peyotism had thrived. Other laws protected religious exercise in the context of prisons or land-use cases. None of them applied to Jack's case.

His lawyers needed to find other defenses. One option, potentially, was state law. After RFRA's collapse at the federal level, a number of states tried to pass similar statutes to correct what the Supreme Court had done in *Smith*. The LGBT left fought them vigorously, for the same reasons they had opposed the new federal statute. Over time, those fights became more and more cantankerous. Some states passed the laws. Others failed. All of the groups on the left that had supported the federal RFRA began labeling the state bills (which were identical to the federal one they had supported) as anti-LGBT statutes. News outlets picked up that theme, mostly out of ignorance. Up to the time David and Charlie walked into Jack's shop and even in the years after, any time a state tried to pass a Religious Freedom Restoration Act, traditional news outlets labeled the laws as antigay or placed the phrase *religious freedom* in scare quotes. Just as in Al Smith's case, the practice again suggested that the statutes were not truly for religious freedom or that the religious beliefs they might protect were not valid. Apparently, it never occurred to any of these reporters that the history behind the RFRAs might be far more complex than they were reporting.

The end result was that only some states had robust protections for religious freedom.

Colorado was not one of them.

If Jack was going to find a defense to battle Charlie and David's charge of discrimination, he would need to find it in the text of the First Amendment. With Scalia's gutting of the Free Exercise Clause, that was no simple task.

As Jack trusted his fate to his God,[7] not far away, his lawyers labored to find arguments on his behalf. There was one blessing in all of their efforts. It was Jack's consistency. His religious objection had never deviated. And in that position, his lawyers found their strongest arguments. They were based in the Religion Clauses, the Free Speech Clause, and even in the Colorado Anti-Discrimination Act itself. The outline of the argument they discovered was fairly straightforward:

> 1. Colorado's statute forbade refusing service "because of" sexual orientation. Jack had not refused Charlie and David "because of" their orientation. He would gladly serve them anything, as long as he didn't have to promote a particular event that violated his religious beliefs;
> 2. Colorado could not constitutionally force Jack to engage in speech with which he disagreed; and
> 3. Colorado could not constitutionally burden Jack's religious exercise by forcing him to violate his religious beliefs.

The first two arguments were relatively simple. The third reflected the jumbled mess Scalia had created with the *Smith* decision.

He had held that if a law was neutral and generally applicable, then it didn't matter under the Constitution if it burdened someone's religion, even if that burden crushed someone's central religious practice. The problem was that no one knew what the terms "neutral" and "generally applicable" actually meant. That's not surprising, since Scalia never defined them.

Once the Supreme Court issues a decision, lower court judges must then apply it as best they can in future cases. As the years passed after *Smith*, every time a case arose for which there was no RFRA protection, judges were forced to apply Scalia's new Free Exercise Clause test. They danced all over the map trying to give it meaning. Some judges blended the two terms together, essentially concluding that "neutral" and "generally applicable" were the same thing. The Supreme Court actually applied the test once and suggested the terms were separate. That is to say, a law had to be both "neutral" *and* "generally applicable" to pass the constitutional test. A law was *neutral* if it didn't target a particular religious group. It was generally applicable if it applied to everyone.

Jack's lawyers blended neutrality and general applicability, likely unintentionally. It was a mistake many judges and lawyers often made. Nevertheless, it appeared to them that the statute didn't apply to everyone. Colorado's law had various exemptions for religious entities, as well as all-male and all-female golf clubs and schools. Government could not, Jack's lawyers argued, exempt secular entities from the requirements of the law and refuse to give religious exemptions. Giving the religious exemptions made the law neither neutral nor generally applicable.[8]

With those arguments, Jack's fate rested in the administrative-law judge's hands.

———————

As Jack's lawyers hunched over their computers finalizing their arguments, Charlie and David's attorneys from the ACLU were doing the same. Their arguments were essentially mirror images of Jack's.

First, they wrote, Jack's distinction between refusing to participate in an event and discriminating "because of" sexual orientation fell flat because the wedding was inextricably tied to Charlie and David's orientation. The two could not be separated.

Second, they contended that Colorado law was neutral and generally applicable not by arguing that it applied to everyone but by contending the secular exemptions didn't undermine the purpose of the law. The exemptions for all-boy or all-girl schools and golf clubs actually expanded access to certain places for minorities, whereas an exemption for Jack would undermine the purposes of the statute. They also argued the law did not target any religions.

Finally, as to Jack's speech arguments, their response could be summed up simply: baking a cake is not speech, even if Jack feels like it is, so the Free Speech Clause doesn't apply.[9]

In the fall of 2013, both sides fired off multiple briefs. More than a year after the incident in Jack's shop, the briefs soared past each other through the ether and into the lap of the administrative law judge. Charlie and David had just celebrated their first anniversary. Jack toiled in anonymity, wondering if the state of Colorado would still shut down the business he had run for so long.

Notes

1. See Garrett Epps, *To an Unknown God: Religious Freedom on Trial* (New York: St. Martin's Press, 2001), 228–29.
2. 42 U.S.C. § 2000bb-1(a).
3. 42 U.S.C. § 2000bb.
4. Bill Clinton "Remarks on Signing the Religious Freedom Restoration Act of 1993," November 16, 1993, Government Publishing Office, https://www.gpo.gov/fdsys/pkg/WCPD-1993-11-22/pdf/WCPD-1993-11-22-Pg2377.pdf.
5. *City of Boerne v. Flores*, 521 U.S. 507 (1997).
6. American Indian Religious Freedom Act, Public Law No. 95-341, 92 Stat. 469 (Aug. 11, 1978) (commonly abbreviated to AIRFA), codified at 42 U.S.C. § 1996. The amendments to correct what happened in *Smith* are Public Law No 103-344.
7. Jack Phillips, in discussion with author, November 8, 2017.
8. Brief in Opposition to Complainant's Motion for Summary Judgment and in Support of Jack Philipps's Cross Motion for Summary Judgment at 40-42, *Charlie Craig and David Mullins v. Masterpiece Cakeshop, Inc.*, no. CR 2013-008 (Colorado Civil Rights Commission May 30, 2014).
9. Complainants' Response in Opposition to Respondents' Cross-Motion for Summary Judgment and Reply Brief in Support of Complainants' Motion for Summary Judgment at 13-28, *Charlie Craig and David Mullins v. Masterpiece Cakeshop, Inc.*, no. CR 2013-008 (Colorado Civil Rights Commission May 30, 2014).

Chapter 37

DESPICABLE

I t was Christmastime, December 4, 2013. In just two days, thousands of parents and children would stream into downtown to watch shining and glittering floats glide through the city's high-rises as part of Denver's Parade of Lights. In a nondescript office building across the street from Colorado's gold-domed capitol, administrative law judge Robert Spencer listened to arguments from lawyers on both sides. On its surface, the case seemed so small that the army of lawyers in the room looked almost comical. Six had come in support of David and Charlie, some local, some from the ACLU, and one from the state attorney general's office. Three stood in the room for Jack, all affiliated with the Alliance Defending Freedom.

Spencer seemed to consider all the arguments.

But just two days later, he issued a thirteen-page, single-spaced order.

Spencer rejected Jack's argument regarding the statute's "because of" language. "The salient feature distinguishing same-sex weddings from heterosexual ones is the sexual orientation of the participants," Spencer wrote. "Only same-sex couples engage in same-sex weddings. Therefore, it makes little sense to argue that refusal to provide a cake to a same-sex couple for use at their wedding is not 'because of' their sexual orientation."[1]

Because Spencer had determined that Jack had violated the state law, the real question was whether the statute, as applied to Jack, violated his free-speech or free-exercise rights. In other words, would the principles of free speech and religious freedom protect Jack from Colorado's law?

As to free speech, Spencer agreed that "government may not compel an individual to communicate by word or deed an unwanted message or expression."[2] This was a long-standing principle of free speech, as was the notion that conduct can be a form of speech. He even acknowledged that "decorating a wedding cake involves considerable skill and artistry." But, he concluded, "the finished product does not necessarily qualify as 'speech.'" His reasoning wasn't based in the notion that food couldn't be speech. He found his hook in a key fact in the case. "The undisputed evidence is that Phillips categorically refused to prepare a cake for Complainants' same-sex wedding before there was any discussion about what the cake would look like."[3] In Spencer's view, this decided the speech issue. Since Jack didn't know precisely what speech he'd be asked to engage in with the cake when he turned it down, the cake was therefore not speech.

To Jack, that reasoning was hollow. Whether it was for Halloween, a bachelor party, a celebration of the occult, adult-themed parties, anti-American cakes, or even an anti-LGBT event, any custom cake was requiring him to use his artistic talents to promote something with which he disagreed. He didn't need to discuss the details of it to know that was true. At the same time, there was never any real dispute that Charlie and David wanted a custom cake with an artistic design. Charlie had held in his hand a binder with ideas.

Spencer wasn't finished. Even if the cake was speech, he concluded, Jack wouldn't win. The forced speech was simply an incidental impact on the state's legitimate regulation of discriminatory conduct. In his view, requiring Jack to use his artistic skill to create a cake for an event with which he disagreed was not the same as forcing someone to display a motto with which they disagreed.[4] He provided little reasoning as to why, other than to suggest that Jack's refusal was more like "objectionable conduct" than it was speech.[5]

Finally, Spencer turned to Jack's religion defenses. Jack's lawyers had argued that both the Colorado state constitution and the First Amendment of the federal Constitution protected him. Spencer didn't really address the state Constitution. As for the test under the Free Exercise Clause, he used Al's case to rule against Jack. Colorado's law, Spencer ruled, was neutral and generally applicable. Under the *Smith* decision, it didn't matter that it was burdening Jack's religious exercise. He concluded that the one exemption for same-gender schools and golf clubs didn't change whether the law was generally applicable.

He then ordered that Jack must:

> (1) Cease and desist from discriminating against Complainants and other same-sex couples by refusing to sell them wedding cakes or any other product Respondents would provide to heterosexual couples; and
>
> (2) Take such other corrective action as is deemed appropriate by the Commission, and make such reports of compliance to the Commission as the Commission shall require.[6]

The first order was enough to ruin Jack's business. He couldn't change his religious convictions and his understanding of what God wanted him to do just because a judge ordered him to do so. He would have no choice but to shut down, at least that part of his business.

As for the second part of the order, Jack could only wonder what other punishments the commission would fire at him.

Charlie and David were ecstatic. In their view, they had won a battle not just for themselves but for anyone who might be turned away from a business. They hoped that no one would have to face a similar rejection in the future.

News outlets picked up the story immediately. Some praised the decision as a ruling against discrimination. Others blasted it as a decision against religious freedom.

A lawyer for the ACLU commented that no one was asking Jack to change his religious beliefs,[7] but in Jack's view, that's precisely what they were doing. In repeated interviews, he emphasized that he simply couldn't sacrifice his religious beliefs for money, safety, or security. If the state forced him to, he would go to prison or shut down his shop before he would violate what he believed was a command from God.

Historically, he was now in the same position as so many who had come before him. He could have his unpopular religious beliefs, or he could have his profession, but he couldn't have both.

A month later, Jack filed an appeal to the Colorado Civil Rights Commission. He submitted a brief in support in April 2014. Several weeks later, Charlie and David filed their brief in response. The Colorado Attorney General's office filed its own brief supporting David and Charlie as well.

On May 30, 2014, everyone from both sides marched up the granite steps of Colorado's grand capitol. Above them, the gilded golden dome reflected a partially cloudy sky. It was cool that day, with a slight breeze. On the steps of the capitol, markers indicated the precise point when someone reached one mile above sea level.

Jack and Charlie and David eventually found themselves traversing marble-tiled hallways until they entered a chamber far grander than anyone might have expected given the dispute's modest beginnings. It was the state of Colorado's old supreme court chambers. Those justices now held court in a different building. This room was used for a variety of other purposes. It was stunning. A grand chandelier hung from the thirty-foot-high decorative ceiling, illuminating the podium where advocates made their cases to the court. The walls were made of red panels and artfully painted columns. It seemed that every doorway, piece of glass, spot of wood, and window had received an artist's touch. In the galley, hundreds of chairs faced the bench so onlookers could watch what transpired.

At the front, the justices' bench loomed large, spanning much of the room, with thirteen high-backed, black chairs behind it.

Jack took his seat.

Charlie and David did the same.

Reporters, lawyers, and supporters filled in the empty chairs. News cameras staked positions to capture Jack and his well-wishers on one side of the room, Charlie, David, and their base on the other.

In time, the commissioners entered. There were seven of them, five women and two men. Their job was to conduct hearings regarding discriminatory practices and, as in this case, to hear appeals from lower government officials. The administrative law judge who had ruled against Jack worked at their direction. They were to determine if he had handled the case properly. Under Colorado law, the commission was supposed to be a balanced group reflective of all the citizens in Colorado.

As soon as they began their deliberations, it was clear that there wasn't a single person on the commission representing Jack's point of view. The statements were quick. The debate short. They all agreed with each other or were silent. The statements also showed a relative lack of understanding of the law, which was not surprising. Traditionally, almost none of the commissioners are lawyers, which means they base their decisions off personal feelings and gut reactions, not legal principles.

When it was over, they affirmed that Jack must comply with Spencer's order. He had to sell cakes for same-sex weddings or give up his business. And they fired off a ruling of their own. It demanded that Jack:

(1) Provide comprehensive training to his staff regarding the Public Accommodations laws of the Colorado Anti-Discrimination Act and change all company policies to come into compliance with the law;

(2) Provide quarterly compliance reports to the government for the next two years; and

(3) Ensure those compliance reports document the number of patrons to whom Jack ever denied service and why.[8]

Once the order was issued, Jack retreated to his home and shop. His lawyers regrouped, grim-faced. How would they save Jack's business? Would Jack have the stomach to appeal? At that moment, they faced nothing but questions.

———

Charlie and David rejoiced. Sitting in those grand chambers, which were indicative of justice and the rule of law, they listened to the commissioners' discussion. David wore a gray shirt and dark tie and watched with interest through half-rimmed glasses. Charlie wore a tan suit with a plaid purple tie against a blue shirt.

As one commissioner commented after another, each against Jack's position, Charlie and David felt a tremendous sense of validation.[9] Their fight had been worth it. It had been a lengthy journey. But at least in Colorado, they believed they had saved others from the harm they had experienced.

———

On June 2, 2014, Jack closed his ovens to wedding cakes. That part of his business represented 40 percent of his income, more than $125,000 per year.[10] But he couldn't do it. His religious beliefs were more than just a simple choice government could force out of him. They were a key part of his core identity, a view of himself and the universe that transcended government regulations and others' religious claims. He couldn't change them, even for money.

Those on the LGBT left argued that it was the price for wanting to do business in a civil society. You could have your beliefs, but not if you wanted to operate a business according to them. To Jack, the government was trying to force upon him its own beliefs regarding the definition and morality of same-sex relationships. He didn't want to violate the law, so his only option was to close that part of his business, pray, and hope the legal system would protect him.

He could also appeal. Fifteen people worked for him in the shop, and if he could keep it operating for them, he would. An appeal would not only allow him to stand for his religious-freedom rights; it would also allow him to request a stay from the commissioners while the case worked its way through the Colorado Court of Appeals.

Roughly a month and a half after the commission issued its final order, Jack's lawyers notified the court of appeals that the appeal was on its way. They also asked the commission to stay its order so Jack could keep operating his shop and keep people employed while the case wound its way through the courts.

On July 25, 2014, a little more than two years after Charlie and David set foot in Jack's bakery, the commissioners met again in the cavernous and ornate chambers in the Colorado capitol. Their purpose: to deliberate Jack's request for a stay.

The room was largely empty. The only person in the audience was one of Jack's attorneys, who was not allowed to speak but wanted to observe.

When the commissioners began their conversation, once again, not a single one advocated or even understood Jack's point of view.

One commissioner said, "In regard to [Jack's] argument, endless argument, . . . it holds no water, as far as I'm concerned, whatsoever. . . . You cannot separate . . . their sexual orientation from the action of wanting to celebrate the marriage."[11]

Others agreed. One other commissioner confirmed that the case was about nothing more than "a gay couple that wanted a cake to celebrate a life event in their life."[12] She said nothing of Jack's side of the case or even acknowledged his arguments.

The meeting culminated with one of the commissioners, Diann Rice, bringing home her point of view:

> I would also like to reiterate what we said in . . . the last meeting: Freedom of religion and religion has been used to justify all kinds of discrimination throughout history, whether it be slavery, whether it be the Holocaust . . . I mean, we can list

hundreds of situations where freedom of religion has been used to justify discrimination. And to me it is one of the most despicable pieces of rhetoric that people can use—to use their religion to hurt others.[13]

No one denounced the statement. With unanimity, they denied Jack's motion for a stay. If he went out of business, so be it. It was, in their view, his choice.

Sometime later, when Jack heard he had been compared to Nazis and slaveholders, he didn't have the words to express his feelings. They choked in his throat. He thought of his own father, who had fought in World War II. Looking back over seventy years, Jack pictured his father storming Omaha Beach in Normandy and then battling his way across France and Germany. The stories his father shared with him of marching upon and liberating Buchenwald Concentration Camp, where it is estimated that somewhere between fifty thousand and sixty thousand people were murdered, echoed in his mind. His father had recounted the stench of decaying bodies, the fleshless skeletons he and other Americans had found clinging to life.

Before his death, he had given Jack a book about World War II that described the Nazi atrocities and how they were far worse than the Nazis had ever admitted. In it, his father had handwritten, "This is true."

As Jack looked upon those words and thought of the commissioner's comments, he wept.[14]

NOTES

1. Initial Decision Granting Complainant's Motion for Summary Judgment and Denying Respondent's Motion for Summary Judgment at 5, *Charlie Craig and David Mullins v. Masterpiece Cakeshop, Inc.*, no. CR 2013-008 (Colorado Civil Rights Commission May 30, 2014).
2. Ibid., at 7.
3. Ibid.
4. Ibid.
5. Ibid., at 8.
6. Ibid., at 13.

7. Associated Press, "Judge Orders Colo. Cake-Maker to Serve Gay Couples," December 6, 2013, https://www.denverpost.com/2013/12/06/judge-orders-colo-cake -maker-to-serve-gay-couples/.

8. Final Agency Order at 2, *Charlie Craig and David Mullins v. Masterpiece Cakeshop, Inc.*, no. CR 2013-008 (Colorado Civil Rights Commission May 30, 2014).

9. Charlie Craig, interview on Denver 7 television broadcast, May 30, 2014.

10. Jack Phillips, in discussion with author, February 23, 2018.

11. Transcript, Colorado Civil Rights Commission Meeting, July 25, 2014, 9, http:// www.adfmedia.org/files/MasterpieceHearingTranscript.pdf.

12. Ibid., 11.

13. Ibid., 11–12.

14. Jack Phillips, in discussion with author, February 23, 2018.

Chapter 38

JUSTICE FOR ALL?

Charlie and David celebrated their second anniversary. For them, life marched on. They continued in their jobs, agreed to interviews when appropriate, and unintentionally became the face of the nationwide LGBT movement. It wasn't something they were seeking. All they had wanted was cake. Now they were seen as LGBT-left activists. Still, they held to the belief that what they were doing was right. It wasn't just for them; it was for everyone who had ever been bullied, turned away, or dismissed by society.

A month later, Jack filed his brief in the Colorado Court of Appeals. For him, life had been a grind. As his employees had departed, he hadn't been able to replace them. The loss of his wedding cake business was just too much. His workers plummeted from fifteen to six. He stayed afloat, mostly from donations and visits by supporters, but times were lean. And troubling. Many times, Jack arrived at his shop to find bags of trash thrown in front of his door. One time, as he stepped to open the shop, a mound of human feces lay on the sidewalk in front of the shop. Often, passersby would spit on his door, leaving it to run down the glass.[1]

His brief reiterated and refined the arguments he had made to the commission. The threats and abuse went unspoken to the courts.

Charlie and David filed their response. By spring, the briefing was complete.

The judges scheduled oral argument for July.

Before then, two events that had been rumbling for some time finally burst forth from the legal landscape. One was across the country. The other was close to home.

On June 26, 2015, Justice Anthony Kennedy of the United States Supreme Court issued an opinion in a case known as *Obergefell v. Hodges*. Its holding: government's refusal to recognize same-sex marriages in the same way it did heterosexual marriages violated the right to liberty the Constitution guaranteed, as well as the Equal Protection Clause. Essentially, Justice Anthony M. Kennedy wrote for a majority of the Supreme Court, if a government was going to recognize marriage, it must treat all couples the same, regardless of orientation.[2]

The opinion itself didn't have any direct bearing on Jack, Charlie, and David's case. To the extent views of marriage were moral, even religious, government couldn't favor one side over another. It represented the swinging of the power pendulum into the middle; yet even then, Justice Kennedy seemed to not want it to swing too far. He went out of his way to refer to people who believed in the traditional definition of marriage as "reasonable and sincere people here and throughout the world" whose beliefs were made in "good faith."[3]

After explaining that there were no practical reasons for government's refusal to recognize same-sex marriage, Justice Kennedy continued, "Many who deem same-sex marriage to be wrong reach that conclusion based on decent and honorable religious or philosophical premises, and neither they nor their beliefs are disparaged here."[4] He then explained that as valid as those beliefs were, government could not constitutionally favor them above other views of marriage without depriving liberty from the second group.

Across the nation, LGBT-rights advocates raised a hearty, collective cheer. They felt as if they were finally experiencing the United States' promise of justice for all. As they did, a large number of people on the religious right shuddered.

As he neared the end of his opinion, Justice Kennedy raised one

final time the fears of religious people. Their concern, expressed countless times in the years before, was that once same-sex marriage was considered a constitutional right, the LGBT left would force churches and
religious people to accept it, even perform or participate in such weddings. That dread, perhaps more than any other concern, was the driving force behind their opposition. Possibly to allay it, Justice Kennedy
explained,

> Finally, it must be emphasized that religions, and those who
> adhere to religious doctrines, may continue to advocate with ut-
> most, sincere conviction that, by divine precepts, same-sex mar-
> riage should not be condoned. The First Amendment ensures that
> religious organizations and persons are given proper protection
> as they seek to teach the principles that are so fulfilling and so
> central to their lives and faiths, and to their own deep aspirations
> to continue the family structure they have long revered. The same
> is true of those who oppose same-sex marriage for other reasons.
> In turn, those who believe allowing same-sex marriage is proper
> or indeed essential, whether as a matter of religious conviction or
> secular belief, may engage those who disagree with their view in
> an open and searching debate.[5]

How these precepts would play out in the case between Masterpiece
Cakeshop and David and Charlie was a complete mystery. For a brief
moment in time, David and Charlie enjoyed the hope and confidence
that springs from equal protection under the law.

Jack looked on with trepidation.

———

That same summer, the Colorado Civil Rights Commission was
processing complaints against a different set of bakers.

A Christian educator named Bill Jack had entered three different
bakeries in the Denver area. At each one, he had requested two sheet
cakes. They each would be in the shape of an open Bible and would
contain Bible verses. On one, he asked for an image of two groomsmen

holding hands with a red "X" over the image. He also asked that three Bible verses and one common saying be spelled out on the cakes:

"God Hates Sin—Psalm 45:7"; "Homosexuality is a detestable sin—Leviticus 18:22"; "While we were yet sinners Christ died for us—Romans 5:8"; and "God loves sinners."

It's hard to know precisely what Bill meant by the messages. Certainly they shared the view that same-sex sexual activity was a sin in his religious tradition, but they also seemed to express the idea that all people were sinners and God loved everyone, including LGBT citizens.

But whatever his intent, all three bakers refused to make the cakes. They explained to Bill that they were happy to sell him any other products for any other occasion, but they could not bake these cakes because they found the messages offensive.

Bill left each shop and eventually filed complaints with the Colorado Civil Rights Commission. The same statute that forbade Jack from discriminating based on sexual orientation also prohibited denials of service based on religion or creed. The bakers pushed the same argument Jack had made. They claimed they weren't discriminating against Bill "because of" his religious creed but because they believed the cakes symbolized derogatory and offensive messages and imagery that they didn't want to promote.[6]

During the same time Jack's appeal was being briefed, the Civil Rights Commission probed the claims in Bill's case. The investigator determined there was no discrimination under Colorado law. The denial of service, she concluded, was not "because of" Bill's creed. It was because the bakers didn't want to bake cakes that conveyed messages with which they disagreed. In all three cases, the investigator found there could not have been discrimination because the bakers were willing to serve Bill in any other setting, as long as the message the goods conveyed didn't violate their beliefs. In all three cases, she determined the offensive messages would be deemed as having come from the cake maker, not the customer.[7]

The decisions fell like a bomb into the middle of the *Masterpiece* case. People on Jack's side spread out across the internet and immediately pointed out what they felt was a double standard. Jack's lawyers submitted the decisions to the court of appeals.

Charlie and David's lawyers scrambled. They did their best in the media to distinguish why the other bakers were different from Jack. Their primary position was that what Bill Jack had requested was offensive and was filled with obscenities. They announced as vociferously as they could that the two cases were entirely different.[8]

Whether anyone believed them was an open question. In reality, the opinions of only three people mattered. Despite all the rants in the media and commenters taking aggressive positions on social media and other websites, all that counted was what the judges on the Colorado Court of Appeals thought.

Bill appealed the investigator's decision to the Colorado Civil Rights Commission, the same seven people who had ruled against Jack.

On June 30, 2015, roughly one week before oral argument in *Masterpiece*, the commissioners denied Bill's appeal. The bakers had not discriminated against him, they ruled. They provided no reasoning. They merely adopted the investigator's report in full.

All of these facts bubbled up to the judges at the court of appeals in Denver. A week later, for the first time, an actual court of law would consider the case.

Notes

1. Jack Phillips, in discussion with author, February 28, 2018.
2. *Obergefell v. Hodges*, 135 S. Ct. 2584 (2015).
3. Ibid., at 2594.
4. Ibid., at 2602.
5. Ibid., at 2607.
6. Joint Appendix at 227–58, *Masterpiece Cakeshop, Ltd. v. Colorado Civil Rights Commission*, 138 S. Ct. 1719 (2018).
7. Ibid.
8. Nathan Woodliff-Stanley, "A Tale of Two Cakes: The Real Truth about Colorado's Cake Wars," Colorado Rights Blog, https://aclu-co.org/blog/a-tale-of-two-cakes-the-real-truth-about-colorados-cake-wars/.

Chapter 39

DEAFENING SILENCE

On the morning of July 7, 2015, Charlie and David bounded up the steps of the Ralph L. Carr Colorado Judicial Center. Both looked confident. It was a pleasant day. David, wearing a gray suit, was in the lead. Both men waved at camera crews and smiled.

Jack followed. In a blue suit with a sky-colored shirt, he walked with a serene look on his face. His lawyers strode beside him, a determined look in their eyes.

As all parties filed into the courthouse and through security, it is likely the judicial center drew a moment of admiration. A grand glass dome above them poured natural light on the expansive lobby. The lower floors were filled with administrative offices, a stunning legal library, an interactive area where lay people could learn about law and government, and several art displays showcasing key historical events in Colorado.

All throughout the building—on rails, in the carpet, etched into redwood, even in a beautiful mosaic of tiles in the main lobby—the Colorado state flower, the columbine, invoked images of mountain meadows and open prairies. The courtroom itself was surprisingly small, but it had a beauty all its own. It was high tech. Cameras allowed people to watch the arguments from computers all over the country. The bench was ornate but simple. Three black leather chairs were behind it, flanked by the United States and Colorado flags, which framed the state seal.

So many cases came and went through the court without fanfare, often with no one in attendance other than the lawyers and the judges. On that day in July, however, reporters had arrived early to stake their positions. Supporters for both sides filled the benches. Extra chairs allowed some visitors to sit along the walls in front of the rows of books that adorned the built-in shelves.

Facing the bench, Jack and his family sat on the right side. Charlie and David, with their legal team, sat on the left. More and more people crammed in. A hush fell over the room. Finally, the marshal rapped the gavel. Once. Twice. "All rise," he said.

As the judges filtered in from behind a white marble wall veined with gray, everyone in the room arose. The marshal continued, "Hear ye! Hear ye! Hear ye! The Colorado Court of Appeals is now in session."

———

Jack's lawyer stood before the court first. He was from Arizona, on staff with the Alliance Defending Freedom, and his name was Jeremy Tedesco. Dressed in a dark suit, white shirt, and light-blue tie, he stood at the podium—perhaps one of the loneliest places in the law—took a deep breath, and introduced himself.

He adjusted the microphone. Then he said, "Your honors, the prosecution of this case against Jack Phillips by the Colorado Civil Rights Commission cannot be reconciled with its recent decisions finding that three Denver bakeries did not violate [Colorado's anti-discrimination law] when they declined to serve a Christian customer when he asked for a cake that celebrated and reflected his religious opposition to same-sex marriage."

Judge Michael Berger, sitting to Tedesco's right on the far side of the bench, immediately interrupted. "What difference does that make?" he asked. "I mean, the other cases might be wrong. Why should we care whether this judgment is inconsistent with two other decisions of the Civil Rights Commission?"

"Because those decisions were correct," Tedesco said. He then launched into all the reasons why the commission had been right to protect the other bakers and wrong not to protect Jack.[1]

But he'd missed an opportunity. Under both the free-speech and the free-exercise laws that had developed after Al's case, the fact that the commission seemed to be treating identically placed individuals differently was a crucial point to make. One of the central tenets of free-speech law is that government may not take sides on debated issues. To do so is viewpoint discrimination. To punish one entity for its speech (or refusal to speak) on one side of an issue but then refuse to similarly punish an entity on the other side places the weighty hand of government on the scales in favor of one viewpoint. Tedesco missed the opportunity to make that point.

Similarly, Justice Scalia's test regarding neutral and generally applicable laws weighed heavy in the courtroom. Tedesco also missed his chance to explain that the commission was not equally applying Colorado's anti-discrimination law to everyone. Perhaps the best way to guarantee that lawmakers and regulators will not oppress people with whom they disagree is to require equal application of the laws they develop and enforce. If they fail to do so, then the law is not generally applicable, and it is highly likely that government officials are not enforcing it in a neutral way. In such a situation, under the test from Al's case, the law must be struck down. Despite all the flaws in the *Employment Division v. Smith* decision, that requirement still stood as a crucial protection for religious freedom for all. When Judge Berger asked why he should care that the commission had failed to enforce the law consistently, he revealed a crucial misunderstanding of federal religious freedom law. Tedesco should have pounced. Instead, he failed to raise the argument.

That was partly because the judges were focused elsewhere. They fired off a series of questions trying to determine what constituted speech and where to draw the line between a baked good and expressive art. They also tried to figure out just how many different types of vendors might be able to deny services to someone if they claimed their work constituted speech. Judge Berger expressed concern that florists, photographers, chefs, interior designers—all might be able to decline to cater a same-sex wedding if the judges ruled for Jack.

Perhaps the most telling part of the oral argument involved Charlie and David's attorney, Ria Mar, from the ACLU. When Judge Berger asked her if a fine-arts painter could be forced under her view of the law to create a painting with which he disagreed, she answered yes, if that painter offered to sell paintings to the public. The implications of her answer were astounding. It would mean that any artist who offered his or her works to the public, including painters, novelists, writers, or sculptors, could be forced to use their artistic talents to create works of art that conveyed messages with which they disagreed.

Aside from the very initial exchange, the judges seemed uninterested in the other cases involving the other bakers. They also didn't ask a single question about the comparison of Jack to Nazis and slaveholders. The vast majority of the argument seemed focused on whether Jack was being forced to engage in speech. The religious-liberty arguments seemed to have mostly fallen by the wayside. That the commission may not have applied the anti-discrimination statute in a neutral way and may not have applied it to everyone generally appeared to be lost on all parties: the judges, Jack's lawyers, and counsel for Charlie and David.

Across the country, the press largely came down hard on Jack. Whatever the requirements were for neutrality among journalists, they weren't being followed here. Later research showed that, when it came to same-sex marriage, traditional newspapers, television stations, and websites were anything but objective. Stories supporting same-sex marriage outnumbered those opposing it by a whopping margin of five to one.[2] This said nothing of the entertainment world, which routinely painted people with Jack's beliefs as hypocrites and bigots. Jack felt that onslaught.

Still, advocates continued to frequent Jack's shop and keep his business afloat. A number of those advocates were LGBT people. The phone rang regularly, and oftentimes the supporters on the other end were folks from the LGBT community who expressed their concern that key freedoms were being eroded.[3] They also let Jack know they supported him. One young couple who happened to be gay frequented Jack's shop on a regular basis. They would come in, buy cookies or brownies, visit with Jack and share support, then go on their way.[4]

Everyone waited for the court of appeals to rule.

More than a month later, on August 13, 2015, the court issued its opinion. It was the first time actual judges had examined the case.

Charlie and David won. The opinion was unanimous.

The judges ruled that sexual orientation was so linked to same-sex marriage that anyone who declined service for an event was necessarily declining service to the category of people who predominately participated in that event: in this case, LGBT individuals.[5] They rejected Jack's argument that he often served LGBT customers in other settings. To comply with the law, businesses needed to offer the full menu of services to LGBT customers, not just a partial menu.

The judges dealt with the other cases, involving the Christian customer who opposed same-sex marriage, in a footnote.[6] There, they explained the bakers had not discriminated against the Christian "because of" his creed but because the message he wanted on the cakes was offensive to them. They didn't address the notion that the messages conveyed by the cakes were inextricably linked to the creed of the person requesting them. And they determined that those bakers could not have been discriminating based on creed because they regularly served Christians for other requests. That Jack served LGBT people in other contexts didn't even receive a mention.

The difference between the treatment of the two sets of cases lingered with the gravity of a black hole. Despite everything else the judges had written, the reality was that every word, every punctuation mark, seemed to swirl around that footnote. It troubled people even in the LGBT community. Whether it would affect anything in later appeals remained to be seen.

After deciding Jack had violated the state anti-discrimination law, the judges turned to whether the Free Speech Clause or the Free Exercise Clause shielded him from the state law. They agreed government could not compel speech except in the rarest of circumstances. They acknowledged that speech could come in many forms and flavors, including through nonverbal conduct.

But they concluded the wedding cake in this case was not speech. In their view, it did not convey a message celebrating a same-sex marriage. And even if it did, "that message is more likely to be attributed to the customer than to Masterpiece."[7] They offered no explanation for why those same principles didn't apply in the cases involving the other bakers.

As for religious freedom, the test from Al Smith's case drove the discussion. The judges were required to determine if the statute was both neutral and generally applicable. They concluded it was neutral because it forbade all discrimination based on sexual orientation and did not target religiously motivated discrimination. The judges didn't address Commissioner Rice's comments that invoking religious freedom as a defense against state laws was "despicable" or her comparison of Jack's behavior to the Holocaust and slavery. They also ignored the commission's targeting of Christian bakers but not going after ideologically opposite ones.

Similarly, they concluded the law was generally applicable because it provided very few exemptions, and the ones it did give, according to the judges, didn't undermine the purpose of the statute.[8] Again, they were silent about the commission's decision not to apply the statute to the other bakers.

That silence would keep all lawyers watching the case awake at night. It invoked an old cliché: it was quiet. Too quiet.

NOTES

1. Video Recording of Oral Argument, *Craig v. Masterpiece Cakeshop*, 2015 COA 115 (July 7, 2015) (No. 14CA1351), https://www.courts.state.co.us/Courts/live/.
2. Paul Hitlin, Mark Jurkowitz, and Amy Mitchell, "New Coverage Conveys Strong Momentum for Same-Sex Marriage," Pew Research Center, June 17, 2013, http://www.journalism.org/2013/06/17/news-coverage-conveys-strong-momentum/.
3. Jack Phillips, in discussion with author, February 23, 2018.
4. Ibid.
5. *Mullins v. Masterpiece Cakeshop, Inc.*, 2015 COA 115, at 282–83 (2015).
6. Ibid., at 282n8.
7. Ibid., at 286.
8. Ibid., at 291–92.

Chapter 40

WAITING

In the legal world, everyone knew the case was marching toward the US Supreme Court with the same inevitability as the rising sun. The only question was whether the justices would agree to hear it.

Given that, it is likely Charlie and David didn't get to celebrate the court of appeals' decision very long. Even the day the ruling came out, David pondered how important it was to him to continue on the path no matter how lengthy or rocky it proved to be.[1] As long as Jack appealed or kept the case alive, they would not give up. In their view, they owed that much to the many people who had been supporting them.

In October of 2015, Jack appealed to the Colorado Supreme Court. The parties briefed the issues. Unlike the court of appeals, the state supreme court was not obligated to take the case. Of the seven justices, three had to agree to review it. If they didn't, the lower court's decision would stand.

On April 25, 2016, the Colorado Supreme Court issued an order denying a review.

The ACLU and other organizations spun it as a complete affirmation of the lower court's decision. That wasn't surprising. In some respects, this was part of their job. But in reality, the decision signified very little. Of the seven justices, two went out of their way to state they would have granted review. For reasons that remain unclear, the third justice most likely to agree with them didn't participate in the decision. Had she been able to, the court likely would have taken the case.

Either way, only one destination remained for both sides. Jack had one last hold that might save his shop from freefall. He was prepared to lunge for it.

Charlie and David needed only to navigate one last section of rapids to seal their victory forever.

Both sides prepared for the United States Supreme Court.

———

On July 22, 2016, Jack's team filed his petition for the United States Supreme Court to take the case. Four years had passed since those twenty seconds in the cake shop.

By December, the briefing was complete. All anyone could do was wait.

For a time, Jack, Charlie, and David's battle fell into anonymity as the world of elections and Supreme Court politics churned. At the same moment in history when their briefs were being delivered to the Supreme Court, the United States presidential election produced an outcome almost no one had seen coming. Additionally, the Supreme Court hobbled along one justice short.

Justice Scalia, whose opinion in Al's case had led to the jumbled state of the law regarding religious freedom, passed away in February 2016. Although President Barack Obama had tried to replace him, the Republicans in the US Senate had refused to vote on his appointee. They argued instead that, since it was an election year, the next president should get to appoint Scalia's replacement. It was a political gamble. But it was one conservative politicians felt necessary. The Supreme Court had been evenly divided for years, with five justices tending to lean toward outcomes conservatives generally favored and four justices tending to lean toward results liberals praised. Whoever replaced Scalia would either keep the court as it had been or would dramatically change the balance of power.

By the time the election rolled around in November, nearly everyone in the country believed the Democratic candidate Hillary Clinton would win by a landslide. The next justice would most certainly be someone who voted with the liberal bloc. As far as Jack, Charlie, and David were concerned, it was highly likely the court would now tilt away from protecting religious liberty rights, at least when they came into conflict with LGBT rights.

Everyone was wrong. When the briefing was finally completed regarding Jack's petition, the president-elect of the United States was Donald Trump.

As winter deepened, near the end of January 2017, Trump nominated Neil M. Gorsuch to replace Justice Scalia. In most everyone's estimation, Gorsuch was ideologically aligned with Justice Scalia in nearly all aspects of the law. Whether he agreed with the test Scalia had developed in Al's case was an open question. Still, Jack's camp surely rejoiced in seeing the Supreme Court's status quo preserved.

David and Charlie and their attorneys likely cast a wary eye upon this new justice, who, as fate would have it, hailed from Denver, just as they did.

In April, Justice Gorsuch officially assumed office. The Supreme Court had returned to its full regiment of nine justices. As he settled into his chambers, it was time for Justice Gorsuch and the other members of the court to get to work.

One of their most unrelenting tasks was to decide which cases to hear.

———

The toll on Jack continued to climb. Years had passed since he'd been forced to give up his wedding cake business. He had lost hundreds of thousands of dollars. Many evenings, he and his wife pored over their books, trying to figure out how to keep their store afloat.[2] Summer, fall, and winter had come and gone since he'd asked the Supreme Court to hear his case. Still, he waited.

Charlie and David, meanwhile, looked for closure. In many respects, their entire marriage had been defined by what had happened in Jack's shop. They had celebrated their fourth anniversary, yet they still hadn't reached the end of the ordeal.

Inside the Supreme Court, often on Fridays, the justices ease into seats around a long table in a library-like conference room to discuss which cases they will agree to take. Getting four justices to take a case is about as statistically probable as getting struck by lightning. Some cases don't even merit discussion and are automatically denied. Of the remainder, the justices often consider them only once or twice before making a decision.

Everyone watched the court to see what they would do with *Masterpiece*. It usually made announcements regarding petitions on Monday mornings, and a popular blog that monitored everything coming from the Supremes began posting news at 7:30 a.m. Colorado time.

Each Monday, Jack would roll into his shop before 7:00 a.m. He would flip on the lights, start some coffee, and put cash in the register. Then he would take a seat at the very desk where he used to consult regarding wedding cakes, open his laptop, and check the blog.

For weeks, the same message appeared on Jack's screen: "DISTRIBUTED for conference."

That meant the justices hadn't made a decision and the case would be considered again at a future conference.

By the time Judge Gorsuch officially became Justice Gorsuch, the case had been distributed for conference ten times. That number was already unusually high. It was clear the justices were considering it because after one conference, they requested some records related to the case. Still, it was anyone's guess what they were doing behind the scenes. It was possible they couldn't muster the four necessary votes but some justices were writing dissents, which meant the denial of the petition couldn't be issued until that process was complete. It was also conceivable they were waiting for Justice Gorsuch to get settled, and he needed more time to weigh in on the various petitions. They may have been watching other cases percolating in lower courts around the country to see how they came out.

The reality was, no one knew. All they could do was speculate.

Beginning February 21, 2017, the justices considered the case essentially every week. Every Friday, they met and conferenced. Every Monday morning, only one sentence bubbled out of the secretive building in Washington, DC: "DISTRIBUTED for conference."

The number of conferences piled into the remarkable. Thirteen, fourteen, fifteen . . .

Every week, Jack watched. Charlie and David did as well. For them, if the court denied Jack's petition, it would have been the ultimate vindication—a confirmation that the Colorado Court of Appeals was correct.

By the time the case had been distributed for the eighteenth time, the court was nearing the end of its term. Never before had it pushed a decision on a petition into the next year. And the number of distributions was so rare that one longtime court observer noted he had only ever seen one other case get distributed more.[3]

Finally, on June 26, 2017, the last day of the court's 2016–2017 term arrived. The court had no choice but to make a decision.

On that Monday morning, Jack walked to his shop. As he approached the door, he greeted a homeless man who regularly slept and hung out around the shopping center. Jack knew him. For years he had allowed the man to come into the shop and enjoy a cup of coffee. In the colder months, he would stay longer, even into the afternoons, just to stay warm.

While the man sat at one of the tables, Jack made him some coffee, slipped the day's money into the cash register, then took his seat in front of his computer. Outside, the sun was already heating up the parking lot and brightening everything.

Jack typed in the address for the Supreme Court blog and waited for 7:30 a.m.

The other man sipped his coffee.

They were the only two there.

Throughout the entire history of the case, Jack hadn't prayed to win. Instead, the focus of his pleas to heaven had been to avoid distraction from his most important goal of being a true disciple of Jesus Christ. That was all he wanted. He didn't want the case, the media, the death threats, or even the outcome of the court decisions to lead him down a path away from his God. If the Supreme Court denied his petition, he simply wanted to keep his faith and trust it was all part of a larger plan.

Across the nation, anyone watching the case knew this was the moment.

As Jack refreshed the screen shortly after the blog went live, three words appeared. They were three words that would change everything. Together, they formed a simple sentence: "Masterpiece is GRANTED."

Jack choked on his own breath. For just a moment, he struggled to take in air. Tears welled in his eyes. He looked around. Aside from the other man, the shop was empty. For three, four, five minutes, Jack sat in shock.

With trembling hands, he sent a text to his wife, "We've been granted!"

She texted back. Neither could believe it.

There was no one in person with whom he could share his thrill who actually appreciated it. But Jack couldn't contain his excitement. He turned to the homeless man. "Hey! I get to go to the Supreme Court!"

With a completely unimpressed face, still sipping his coffee, the man responded, "Yeah, I gotta go to court on Wednesday."[4]

NOTES

1. Jordan Steffen, "Appeals Court: Lakewood Baker Discriminated against Same-Sex Couple," *Denver Post,* August 13, 2015, https://www.denverpost.com/2015/08/13/appeals-court-lakewood-baker-discriminated-against-same-sex-couple/.
2. Jack Phillips, in discussion with author, February 23, 2018.
3. John Elwood, "Relist Watch," SCOTUSblog, June 8, 2017, http://www.scotusblog.com/2017/06/relist-watch-107/.
4. Phillips, discussion with author.

Chapter 41

MUTUAL TOLERANCE

The threatening phone calls poured in almost immediately. For the first couple of weeks, a seemingly nonstop stream of threats and tongue-lashings kept Jack's phone ringing nearly constantly. Some he answered, some he didn't. Often, he simply listened. He knew he would never convince those who opposed him over the phone.[1]

At the same time, the public-relations machines for both camps revved up in earnest. As important as winning in the Supreme Court would be, both sides recognized that gaining public support was perhaps even more crucial. What had been lingering as a quiet dispute known only to a few in the legal channels of Denver had just been launched into the national spotlight. Charlie and David had a decided advantage. Traditional media outlets, reporters, newspaper editorial boards, journalists—the vast majority favored David and Charlie. Their religious views opposed Jack's, and that meant he faced a steep slope on the mountain of public opinion. For the next many months, nearly every interview Jack did, he went in knowing the reporter was likely to be against him, if not downright hostile.

Of course, most of these reporters didn't understand the nuances of the case, as would be evident almost immediately. Just days after the Supreme Court made its announcement, the hosts of *The View* on ABC invited Jack and his attorney Kristen Waggoner onto their show.

It was Jack's first time on television to talk about the case. It portended the coming storm.

When the segment launched, Jack sat at the center of the hosts' table. To his right were Sunny Hostin, Paula Faris, and Joy Behar. To his left were Ms. Waggoner, followed by Sara Haines and Jedediah Bila. Jack was clearly out of his element. His gray goatee clashed with his ruffled and thinning brown hair. The wrinkles in his worn blue shirt revealed both his financial situation and his complete lack of interest in fashion. This was clearly a man thrust into the spotlight who neither wanted it nor had prepared for it. There on the set, where producers fretted over even a minor speck of dust on the hosts' table, surrounded by people molded after Manhattan's obsession with fashion, Jack couldn't have looked more out of place if he'd tried.

Yet his lack of polish was also endearing. At one moment, Joy Behar, who spoke with the volume and confidence of someone who has spent a lifetime in the entertainment world, asked Jack to speak up. He was so soft-spoken, she struggled to hear him. "Can you speak up just a little bit?" she asked.

"Yeah," Jack said. "People tell me that all the time."[2] A year later, the hosts of *The View* would describe him as a "very lovely man, and very rooted in his beliefs."[3]

In his initial interview, however, the conversation was as frustrating as watching aliens trying to communicate with earthlings for the first time. Everyone was speaking a different language.

When Joy Behar tried to understand Jack's position, he did his best to explain that he did not reject the couple. He would welcome them into his store and serve them anything. He simply couldn't make cakes for certain events, and he wouldn't sell those cakes to anyone, no matter their identity. "It's a difficult thing to be in my position," he explained to Behar, "and know that somebody is requesting me to do something that I can't in good conscience do. I'm not turning them away. It's just this event. Please understand that."[4]

They didn't. Jedediah Bila immediately followed up with a

question that showed she simply didn't understand Jack's position. Her hair gathered in a loose bun on the crown of her head, she said, "I understand the concern people have about government dictating to private businesses what their business should look like, but on this religious freedom argument, I struggle. If it violates your religious freedom to sell a wedding cake to a gay couple, for example, do you then when straight couples come in, do you ask them if they've had a child out of wedlock, . . . if they participate in premarital sex, . . . because where do you draw the line?"[5]

The crowd immediately burst into applause, as if she were making a powerful rhetorical point. In reality, she had completely missed Jack's message. The premise of her question—that it violated Jack's religious freedom to sell a wedding cake to a gay couple—was precisely what he had just asked them to understand was *not* his position. If they had been purchasing a wedding cake for a traditional marriage, he would have happily sold it to them. His position was not that he couldn't sell products to sinners. It was that he couldn't participate in certain events.

In his gentle voice, Jack tried to explain, "Again, I don't judge people when they come in. I try and serve everybody. I just don't make cakes for every event that's asked of me."[6] He emphasized his opposition on Halloween cakes, adult-themed party cakes, and cakes disparaging others.

A smattering of applause responded.

The hosts then pivoted. Behar asked precisely what Jack's religious beliefs were that prevented him from baking this cake.

When Jack explained that he believed marriage should be between one man and one woman, Behar and others challenged that. The rest of the conversation devolved into the hosts trying to explain to Jack why his religious beliefs were wrong and why he was misinterpreting the Bible.

At one point, Behar exclaimed, "Jesus would have made the cake," nodding her head emphatically. "Jesus . . . that's a deal breaker. Jesus is gonna make the cake."[7] She raised her hands to signal the end of the debate. It was partly in jest, but it peeled back the layers and revealed the thrust of what this case was truly about: one side agreed with Jack's religious beliefs, and one didn't. And in interview after interview, the most common argument thrust against Jack was not *legal* but *theological*. It was the notion that Jack's religious understanding was simply wrong.

The problem, of course, is that religious disagreement cannot serve as a justification to use the law to tell someone they cannot serve in their chosen profession because of their religious beliefs. If that were allowed, the religious majority would always crush those with different views. Part of the very essence of religious freedom is to prevent that from happening.

As summer faded to fall and the interviews piled up for both sides, that key point would be lost on reporter after reporter. The more important question was whether it would be lost on the justices.

———————

Across the country, kids returned to school, the college football season roared to life, and briefs from all over the United States streamed into the Supreme Court. In total, fifty amicus briefs in support of Jack reached the court, including one from the United States government itself.

The thrust of Jack's legal argument, now honed over five and a half years was this: (1) the Colorado Anti-Discrimination Act, as the Colorado Commission had applied it, violated his free speech rights by compelling him to engage in speech with which he disagreed; (2) the Act violated Jack's free-exercise rights because the commission had not applied it in a neutral way that was generally applicable to everyone (this was the test Justice Scalia had developed in Al Smith's case); and (3) because the commission's behavior burdened both free-speech and religious-liberty rights, the court should be even more dubious of it. He concluded by emphasizing that the commission simply could not show it had a compelling interest for doing what it did.

In October, the justices set a date for oral arguments: December 5, 2017.

A few weeks later, Charlie and David filed their response, as did the commission. An additional forty-five briefs arrived in support of their positions.

In the media, the sniping continued. People pushed op-eds, advocacy groups for both sides made heartwarming videos showing why their side was more sympathetic, people raged on social media. It seemed everyone, everywhere, had an opinion. In contrast to the days of Roy Torcaso or Al Smith, where newspaper editors served as gatekeepers for public commentary, the internet allowed anyone with an opinion to voice it. And they did. People on both the far left and the far right fired off misinformed, vulgar accusations at one another and at the parties in the case. As much as those two groups hated one another, the remarkable thing was how similar their behavior was. In many respects, they were mirror images.

For Jack, the days and weeks melted into a familiar routine: open his shop, bake something, do an interview, put something in the oven, do another interview.[8]

For Charlie and David, the interview regimen was similar. While the justices hunkered in their chambers with their clerks, reviewing the briefs and debating the law, the dueling media strategies played out across the airwaves, in the papers, and on the internet. In reality, all that mattered were the opinions of nine men and women at 1 First Street NE in Washington, DC.

––––––––

Beneath a semitransparent cloud cover on the morning of December 5, 2017, Jack and his family marched up the steps of the Supreme Court. Nearby, Charlie and David navigated the same stairs with their supporters. At long last, the case had arrived. Somehow, this small dispute that had lasted fewer than twenty seconds had become, six years later, the day's biggest newsmaker. It had morphed into nothing short of an iconic symbol of the so-called culture wars. Every newspaper and news website in the country highlighted it prominently above all else. Editorial boards from *The New York Times*, *USA Today*, the *Los Angeles Times*, the *Chicago Tribune*, and dozens of other news outlets offered their opinions. Most had no idea what they were talking about or intentionally avoided the nuances of the case to score points with their supporters. When an editorial board begins its discussion of a key First Amendment case with the title "Baker's case is not about the First Amendment," it loses whatever credibility it had in the first place.[9] Nevertheless, the news media spilled their views onto their pages with vigor. And they weren't alone. People with dueling sentiments sparred in opinion sections, in rallies, and on social media across the country. As usual, both sides were completely talking past each other. The theme from Charlie and David's supporters was that the case was about discrimination, pure and simple; religion had nothing to do with it. From Jack's side, the case was about religious liberty and freedom of speech, not discrimination.

It was almost as if the two sides were involved in two completely different cases. Refusing to compromise, insisting they could never achieve common ground, they raged against one another while the nation watched.

––––––––

The buzz in the vaunted Supreme Court chamber reflected the magnitude of the case. Outside, people who weren't parties had waited in line for days, hoping to catch a live glimpse of the argument.

Jack had arrived early. Wearing a black suit and navy-blue tie against a white shirt, he had positioned himself with his family in the third row of the middle section, not far from where Roy Torcaso and Al Smith had both sat.

A short time later, Charlie and David entered the courtroom with Charlie's mom. They also sat in the third row but in a different section, across the aisle from Jack. Charlie wore a blue suit with a purple shirt and tie. David's slim-fit purple suit magnified his white tie. The lawyers spilled in, as did various dignitaries. When it was all said and done, the United States Solicitor General, US senators, representatives from every major media outlet, the highest officials from the Alliance Defending Freedom and the ACLU, and dozens of others packed into the pews.

Up on the justices' bench, aides scurried between the empty chairs. In total, more than one hundred briefs had been filed in the case. The aides struggled to carry them to their bosses' seats. Some managed to heft the entire stack; others used magazine holders and made more than one trip. All of them broke the stack into smaller piles that they spread out on the mahogany. Otherwise, the briefs would have dwarfed the justices and blinded their views.

At the appointed time, the jurists emerged from behind the curtain and took their seats, the same way they had for Roy Torcaso, and just as they had for Al Smith. Though the three cases spanned nearly sixty years and the Supreme Court had heard numerous other religious-liberty issues during those decades, for longtime observers of the court, there was something familiar about the situation. The names had changed, the facts were different, but the justices were still grappling with the same basic question Americans had been experimenting with since the country's founding: Did the Constitution of the United States protect religious dissenters from laws driven by the majority in power?

When Chief Justice John Roberts finished some preliminary procedural matters, all eyes rested on the nine men and women donned in black, sitting in the high-backed leather chairs. Once again, they would answer that question.

"We'll hear argument this morning in Case 16–111, Masterpiece Cakeshop versus Colorado Civil Rights Commission," Justice Roberts said. His treble voice was so flat he may as well have been announcing the beginning of a colloquium on the nuances of the latest accounting regulations, not the most widely watched Supreme Court case in recent memory. But that was part of the decorum. With the slight nod of his head, he turned to the primary attorney representing Jack, "Ms. Waggoner."

Kristen Waggoner stepped to the podium, which was almost as tall as she was. To the people in the audience who had never seen her before, she must have been quite a sight. Nearly everything about her suggested diminutive. At forty-five, she wasn't much taller than some elementary school kids. When she spoke, her voice was nearly that of a small child reading bedtime stories. It was both pleasant and disarming. It was also confident. No one would have guessed that she was arguing before the Supreme Court for the first time.

"Mr. Chief Justice, and may it please the Court," she began smoothly. "The First Amendment prohibits the government from forcing people to express messages that violate their religious convictions. Yet the commission requires Mr. Phillips to do just that, ordering him to sketch, sculpt, and hand-paint cakes that celebrate a view of marriage in violation of his religious convictions."[10] It was no doubt an opening line she had rehearsed hundreds of times.

It was also the last sentence she would utter that didn't involve some interplay with the justices.

And anyone interested in the religious-liberty arguments would have been disappointed. In the buildup to oral arguments, the parties had focused most of their attention on Jack's claims under the Free Speech Clause. This was a strategic decision by both camps. Jack's attorneys felt the justices were more likely to stop the government from compelling speech than to protect religious freedom under the *Smith* test. Charlie and David's lawyers feared the same. So did the state of Colorado. In the media, almost all of the discussion had been on whether a cake was speech. Since the vast majority of commentators in print and television favored Charlie and David, they argued it was not—for if the justices determined it was, then Jack would mostly likely win.

Not surprisingly, then, the very first question out of the gate, from Justice Ruth Bader Ginsburg, involved where the justices should draw the line when determining what was speech and what was not. Unlike the media commentators, to the justices, the line was not obvious. It held profound implications. And they needed to get it right.

They lobbed question after question to Waggoner. With the verbal dexterity of a professional baseball player, she batted each one away. But the case was not easy. If a custom cake was speech, why not a haircut for a wedding, or a floral arrangement, or a menu, or a plate of finely cooked cuisine, or an architectural plan? How were the justices supposed to decide? Waggoner, like everyone else, struggled to answer.

What never came up, what no one ever raised, were the questions relating to the religious freedom test Justice Scalia had created in Al Smith's case. Was the Colorado Anti-Discrimination Act, either as written or as applied to Jack in this case, "neutral" and "generally applicable"? That was the question the Supreme Court was supposed to apply when a law burdened someone's religious exercise. Yet the state of Colorado had dedicated only six pages of its sixty-two page brief to the question. David and Charlie had included only five, despite a brief fifty-seven pages long.

The question of what constituted speech consumed everyone so fully that when Waggoner's time had dwindled to nothing, she never even got to address the religious freedom arguments.

When she finished, Chief Justice Roberts turned the podium over to United States solicitor general Noel Francisco. Of Filipino descent, Francisco was familiar with the court and its ways. Earlier in his career, he had served as a law clerk to Justice Scalia. With striking silver streaks punctuating his dark hair, he was, in many respects, the eldest of the advocates arguing that day. His role was to represent the interests of the United States government in the case. It was not a party, but it is common for the United States to take sides on key cases, and when it does, the justices often afford it an opportunity to argue.

Near the end of his argument, General Francisco summed up why the United States had sided for Jack in the case:

> [Y]ou really are envisioning a situation in which you could

force, for example, a gay opera singer to perform at the Westboro Baptist Church just because that opera singer would be willing to perform at the National Cathedral.

And the problem is when you force somebody not only to speak but to contribute that speech to an expressive event to which they are deeply opposed, you force them to use their speech to send a message that they fundamentally disagree with.

And that is at the core of what the First Amendment protects our citizenry against.[11]

It was a compelling point. Surprisingly, the justices actually let him finish his thought without interruption. Still, he was no more successful than anyone else when it came to providing a test for what constituted speech.

He volleyed back and forth with the justices. In the end, he pushed for a line that would make something speech if it was "predominantly expressive" and not speech if it was "predominantly utilitarian."

Of the cake Charlie and David were requesting Jack to create, General Francisco argued, "And here you have a cake that is essentially synonymous with a traditional sculpture except for the medium used."[12]

When he was finished, it wasn't clear if any of the justices were satisfied.

Once again, no one discussed the religious-freedom issues. It was almost as if the one issue that mattered most to Jack Phillips, that had spurred his behavior in the first place, had been forgotten by everyone.

―――――――

"Mr. Yarger," Roberts said, referring to the solicitor general of the state of Colorado.

Frederick R. Yarger had traveled from Denver to represent the state of Colorado, in particular the Colorado Civil Rights Commission. It was his job to defend their rulings against Jack. The youngest of the attorneys to stand at the podium that day, he spoke with a soft, kind tone.

After his preliminary introduction, he lunged into his argument with confidence: "Masterpiece Cakeshop is a retail bakery that is open to the public and subject to the Colorado Anti-Discrimination Act. Yet, Petitioners claim that they can refuse to sell a product, a wedding cake of any kind in any design to any same-sex couple."[13]

It was a strawman argument. Anyone watching the case carefully—and the justices certainly were at this point—knew that Jack's position was not what Yarger claimed. The state solicitor general was framing the facts as he hoped them to be—that Jack refused service to a same-sex *couple*; not as they actually were—that he refused service connected to a same-sex *wedding*.

The justices pounced. Justice Roberts hit first: "I think there are many different faiths, but Catholic Legal Services, they provide pro bono legal representation to people who are too poor to afford it and they provide it to people of all—all different faiths. So let's say someone just like [Charlie and David] here, except needing the pro bono assistance, goes into Catholic Legal Services and say, we want you to take this case against Masterpiece Cakeshop. And the . . . lawyers say: 'Well . . . we're not going to, because we, we don't support same-sex marriage. Are they in violation of the Colorado law?"

It was a carefully crafted hypothetical designed to paint Yarger into a corner.

"No," Yarger began. "Chief Justice, Mr. Chief Justice, they are not. Refusing to offer a particular service in that case, when they wouldn't provide it to any other customer—"

"No, no," Justice Roberts interrupted, "They would provide it. If a heterosexual couple comes in and says we need particular services in connection with our marriage, they would provide it. It's only because, and they say this, it's only because it's a same-sex marriage that we're not going to provide pro bono legal services to you."

After he and Yarger stumbled over each other, Roberts provided more clarity to his example, "You know, they're having a . . . contract dispute with somebody in connection with their marriage, and the lawyer says we're not going to provide services in connection with same-sex marriage because we have a religious objection to that." It was clear Roberts understood the distinction Jack had made between the couple and the marriage.

It was easy to understand why Yarger would be hesitant to answer. First, lawyers hate to answer how the law would apply to a hypothetical they haven't had time to truly consider. Second, Roberts was pushing Yarger to state a conclusion that made Colorado's law seem unpalatable.

When Yarger finally committed and at least suggested the law would apply, Roberts asked, "So Catholic Legal Services would be put to the choice of either not providing any pro bono legal services or providing those services in connection with the same-sex marriage?" It was a rhetorical question. Yarger struggled to respond. It didn't matter. The chief justice had made his point: here was an entity known for providing an almost incalculable public good—free legal services for the poor and indigent—and Colorado would shut down those services because of the entity's religious opposition to same-sex marriage.[14]

"The Chief Justice," Justice Kennedy said, "has introduced the question of the Free Exercise Clause in this case." Kennedy acknowledged what anyone interested in the religious freedom law in the case was thinking. He then struck directly at the question of whether the Colorado Commission had behaved in a neutral way when applying the Colorado Anti-Discrimination Act.

He raised the statement of Commissioner Rice comparing Jack to Nazis and slaveholders and referring to religious freedom as "a despicable piece of rhetoric."

"Did the Commission ever disavow or disapprove of that statement?" Kennedy asked.

"Uh," Yarger hesitated. "There were no further proceedings in which the Commission disavowed or disapproved of that statement."

In his deep, pointed voice, Kennedy asked, "Do you disavow or disapprove of that statement?"

"I would not have counseled my client to make that statement."

"Do you *now* disavow or disapprove of that statement?" Kennedy said, frustration lingering in his voice.

"I, I, I do, yes, Your Honor," Yarger said. "I think . . . I need to make clear that what that commissioner was referring to was the previous decision of the Commission, which is that no matter how strongly held a belief, it is not an exception to a generally applicable anti-discrimination law. And if, if the assertion that what is engaging in is speech is enough to overcome that law, you're going to face a situation where a family portrait artist can say I will photograph any family but not when the father . . . is wearing a yarmulke because I have a sincere objection to the Jewish faith. That would be discrimination."[15]

It was a crafty argument. And Yarger did his best to deal with the facts his client had given him. There was just one problem. His example was, again, not what Jack was arguing. Yarger was talking about rejecting someone because of their status—as an LGBT person, as a Jewish person, or even as a Christian. Jack was concerned with participating in an *event*—about facilitating behavior his religion taught was sinful. So the ruling Jack sought would not result in the outcome Yarger was posing.

It was also misdirection in that it didn't address whether the commission had behaved in a neutral way when applying the Colorado Anti-Discrimination Act. Justice Kennedy refused to follow Yarger's red herring. "Suppose we thought that in significant part at least one member of the Commission based the commissioner's decision . . . on the grounds of . . . hostility to religion. . . . Could your judgment then stand?"

"Your Honor, I don't think that *one* statement by the commissioner, assuming it reveals bias—"

Kennedy would not allow Yarger to avoid the question. With a bit more force, he repeated himself, "Suppose we thought there was a significant aspect of hostility to a religion in this case. Could your judgment stand?" Again, he was getting at the key question of neutrality under the test Justice Scalia had created in Al's case.

Yarger again answered without answering, "Your Honor, if—if—if there was evidence that the entire proceeding was begun because of a—an intent to single out religious people, absolutely, that would be a problem."

Justice Sotomayor then jumped into the fray. On the surface, given the facts of the case, Yarger could be forgiven for thinking she was diving in to save him.

"How many commissioners are there?" she asked.

Yarger was still hitting his previous point and talked over her question. "Excuse me, Justice Sotomayor."

"I'd like you to answer Justice Kennedy's question," she said first. Then she repeated, "How many commissioners are there?"

"There are seven commissioners, Your Honor," Yarger said.

"All right," she said. Then her tone turned stiff. "If there was a belief—not yours—stop fighting the belief; accept the hypothetical—that this person was improperly biased, what happens then? I think that's what Justice Kennedy is asking you."

"If there is one person that's improperly biased?"

"One of the commissioners is improperly biased," she said.

"I think you're going to have to ask whether the complaint filed with the division which was filed by a customer who was referred to a bakery to receive a product, and the ALJ and the commission in the appeal were all biased in the sense that this was a proceeding meant to single out a religious person for his views. And that is not the fact here."

Chief Justice Roberts didn't like the answer. "We've had this case before," he said. He then pointed out that the Supreme Court had, in its past, overturned decisions by three-judge panels where one biased judge might have influenced the views of the other two.

Yarger fell back to his initial comment. "And, Your Honor, again,

I don't think that this—that particular phrase—I wouldn't advise my client to make that statement, but it was referring back to the previous decision—"[16]

The justices kept hammering. The newest among them, Neil Gorsuch, pointed out that a second commissioner had made statements hostile toward religion. On some level, that wasn't surprising. With the makeup of the court at the time, Yarger knew that four of the justices—Gorsuch, Thomas, Alito, and Roberts—were going to vote against him. Kennedy was a question mark. He had traditionally voted in favor of LGBT rights, but this case was different. It represented perhaps the first time that the LGBT left wanted to force its view of sexual morality on someone else, and it wasn't clear how Kennedy would feel about that.

What had to have been even more concerning for Yarger, however, was that the attacks weren't coming only from the justices he had expected to be hostile.

Justice Breyer launched into a lengthy soliloquy, "The reason I want you to continue this is that many of the civil rights laws, not all public accommodations laws, though—there are exceptions, like, for example, with housing, a person's own room, for example. And what people are trying to do with exceptions is take the thing you're worried about, where there are genuine, sincere religious views or whatever it is, and minimize the harm it does to the principle of the statute while making some kind of compromise for people of sincere beliefs on the other side. And we find that in—in a lot of them, but that's primarily a legislative job. And my impression of this is there wasn't much effort here in Colorado to do that."[17]

The justice had revived an itch that had been annoying people in the middle of this debate: was there a way to achieve fairness for all? To enact laws that protected LGBT citizens while also protecting sincerely religious people like Jack Phillips in narrow circumstances? Justice Breyer believed it was a question that must be asked and explored, regardless of how difficult it was to do.

Yarger disagreed that Colorado hadn't tried to protect everyone, but he offered no evidence to support his view.

At that, Justice Samuel Alito jumped. "I mean, one thing that's disturbing about the record here, in addition to the statement made, the statement that Justice Kennedy read, which was not disavowed at the time by any other member of the Commission, is what appears to be a practice of discriminatory treatment based on viewpoint.

"The, the Commission had before it the example of three complaints filed by an individual whose creed includes the traditional Judeo-Christian opposition to same-sex marriage, and he requested cakes that expressed that point of view and . . . there were bakers who said no, we won't do that because it is offensive.

"And the Commission said: That's okay. It's okay for a baker who supports same-sex marriage to refuse to create a cake with a message that is opposed to same-sex marriage. But when the tables are turned and you have a baker who opposes same-sex marriage, that baker may be compelled to create a cake that expresses approval of same-sex marriage."[18]

Every important fact that the Colorado Court of Appeals had missed now sat front and center before the justices. The biased statements from the commissioners, the other bakers—the lower court had failed to see their significance. These justices clearly had not.

Yarger played the only card he had left. One maneuver every litigator learns is "distinguishing"—the ability to explain why other cases that establish precedents not in their favor are actually different and shouldn't apply. When it came to the other bakers the commission had treated so differently, the ACLU and Yarger began pushing that skill to the limit. And sacrificing credibility along the way. Yarger tried to explain why the other cases were different from this one, but Justice Alito didn't buy it.

As Yarger fumbled through a response, Justice Sotomayer twice demanded that he answer Justice Alito's question. He tried. For anyone who knew the facts of the case, his answers were wholly unsatisfying.

The exchange culminated in a lecture from Justice Kennedy, "Counselor, tolerance is essential in a free society. And tolerance is most meaningful when it's mutual. It seems to me that the state in its position here has been neither tolerant nor respectful of Mr. Phillips's religious beliefs."

"And, Your Honor, I, I—" Yarger interrupted.

Justice Kennedy continued as if Yarger hadn't spoken. "And because accommodation is quite possible, we assume there were other shops that, other good bakery shops that were available."[19]

The arguments continued along the same line.

Yarger's time was running out. The barrage of questions had been brutal.

After Chief Justice Roberts had asked him one more question, Yarger, thinking his time was about to expire, said, "Well, Mr. Chief Justice—may I answer?"

"You have five more minutes," Roberts said.

"Oh," Yarger said.

"If you want," Roberts quipped.

A rare moment of laughter washed over the chamber, but Yarger took the time. He repeatedly insisted that Jack had discriminated based on identity.

Justice Alito pointed out that he was mischaracterizing Jack's argument.

Other justices chimed in on more technical legal questions, including whether it mattered that Colorado had not even legally recognized same-sex marriage in 2012 when the case began. The notion of whether the cake was speech largely fell by the wayside. Religious freedom had stormed into the chamber and taken center stage.

Yarger's time finally did run out. As he stepped from the podium, his gut told him he was going to suffer a narrow defeat. But the arguments were not over. Up next was the far more seasoned David D. Cole, legal director for the ACLU.

David Cole's résumé was formidable: a renowned constitutional law professor at Georgetown with nearly forty years of experience litigating civil rights cases, authoring numerous books, writing dozens of law-review articles, and trying multiple cases before the Supreme Court. When he stood to the podium, he spoke smoothly, with confidence. He sounded kind but firm. His role was to represent the interests of David and Charlie.

His argument also focused on the speech aspects of the case. He gave almost no time—and the justices demanded very little—to the religious-liberty claims. His major thrust was that it just wasn't possible for the Supreme Court to rule that wedding cakes in this context were speech without creating a world of problems. The lines, in his view, were just too difficult to draw.

But that position was just as problematic for the justices as was Jack's. No matter what, if the justices waded into the waters of free speech, they were going to drown in a sea of potentially negative outcomes.

In response to one of Cole's arguments, Justice Alito flagged the concern. "What you just said . . . is that someone can be compelled to write particular words with which that person strongly disagrees. . . . That *is* your position, isn't it?"[20]

Cole confirmed it was.

Just like Kristen Waggoner, Cole fielded question after question from the justices. What if the government forces a baker to create a cake for the Ku Klux Klan? A Jewish baker for Nazis? A black baker for a religious group with the same beliefs as the KKK? Would the cakes be considered speech in those cases?

Cole struggled to answer. Like Yarger, he insisted Jack had discriminated against David and Charlie based on their identity, not the event, but he too was stating as fact something the justices had yet to accept.

At one point, Justice Kennedy explicitly rejected the mischaracterization. "It's not their identity," the eighty-one-year-old jurist said, "it's what they're doing. . . . Your identity thing is just too facile."[21]

Cole did his best to answer, but the reality was that no matter what the justices did, if they ruled on Jack's freedom-of-speech claim, they would unsettle waters that would then be difficult to contain.

The closest Cole came to truly delving into the religious freedom argument involved hypothetical cases he insisted were not before the justices or involved his repeated arguments that the Colorado law in this case was neutral and generally applicable. None of the justices challenged him on that.

At one point, as Cole's time was running out, Justice Alito questioned whether, under Cole's view of the law, the state of Colorado could compel a religious university with objections to same-sex marriage to provide married student housing to same-sex couples.

Cole then launched into his most comprehensive argument regarding the religious-freedom aspects of the case:

> Well, I think under this Court's doctrine in *Employment Division versus Smith*, the question would be, is it a generally applicable neutral law? And if it's a generally applicable neutral law, there would not be a free exercise question at all. Right?
>
> And so . . . the reason for that, as Justice Scalia said in *Employment Division versus Smith*, is equally applicable here.
>
> Once you open this up, once you say generally applicable regulations of conduct have exceptions when someone raises a religious objection, or in this case have objections where someone raises a speech objection, you're in a world in which every man is a law unto himself.
>
> And so the only sensible way to approach this is to say if the state is targeting religion, then we're going to be very careful about protecting religion. And if the state is targeting the message, is targeting the content of speech, then we're going to be very careful about protecting.
>
> But when the state is regulating conduct neutrally, unrelated

to expression, which is what this Court has already said is the case with respect to public accommodations, then we can have a world in which everybody who raises an objection—otherwise we would live in a society in which businesses across this country could put signs up saying we serve whites only, music lessons for Muslims need not apply, passport photos not for the disabled.[22]

He had clearly lost his train of thought near the end. His point was that if a public-accommodations law like Colorado's, when applied in a neutral and generally applicable way, allowed for exemptions for religious people, then a parade of horribles would follow. He had one problem. He never addressed Jack's argument that the Colorado Commission had failed to apply the law neutrally, that it had targeted Jack's message and no one else's. Those questions still lingered.

By the time Cole finished, he had ventured no closer than anyone else to helping the justices resolve the dilemma regarding speech. If he had wanted to challenge Jack's religious-freedom arguments, his opportunity was gone.

Chief Justice Roberts cut him off with a simple but firm, "Thank you. Thank you, counsel."

He then turned back to Jack's attorney. "Ms. Waggoner, five minutes."

It was a short walk to that lonely podium. Waggoner traversed the distance in a few seconds. Before she even had a chance to open her mouth, Justice Sonia Sotomayor began peppering her with questions relating to certain technical aspects of the law and the relationship between Masterpiece Cakeshop the entity and its owner Jack Phillips.

Waggoner tried to sidestep them quickly, but they ate up a good chunk of her time. Perhaps now sensing the importance of attacking the question of neutrality, she hit the concept hard:

> I have three brief points in rebuttal:
> First of all, the bias of the Commission is also evidenced in the unequal treatment of the cake designers, the three other cake designers who were on the squarely opposite sides of this issue.

If, if the Court looks at the analysis that was provided by the Colorado Court of Appeals, line by line they take the opposite approach to Mr. Phillips that they do to those who are unwilling to criticize same-sex marriage.[23]

She was in her groove now. Justice Ruth Bader Ginsburg interrupted her only once. Otherwise, the justices, in uncharacteristic fashion, allowed her to talk. She made the best of it.

The Colorado Court of Appeals said that [other bakers] could have an offensiveness policy, and they said that those three cake designers were expressing their own message if they had to design that cake.

In Mr. Phillips's case, they said it wasn't his message. It's simply compliance with the law.

In the other case, they said that the cake designers, because they served Christian customers in other contexts, that that was evidence it was a distinction based on the message, but in Mr. Phillips's case, they ruled the opposite way. . . .

Second, the Compelled Speech Doctrine and the Free Exercise Clause is anchored in the concept of dignity and speaker autonomy. And in this case, dignity cuts both ways. The record is clear on that.

Demeaning Mr. Phillips's honorable and decent religious beliefs about marriage, when he has served everyone and has a history of declining all kinds of cakes unaffiliated with sexual orientation because of the message, he should receive protection here as well.

This law protects the lesbian graphic designer who doesn't want to design for the Westboro Baptist Church, as much as it protects Mr. Phillips.

Lastly, political, religious, and moral opinions shift. We know that. And this Court's dedication to Compelled Speech Doctrine and to free exercise should not shift.[24]

Justice Sotomayor had heard enough. "Counsel," she began sternly, "the problem is that America's reaction to mixed marriages and to race didn't change on its own. It changed because we had public-accommodation laws that forced people to do things that many claimed were against their expressive rights and against their religious rights.

"It's not denigrating someone by saying, as I mentioned earlier, to say: If you choose to participate in our community in a public way, your choice, you can choose to sell cakes or not. You can choose to sell cupcakes or not. Whatever it is you choose to sell, you have to sell it to everyone who knocks on your door, if you open your door to everyone."

The statement was an oversimplification of the law and of history. But Waggoner was out of time. She looked to Roberts. "Mr. Chief Justice?"

"You can respond, if you'd like," he said.

"Justice Sotomayor," Waggoner said. "I think that the gravest offense to the First Amendment would be to compel a person who believes that marriage is sacred, to give voice to a different view of marriage and require them to celebrate that marriage. The First Am—"

"Then—don't—participate—in weddings," Justice Sotomayor said, emphasizing each word, "or create a cake that is neutral, but you don't have to take and offer goods to the public and then choose not to sell to some because of a protected characteristic. That's what the public anti-discrimination laws require."[25]

There, at the end, Justice Sotomayor had revealed her position: people could have religious beliefs, but if the rest of society decided they weren't appropriate, then they couldn't have them along with the profession of their choice. She also laid bare how she viewed the case. Jack's argument that he was not denying service based on a protected characteristic but instead because he didn't want to be forced to participate in an event didn't persuade her. It wasn't surprising to anyone who watched the court carefully, but she accepted the state's and David and Charlie's argument.

"A brief last word, Ms. Waggoner," Chief Justice Roberts said.

"A wedding cake expresses an inherent message," Waggoner said, "that is that the union is a marriage and is to be celebrated, and that message violates Mr. Phillips's religious convictions. Thank you. This Court should reverse."

"Thank you, counsel," Roberts said. "The case is submitted."[26]

NOTES

1. Jack Phillips, in discussion with author, February 23, 2018.
2. "Baker in Supreme Court Gay Wedding Ca[s]e Jack Phillips Shares His Story," *The View*, June 29, 2017, https://playtube.pk/watch?v=coBIZle18kM, at 4:48.
3. "Supreme Court Sides with Christian Baker," *The View*, June 4, 2018, https://www.youtube.com/watch?v=9JYbwpSij8E, at 1:50.
4. "Baker in Supreme Court Gay Wedding Ca[s]e Jack Philips Shares His Story," *The View*, June 29, 2017, at 1:03.
5. Ibid., at 1:17.
6. Ibid., at 1:48.
7. Ibid., at 5:00.
8. Jack Phillips, in discussion with author, February 23, 2018.
9. "Baker's Case Is Not about the First Amendment," *USA Today*, December 4, 2017, https://www.usatoday.com/story/opinion/2017/12/04/supreme-court-baker-case-not-first-amendment-editorials-debates/911452001/.
10. Transcript of oral argument, *Masterpiece Cakeshop v. Colorado Civil Rights Commission*, 138 S. Ct. 1719 (2018) (No. 16-111), 2017 U.S. Trans. LEXIS 64, at *1–2.
11. Ibid., at *34–35.
12. Ibid., at *30.
13. Ibid., at *35.
14. Ibid., at *35–38.
15. Ibid., at *39–40.
16. Ibid., at *40–43.
17. Ibid., at *43–44.
18. Ibid., at *45.
19. Ibid., at *48.
20. Ibid., at *63.
21. Ibid., at *68.
22. Ibid., at *74–75.
23. Ibid., at *77.
24. Ibid., at *77–79.
25. Ibid., at *79–80.
26. Ibid., at *80.

Chapter 42

HOSTILITY

The early morning of June 4, 2018, was baking time. It had been six months since the oral argument. From the court, not a single peep about the case had leaked. At Masterpiece Cakeshop, all was quiet. Immediately after oral argument, Jack and Charlie and David had skittered from one media outlet to another to continue the thrust and parry of dueling interviews. But much of that had now subsided as the nation waited for the justices to rule. On a day that was shaping up to be one of the hottest of the year so far, Jack went about his normal routine.

Neither he nor anyone else expected anything from the court. In theory, the justices could have ruled anytime after oral argument, but almost everyone suspected they would wait until the end of June, perhaps until even the very last day of the term. That's what they often did with closely divided cases.

Still, Jack couldn't help but keep a careful watch on the news coming out of DC. As he did every morning, he fired up the computer resting on the very table where he had sat across from David and Charlie six years earlier. In many respects, the shop had become a testament to the lengthy battle Jack and Charlie and David had endured. On the wall, he had hung plaques and pictures memorializing his trip to the Supreme Court, including one signed by hundreds of supporters. On one of the tables where his grandchildren engaged in their homeschooling, a picture book of his family's trip to DC lay open for visitors to peruse.

No one quite knew how the justices would rule. From oral argument, many guessed that Justice Kennedy might sway in Jack's favor, and he would eke out a narrow five-to-four victory. Others figured Justice Kennedy's history of protecting LGBT citizens would rule the day. But that wasn't entirely clear either, especially since this case seemed to cross the line from protecting LGBT citizens to forcing the belief that same-sex marriage was moral on others. Above all, trying to guess rulings based on what the justices said at oral argument was an inexact science at best. Oftentimes they hinted at one thing, then veered an entirely different direction after discussing the case with each other and their clerks.

Jack himself was at peace with whatever happened. From the beginning of the litigation, what he had prayed for each day was that he wouldn't allow the case to distract him from his relationship with Jesus Christ. He drew on the Bible daily to secure that foundation. As important as the issues were on a societal level, what was more important for Jack was his faith and ensuring that he walked with his Lord. If he wasn't allowed to create wedding cakes again, he would accept that as God's will. He would trust what God did without apprehension for his future. His certainty that God watched over him and that everything happened for a reason gave him a quiet dignity even in the face of instability and hardship.[1] Every night, he lay his head on his pillow and slept in the peace that comes to those with deep conviction.

As he had so many times before, he clicked his way to the blog that reported on Supreme Court decisions. His expectation was that there would be no news and he would move on with another day of not knowing. On the website, he read the words "We have Masterpiece." He immediately called his wife. Together they tried to find the result. Eventually, he saw the following:

Judgment REVERSED. Kennedy, J., delivered the opinion of the Court, in which Roberts, C. J., and Breyer, Alito, Kagan, and Gorsuch, JJ., joined.

It would have taken a moment to process what it meant, but it slowly sank in. The decision of the Colorado Court of Appeals had been reversed. And the justices hadn't waited until the last day of the term to issue a bitterly divided opinion, as most everyone had suspected they would. Instead, seven justices had ruled in Jack's favor. Only two had dissented.

Jack hadn't read the opinion yet. He might not have fully understand its nuances even if he had. But he knew one thing for certain. After six years, *Masterpiece Cakeshop, Ltd. v. Colorado Civil Rights Commission* was over.

Not too far away, in their home in Denver, David and Charlie checked the same blog. Like Jack, they weren't expecting anything from the court. Still, the case had defined their marriage. It had turned them into gay-rights activists, whereas before they had simply wanted to live their lives in private. When they saw the decision, when the realization sunk in that they had lost, David swore.

He and Charlie hugged each other. A wave of emotions flooded over Dave, so much so that he couldn't process them.[2] They were both shocked and disappointed.

They assured one another that everything would be okay.

Within hours, before they even had a chance to process the significance of the ruling or what it meant, they were whisked away to media interviews and rallies and efforts by the ACLU to spin the decision as best it could. Once again, the public relations machines revved to life.

In the Supreme Court, a seven-justice victory is a rout. Still, *why* the justices ruled the way they did is just as important as how many joined an opinion. A technical victory could still be a loss if the justices included reasoning harmful to one side or the other.

So as soon as it was issued, lawyers for both sides pored over Justice Kennedy's opinion. Despite all the focus on speech in the buildup to the case, the vast majority of the court determined that Jack should win based on his religious freedom arguments. In fact, his victory on that ground was so decisive there was simply no reason to trouble the Free Speech waters.

To begin with, Justice Kennedy acknowledged that the "free speech aspect of this case is difficult."[3] After explaining why, he reached the crux of the ruling: "Whatever the confluence of speech and free exercise principles might be in some cases, the Colorado Civil Rights Commission's consideration of this case was inconsistent with the State's obligation of religious neutrality."

Kennedy acknowledged that under the precedent set by Al Smith's case, it may well be there were certain situations when someone's "free exercise of his religion must yield" to a law that was neutral and generally applicable. "That requirement, however, was not met here," he wrote. "When the Colorado Civil Rights Commission considered this case, it did not do so with the religious neutrality that the Constitution requires. . . . The Commission's actions here violated the Free Exercise Clause; and its order must be set aside."[4]

Kennedy provided the lengthy history of the case, a common practice. In the body of the opinion, he spoke of the broad issues at stake in the case. "Our society has come to the recognition that gay persons and gay couples cannot be treated as social outcasts or as inferior in dignity and worth. For that reason the laws and the Constitution can, and in some instances must, protect them in the exercise of their civil rights. The exercise of their freedom on terms equal to others must be given great weight and respect by the courts."

It sounded like a prelude to a resounding victory for Charlie and David.

But Kennedy pivoted. "At the same time," he wrote, "the religious and philosophical objections to gay marriage are protected views and in some instances protected forms of expression." He then confirmed that he had meant what he wrote in his 2015 opinion declaring that government must recognize same-sex marriages on equal par with opposite-sex ones—that "'the First Amendment ensures that religious organizations and persons are given proper protection as they seek to teach the principles that are so fulfilling and so central to their lives and faiths.'"5

LGBT citizens, Kennedy explained, certainly had a right under the law to receive goods and services on the same terms as everyone else. That was unremarkable. And, he emphasized, Jack was not arguing otherwise. Jack's position was "narrower" and implicated important First Amendment concerns.

The table was set, and the interests of both sides laid bare for all to see. They each had compelling arguments. On the one hand, LGBT citizens deserved protection to avoid a "serious stigma" being thrust upon them. On the other hand, Jack "likely found it difficult to find a line where the customers' rights to goods and services became a demand for him to exercise the right of his own personal expression for their message, a message he could not express in a way consistent with his religious beliefs."6

It was a difficult problem, to be sure. But one thing was clear, whatever arguments either side wielded, "Phillips too was entitled to a neutral and respectful consideration of his claims in all the circumstances of the case."

He didn't receive it, Kennedy found. "The Civil Rights Commission's treatment of his case has some elements of a clear and impermissible hostility toward the sincere religious beliefs that motivated his objection."

"That hostility surfaced" when the "commissioners endorsed the view that religious beliefs cannot legitimately be carried into the public sphere or commercial domain, implying that religious beliefs and persons are less than fully welcome in Colorado's business community."

Through all the media blitz and attempts at obfuscation, Kennedy and the six justices who joined him had perceived the problems with the commission that the Colorado Court of Appeals had completely missed. "One commissioner," Kennedy wrote, "suggested that Phillips can believe 'what he wants to believe,' but cannot act on his religious beliefs 'if he decides to do business in the state.' A few moments later, the commissioner restated the same position: '[I]f a businessman wants to do business in the state and he's got an issue with the—the law's impacting his personal belief system, he needs to look at being able to compromise.'"

Justice Kennedy pointed out that these comments could be seen as "inappropriate and dismissive . . . showing a lack of due consideration for Phillips' free exercise rights and the dilemma he faced."[7]

But Kennedy wasn't finished. He also pointed out the comments by a different commissioner that compared Jack to Nazis and slaveholders and called his religious positions "despicable pieces of rhetoric."

"To describe a man's faith as 'one of the most despicable pieces of rhetoric that people can use,'" Kennedy said, "is to disparage his religion in at least two distinct ways: by describing it as despicable, and also by characterizing it as merely rhetorical—something insubstantial and even insincere. The commissioner even went so far as to compare Phillips' invocation of his sincerely held religious beliefs to defenses of slavery and the Holocaust. This sentiment is inappropriate for a Commission charged with the solemn responsibility of fair and neutral enforcement of Colorado's anti-discrimination law—a law that protects discrimination on the basis of religion as well as sexual orientation."[8]

Kennedy went on. In a less-than-subtle way, he blasted the other commissioners, the Colorado Court of Appeals, and even the lawyers for the state: "The record shows no objection to these comments from other commissioners. And the later state-court ruling reviewing the Commission's decision did not mention those comments, much less express concern with their content. Nor were the comments by the commissioners disavowed in the briefs filed in this Court."[9]

Kennedy acknowledged that the justices have disagreed over the years about whether they should consider comments made by lawmakers when they are passing a law to determine whether the law has discriminatory intent. "In this case, however," he wrote, "the remarks were made in a very different context—by an adjudicatory body deciding a particular case."

And that was not all. "Another indication of hostility," Kennedy wrote, "is the difference in treatment between Phillips' case and the cases of other bakers who objected to a requested cake on the basis of conscience and prevailed before the Commission."

He recounted the cases of the other bakers who had refused to bake cakes opposing same-sex marriage. Then he explained what the lower-court judges had completely missed.

> The treatment of the conscience-based objections at issue in these three cases contrasts with the Commission's treatment of Phillips' objection. The Commission ruled against Phillips in part on the theory that any message the requested wedding cake would carry would be attributed to the customer, not to the baker. Yet the Division did not address this point in any of the other cases with respect to the cakes depicting anti-gay marriage symbolism. Additionally, the Division found no violation of CADA in the other cases in part because each bakery was willing to sell other products, including those depicting Christian themes, to the prospective customers. But the Commission dismissed Phillips' willingness to sell "birthday cakes, shower cakes, [and] cookies and brownies," . . . to gay and lesbian customers as irrelevant. . . . In short, the Commission's consideration of Phillips' religious objection did not accord with its treatment of these other objections.[10]

And the Colorado Court of Appeals, Justice Kennedy wrote, "addressed the disparity only in passing and relegated its complete analysis of the issue to a footnote." Even in that footnote, its reasoning was improper. The Colorado Court of Appeals deemed those other cases to be different because those bakers had not discriminated based on religion but because they found the messages opposed to same-sex marriage to be "offensive."

The seven justices tore that reasoning apart. "A principled rationale for the difference in treatment of these two instances cannot be based on the government's own assessment of offensiveness," they wrote. "The Colorado court's attempt to account for the difference in treatment elevates one view of what is offensive over another and itself sends a signal of official disapproval of Phillips' religious beliefs." This was a crucial point. So much so that the justices took on a note of impatience toward the lower court, the state, and its attorneys, sounding almost like parents tired of repeating themselves: "[I]t is not, as the Court has repeatedly held, the role of the State to prescribe what shall be offensive."[11]

From there, Kennedy provided broad principles relating to religious freedom. As bad as the test was from Al Smith's case, it still protected religious liberty. Government, Justice Kennedy wrote, "cannot act in a manner that passes judgment upon or presupposes the illegitimacy of religious beliefs or practices. The Free Exercise Clause bars even subtle departures from neutrality on matters of religion. . . . The Constitution commits government itself to religious tolerance, and upon even slight suspicion that proposals for state intervention stem from animosity to religion or distrust of its practices, all officials must pause to remember their own high duty to the Constitution and to the rights it secures."[12]

After listing various factors lower courts could consider when determining if a law truly was neutral (or was being applied in a neutral way), Kennedy explained that the commission in Colorado had clearly based its behavior on hostility to Jack's religious views. "It hardly requires restating," the justices wrote, "that government has no role in deciding or even suggesting whether the religious grounds for Phillips' conscience-based objection is legitimate or illegitimate." And yet it clearly did need restating. These basic principles of constitutional law, of freedoms so cherished in the United States, had been lost on nearly everyone throughout the entire case. If laws could stand based on whether the lawgivers or judges agreed with the religious beliefs of one of the parties or found them offensive, then the only party who could ever win would be the one whose beliefs aligned with the people in power. That would be the end of religious freedom.

With that, the justices reversed the judgment from the Colorado Court of Appeals.

———————

For the ACLU, the day was one of damage control. They hosted a rally at the Colorado State Capitol. They set up interviews for David and Charlie, who spoke about the importance of nondiscrimination laws and how significant it was that Colorado's law remained intact.

"The bakery wins the battle but loses the war," the ACLU said in response to the loss at the Supreme Court.[13] The statement strained credulity; but it is a common tactic used by interest groups in such situations. A key aspect of today's "culture wars" is controlling the narrative for people who are only barely paying attention. After the stinging loss, the ACLU engaged in that practice with gusto. It did everything it could to spin the decision in its favor, including trying to convince people that the loss was actually a win.

In statement after statement, they declared it a victory because the Supreme Court had kept the Colorado Anti-Discrimination Act in place. Of course, Jack had never asked that it be struck down. He had only asked for an exemption from it because, as applied in his case, it burdened his religious exercise. And that was what he got.

The ACLU also worked overtime to suggest the ruling had no precedential value—that it was so narrow it could never be applied to any future case. It was a valiant effort, and many in the media picked up on the theme. It was also wrong. It was certainly true that once the justices decided the state had not acted in a neutral manner, they didn't need to address free speech or general applicability. But it was also true that they had created a standard for neutrality that would be a powerful check on governments' intent on oppressing people with whom they disagreed. First, the ruling would drive negative discourse underground. That, by itself, would simply mean that the rhetoric used by state officials would be more civil. It was a minor effect but a much-needed one. Second, and more important, the justices required state actors to treat everyone the same. In other words, if government regulators wanted to enforce laws against their enemies, they must also enforce them against their allies. Otherwise, the law was not neutral. That requirement became a powerful check on regulators bent on oppressing their ideological opposites.

Finally, the Supreme Court also sent a dramatic message regarding religious beliefs supporting traditional marriage. An unfortunate irony lingered in the culture war between the LGBT left and those on the religious right. For years, the far religious right had sought to force LGBT citizens to remain hidden as if they were not a part of the broader society. Now that the balance of power had shifted to the LGBT left in many respects, they sought to do the same to the far religious right. The commission certainly had reflected that view. Such believers could have their beliefs, but they weren't welcome in the public marketplace. They had to remain in the closet. This is a classic human instinct: the oppressed often become the oppressors.

The Constitution acts as a check against that universal human instinct. And the justices once again ensured that it did its job.

For Jack and his supporters, it was a day of joy. Though the shop, for the moment, still wasn't selling the wedding cakes that had defined it for so long, it shined with a euphoria it hadn't seen in years, if ever. Jack and his wife dashed between the kitchen and the counter, struggling to bake cookies and other goods amidst nonstop phone calls, texts, and well-wishers. Outside, cameramen, reporters, journalists, and even casual onlookers began to gather.

Jack donned a black Masterpiece Cakeshop T-shirt and tied a white apron around his waist. In his typical subdued fashion, he celebrated the victory with a peaceful smile under a goatee dotted with a little more gray than it had held six years before.

Notes

1. Jack Phillips, in discussion with author, February 23, 2018.
2. "Same-Sex Couple Reacts to Supreme Court Decision in Favor of Baker," NPR, All Things Considered, June 4, 2018, https://www.npr.org/2018/06/04/616917862 /same-sex-couple-reacts-to-supreme-court-decision-in-favor-of-baker.
3. *Masterpiece Cakeshop, LTD., v. Colorado Civil Rights Commission*, 138 S. Ct. 1719, 1723 (2018).
4. Ibid., at 1723–24.
5. Ibid., at 1727; Justice Kennedy quotes here from *Obergefell v. Hodges*, 135 S. Ct. 2584 (2015).
6. Ibid., at 1728.
7. Ibid., at 1728; alterations in original.
8. Ibid., at 1729.
9. Ibid., at 1729–30.
10. Ibid., at 1730.
11. Ibid., at 1730–31.
12. Ibid. at 1731; quotation marks omitted.
13. https://www.aclu.org/blog/lgbt-rights/lgbt-nondiscrimination-protections/master piece-bakery-wins-battle-loses-war.

EPILOGUE

Mary Stinemetz died. At sixty-six, on October 21, 2012, the devout Jehovah's Witness passed away at the University of Colorado Hospital from complications stemming from primary biliary cholangitis and liver failure.

Her death was the predictable biproduct of the jumbled state of religious liberty law in the United States. In many respects, her case was a race against time. When she sued the state of Kansas in 2010 for refusing to transfer her to a different facility that could perform a bloodless liver transplant, she was already dying. She would have needed a very quick decision.

It didn't come. The ruling in Al Smith's case had confused the law. The federally drafted Religious Freedom Restoration Act didn't apply to claims challenging state laws. Most important, the ongoing fight between the far right and the far left over LGBT and abortion rights had made it impossible to pass any sort of religious-freedom protections for someone like Mary. The unending battles between those two camps continued to leave in their wake a trail of confusion and vulnerability for everyone else.

In states like Kansas, it was unclear precisely what the law was for a claim like Mary's. She was asking for the same relief Anthony Kohlmann, Roy Torcaso, Al Smith, and Jack Phillips sought: a religious exemption to the normal rules. Had Justice Scalia not changed the law with his opinion in *Smith*, the analysis would have been simple. Had the Supreme Court not struck down the original federal Religious Freedom Restoration Act as applied to state and local governments, the outcome would have been clear. Had the far left and the far right simply been willing to compromise with one another to help states pass statutes that achieved fairness for all, there would have been no question regarding how Mary's claim should be handled.

Instead, it needed to be litigated. It had to traverse numerous levels of administrative hearings. It crawled its way to a Kansas trial court, eventually settling in the Kansas Court of Appeals. There, the appellate judges finally determined that Mary should win under the *Smith* test (because the law was not generally applicable) and under the Kansas State Constitution. The decision came down on May 4, 2011.[1] The state announced they wouldn't appeal.

It was too late. By then, the doctors had determined that her condition had deteriorated to the point that a transplant could no longer help her. Had it been granted sooner, she would have survived. In the months that followed, as she slipped away from this life, she expressed peace in knowing that her case could ensure others would not die for their beliefs. In her faith that she would one day live again, she found comfort and solace.

After Mary's passing, across the United States, religious liberty continues in its position as a lonely and misunderstood freedom. Every time a state attempts to pass a law restoring the test that existed before the Al Smith case, it is labeled as nothing more than a pretext for discrimination, the term "religious freedom" placed in scare quotes. There are groups in the middle seeking to achieve an understanding between those on the far right and those on the far left, but they are often demonized by both extremes. In keeping with the goal of trying to achieve fairness for all, these groups continue to engage in talks with reasonably minded representatives of both camps.

But the spirit of reconciliation only rarely triumphs and quickly gets drowned out by louder, less conciliatory voices. Perhaps recognizing that, at the end of the opinion in *Masterpiece*, the seven justices provided one, final admonition. It was more parental than legal. Most media outlets and legal scholars ignored it. The justices spoke of the importance of resolving "these disputes . . . with tolerance, without undue disrespect to sincere religious beliefs, and without subjecting gay persons to indignities when they seek goods and services in an open market."[2] That message was an important one. It had served as the foundation of religious freedom in the United States since the country's founding. Through two and a quarter centuries, every time religious freedom won, it was because a judge or government official recognized the need for mutual tolerance.

At the very beginning, it was reflected in a letter George Washington penned to the Quakers when they asked for his assistance. At the time, the new nation required all able-bodied men to join the military. The Quakers had asked for an exemption to that general requirement because fighting in war violated their religious beliefs. On October 13, 1789, President Washington penned a letter to them. In part, it read:

> Gentlemen,
>
> I receive with pleasure your affectionate address, and thank you for the friendly Sentiments & good wishes which you express for the Success of my administration, and for my personal Happiness.
>
> We have Reason to rejoice in the prospect that the present National Government, which by the favor of Divine Providence, was formed by the common Counsels, and peaceably established with the common consent of the People, will prove a blessing to every denomination of them. . . .
>
> I assure you very explicitly that in my opinion the Consciencious [*sic*] scruples of all men should be treated with great delicacy & tenderness, and it is my wish and desire that the Laws may always be as extensively accomodated [*sic*] to them, as a due regard to the Protection and essential Interests of the Nation may Justify, and permit.[3]

It was a sentiment the Supreme Court echoed 229 years later. When faced with the same dilemma, they had called for the same solution. Perhaps the only question was whether all citizens—of whatever background—would have the deep conviction necessary to heed the call.[4]

NOTES

1. *Stinemetz v. Health Policy Authority*, 45 Kan. App. 818 (2011).
2. *Masterpiece Cakeshop, LTD. v. Colorado Civil Rights Commission*, 138 S. Ct. 1719, 1732 (2018).
3. From George Washington to the Society of the Quakers, October 13, 1789, Founders Online (website), https://founders.archives.gov/documents/Washington /05-04-02-0188. See also Michael W. McConnell, "Freedom from Persecution or Protection of the Rights of Conscience: A Critique of Justice Scalia's Historical Arguments in *City of Boerne v. Flores*," *William and Mary Law Review* 39, no. 3 (1998): 819, 838.
4. Just two weeks after the Supreme Court issued its opinion in *Masterpiece*, the state of Colorado again charged Jack with discrimination in a case with some similarities to the one involving David and Charlie. This time, an LGBT-left activist had called Jack's shop asking him to bake a cake celebrating a gender transition ceremony. The call had come on the same day that the Supreme Court had agreed to hear Jack's case. By then, Jack had been in the spotlight for five years. He politely declined to bake the cake. The State of Colorado waited until a ruling in *Masterpiece* had been made before deciding what to do, then they largely ignored that ruling and came after Jack again. Jack sued the state in federal court, and the federal judge allowed Jack's lawsuit to proceed. Roughly eight months later, in March 2019, when additional discovery revealed the state's continued hostility toward Jack's religious beliefs, the state of Colorado backed down. It finally agreed, after six years, to allow Jack to run his tiny shop in Lakewood in peace.

ACKNOWLEDGMENTS

When I first considered a book on religious liberty, my biggest worry was that no one would find it interesting. The issues affect every single one of us, even if we don't realize it, but seeing how to bring those issues to life in an engaging way was not obvious to me at first. I have long since run out of words of gratitude for my editor, Chris Schoebinger, who helped conceive the concept and stories in this book. His brilliance goes unmatched. And I will forever be thankful for the elite professionals at Shadow Mountain Publishing to whom Chris introduced me: Ilise Levine, Lisa Mangum, Heidi Taylor Gordon, Janna DeVore, Jill Schaugaard, David Brown, Jack Newman, and many others working diligently behind the scenes.

Bringing historical figures to life, with their quirks and personal moments, is not easy. At first blush, their stories seem lost to us. In reality, they still exist, but they are scattered across the world like pieces of a treasure that need discovering and reconstructing. I found the basic framework for each story where I expected: in court filings, newspapers, online archives, and decisions from judges. But the salient facts, the little details that allowed the narratives to come alive, came from so many other places, sources, and people, for which I will always be thankful. These included the Special Collections Research Center at the Syracuse University Library, the University of Denver's Law Library, historians at St. Peter's Catholic Church in Manhattan, the organist and historians at St. Patrick's Old Cathedral, Bill and Donald Torcaso, Linda Bernstein, Jane Farrell, Kaila Farrell-Smith, the Department of Records in the Municipal Archives for New York City, the kind young man who taught me how to use the microfilm machine, the staff of St. Paul's Chapel, the many families who buried their loved ones there, Jack Phillips, Jeremy Tedesco, Kristin Waggoner, Paula Greisen, Bessie M. Decker of the Maryland Court of Appeals, Tammy Kiter of the New York Historical Society, Steven Moore and John Echohawk of the Native American Rights Fund, Walter Walsh, and so many previous authors whose research into a vast array of topics—from peyotism to the condition of early Manhattan's streets—informed this book.

To Professor Douglas Laycock, the amount of praise I have heaped on you in recent years is almost embarrassing, but it still isn't enough. Thank you for laying the foundation.

Special thanks goes to Sam Feldman, who provided me excellent research assistance, tracking down letters and items that no one had any business finding.

Many people assisted me in crafting the narratives in this book, providing feedback as I slogged through draft after draft. Tonya Wendel, Taani Secrist, Stephen Craig, Jerusha Collis, Adele Lee, all my editors—I took to heart every piece of feedback you gave me. Thank you for serving as beta readers. Thank you, also, to Elise McMullen-Ciotti, for her careful and helpful review of Al Smith's story.

Perhaps the greatest kindness shown to me in the creation of this book came from the exceptionally skilled and unflappable Wendy Pifher and Amy Bowler. They are two of the most talented lawyers I know.

No book reaches the finish line without tremendous sacrifice, not just by authors, but by everyone in their circle. To my wife and children, thank you for helping me make this a reality. On those long nights and early mornings, when no one else knew the sacrifice we were making, I'm so thankful you were by my side. Your encouragement and enthusiasm kept me going even when I'd reached my limits. I express the same gratitude to my parents, whose selfless sacrifice never ends.

Finally, page limitations prevent me from truly expressing how deeply grateful I am to each person who contributed to this book. I hope you know how appreciative I am, even if I don't have the space to express it here.

Additional information and resources about
this book (including historical photographs and
illustrations) are available at **steventcollis.com**.

INDEX